Vernacular Architecture
An Illustrated Handbook

R. W. Brunskill

faber and faber

To Lorna, Cameron and Rory,
my grandchildren

First published in 1971
by Faber and Faber Limited
3 Queen Square London WC1N 3AU
Second edition, 1978
Third edition, 1987
Fourth edition (retitled), 2000

Photoset by Parker Typesetting Service, Leicester
Printed and bound in Great Britain by Butler and Tanner Ltd, Frome

A CIP record for this book
is available from the British Library

ISBN 0−571−19503−2

CONTENTS

ILLUSTRATIONS

ROOFING: SHAPE, CONSTRUCTION AND MATERIALS

URBAN VERNACULAR AND MINOR INDUSTRIAL BUILDINGS, CHAPELS

NOTE. Items marked M.U.S.A. are from the collections of the Manchester University School of Architecture.

Items marked NMR are from the National Monuments Record for England.

Items marked NMRW are from the National Monuments Record for Wales and are Crown Copyright: Royal Commission on the Ancient and Historical Monuments of Wales.

Preface and Acknowledgements

Like so many of my age-group (the young middle-aged) I am only one generation removed from the land. I have therefore had the privilege, which may not be available to my own children, of spending school holidays on the farms of my grandparents, uncles and cousins, and taking part in a way of life which, as recently as thirty years ago, retained intact many of the traditions accumulated over several centuries. It was during such holidays spent in remote parts of Cumberland and Westmorland that I first became aware of differences of walling material, roofing material, plan form and architectural detail, and it was from practical if inexpert activities that I began to realize the significance in different forms of farmstead layout and farm building design.

As a student at the School of Architecture in the University of Manchester my interest was detected by Professor R. A. Cordingley, encouraged and guided until I was ready to participate in the postgraduate study of vernacular architecture which he had initiated in the late 1940s. I played my part between interruptions of military and professional activity in the extension of the study during the following decade, building on the experience of my predecessors and helping to develop techniques which have been adopted by succeeding graduate students. We had all assumed that, on his retirement in 1963, Professor Cordingley would draw together our various regional studies and use them as the basis for a comprehensive and authoritative account of vernacular architecture in England. His sudden and untimely death within a few months of retirement cruelly shattered that assumption.

However, it had become apparent that interest in vernacular architecture had been growing simultaneously and independently in other, and perhaps more appropriate centres than Manchester, and in 1954 the Vernacular Architecture Group had been founded to bring together in an informal study group the widely scattered and diverse interests of architects, archaeologists, historians and museum curators. The rapid growth in the numbers and authority of the Group showed that there was a wide general interest in the subject and a largely untapped enthusiasm for the study of the surviving buildings of a rather changing rural economy. With this in mind I began to adapt the rather ambitious objects and somewhat elaborate techniques of Professor Cordingley's study to the more limited objectives and lesser capabilities of architectural students. With the encouragement of Professor N. L. Hanson, this was done and seemed successful. I then began to make the further adaptation needed to extend the study amongst members of archaeological societies and extra-mural classes who had no architectural training but considerable enthusiasm. This further adaptation included the publication by the Ancient Monuments Society of the 'Systematic Procedure for Recording English Vernacular Architecture', and, from this, there developed the suggestion that some simple handbook might be produced which would amplify the basic information collected through completing record cards and would also assist in full understanding of the accounts of vernacular architecture based mainly on documentary sources which were now becoming available. The preparation of this handbook was the result.

Although I have taken most of the photographs and prepared all the diagrams specifically for this book, and must take responsibility for the facts recorded and opinions expressed, its preparation would have been quite impossible without the published work noted in the list of references and recommended for further reading. The help of my colleagues in the University of Manchester, especially Dr Wood-Jones and Dr Marsden, is gratefully acknowledged, and my former colleague, J. H. G. Archer, was kind enough to approve my comments on the Vernacular Revival and allow me to use his photograph of the Edgar Wood drawings. The discussions during many conferences of the Vernacular Architecture Group have opened my eyes to many unfamiliar parts of the country and sharpened my understanding of what I had thought familiar; special mention must be made of the following who have helped on specific points: Dr P. Eden, Dr E. Gee, R. A. Foster, Sir Robert Hall, T. M. Owen, S. R. Jones, E. Mercer, Miss V. Parker, Dr J. E. C. Peters, P. Smith, J. T. Smith, and W. J. Smith. I must thank students of the School of Architecture for the drawings and photographs which have been adapted and Professor Hanson for permission to make use of them. Some of the sections include information gained with the benefit of the Neale Bursary and a Research Grant of the R.I.B.A., and, in the case of American material, as one of the by-products of a Commonwealth Fund Fellowship of the Harkness Fund and a Staff Travel Grant of Manchester University. I must also thank the Breconshire Education Committee and Deiniol Williams, their Chief Education Officer, for the opportunity to conduct research into farm buildings in the county. The students at the Vernacular Architecture Summer Schools which I have conducted for several years as part of the programme of the Institute of Advanced Architectural Studies, University of York, have been willing guinea pigs for recording techniques, and sharp critics of my theories, and I am grateful to them and to Professor P. Nuttgens for this opportunity.

Finally I must thank my wife for typing the draft manuscripts and Mrs Johnson and Miss Beck for the final typing; and also Mr Peter Crawley and his colleagues for humouring an architect who insisted on trying to design a book rather than write it.

R. W. BRUNSKILL
Wilmslow, Cheshire, February 1969

Preface to Fourth Edition

A second edition of this book was published in 1978 with additions to many parts of the text and diagrams – especially in the section on urban and rural house plans – and with major additions to the Notes and References section to reflect the amount of additional published material.

A third edition was published in 1987. The Notes and References section was completely rewritten, a brief introduction to the vernacular architecture of Scotland was added, some maps and diagrams were redrawn and minor corrections were made.

The opportunity has now arisen for a fourth edition. The basic organization of text, photographs, diagrams and maps has all been retained though parts have been corrected, modified or rewritten. Extra double-page spreads have been added on cottages, staircases, minor textile buildings and chapels, while extra pages have been included on bank barns, American vernacular architecture and the traditional buildings of Scotland. The glossaries of room names and farm-building terms have been rewritten and extended. The Notes and References section has been completely rewritten and considerably amplified while a separate Bibliography has now been included. However, there are limits to what can be rewritten and I hope regular users will be tolerant of the limitations of the book.

The title has been changed to *Vernacular Architecture: An Illustrated Handbook* to reflect the way in which most readers refer to the book.

The traditional counties have been retained – some of the 1974 creations have proved short-lived – and imperial measures have been used here as they were used in the past by the builders of the works of vernacular architecture about which I have written.

I continue to be grateful for the comments of reviewers and others and I appreciate the faith of the publishers in the demand for a new edition.

R. W. BRUNSKILL
Wilmslow, Cheshire, November 1998

INTRODUCTION

Forty years ago, the serious study of vernacular architecture in Great Britain had scarcely begun. True, three of the pioneering studies, Addy's *Evolution of the English House*, Innocent's account of *The Development of English Building Construction*, and Peate's *The Welsh House*, had long been completed, and certainly many books describing in a general way the characteristics of selected farm-houses and cottages had been published. But the careful investigation of individual buildings and the classification of comparable examples which has now made the subject such a hive of academic industry is a pursuit which has only just reached its maturity.

During the past forty years or so the study of vernacular architecture has engaged the interest of scholars in many fields and each one has contributed the techniques of his discipline to the general inquiry. Among the foremost have been the social and economic historians, looking to the buildings of the countryside to help describe the activities they were designed to house, and relating periods of intense building activity to the opportunities for the accumulation of capital. The new topographers, seeking to find the historical explanation for the intricately organized landscape of the British countryside, have related rural buildings to their wider setting. The medieval archaeologists have discovered in the study of roof construction in vernacular buildings a rich field for investigation and comparison. The Royal Commissions on Historical Monuments have, during the past three decades, turned an increasing proportion of their resources to the study of vernacular architecture. Geographers, in the transformation of their own subject, have seen in vernacular architecture evidence of the significance of quite localized geographical factors in the development of the different regions of the country. Sociologists, in their intensive surveys of individual communities, have discovered that the buildings of the people and the way they were erected, ranked with their churches and forms of religious observance in expressing their social organization. The students of folk life, in their allied field, have shown, for instance, how often architectural details and building practices have perpetuated customs whose origins were thought lost, and whose technical basis had long been transformed. Vernacular architecture has been seen as one of the ways in which regional and national character survived the various political amalgamations which make up the present nation. And to end a list which could most probably be extended, the architectural historians have recently devoted some of their attentions to the study of the many minor architectural monuments, the houses of the people, the barns of their crops, and the factories of their early industrial efforts, which their brothers in practice are now so rapidly replacing.

Following on the increasing academic interest in the subject of vernacular architecture there has been an increasing public interest. This has taken the form of individual interest expressed, for instance, in the current enthusiasm for converting cottages for weekend use, as well as in the protests at planning proposals which threaten the quality of village life. It has included group interest, particularly on the part of the WEA classes who are making systematic studies of their own villages. It is now taking on a national scale in the development of environmental studies in the schools, for the study of vernacular architecture is being recognized as a major part of the study of both the urban and rural environment.

Official interest in vernacular architecture has also developed through the building conservation movement. The recently expanded lists of buildings of special architectural and historical interest include many examples of vernacular architecture while most conservation areas consist mainly of vernacular buildings. Among large landowners, the National Trust has begun a survey of its vernacular building stock.

As a consequence of the academic work carried out during the past forty years there has been a respectable trickle of books and articles on vernacular architecture which can provide background reading and specific information to feed the popular interest in the subject. But a need has been established for a handbook to provide basic information on the buildings and for use in the field, and the present work is intended to go some way to filling that need. Its pretensions are modest; it will contain little that is new to the established workers in the subject, it certainly is not intended to anticipate the definitive work which the study has now justified, but if it helps the enthusiastic amateur to increase his own awareness of vernacular architecture and encourages him to add his own contribution to the national stock of knowledge of the subject, then its preparation has been worth while.

The Introduction remains basically as it was written nearly thirty years ago.

The first few words 'Twenty years ago' have already been updated in the Third Edition to 'Forty years ago' and now must be extended to 'Fifty years ago' with corresponding changes to the other periods quoted. The work of the Royal Commissions on Historical Monuments, of the National Trust and of English Heritage, Cadw and Historic Scotland in the study of vernacular architecture has continued apace. The 'respectable trickle of books and articles' has now become something of a flood. Serious students of vernacular architecture have become ever more numerous and even more knowledgeable. But year by year the subject continues to attract new enthusiasts while developments in education at all levels foster interest in our vernacular environment. A book such as this will, one hopes, continue to foster both interest and enthusiasm.

Types of Vernacular Architecture

Examples of vernacular architecture may be broadly divided into domestic, agricultural, and industrial categories. Some other building types provide examples which have been described as vernacular, for instance the small, simple churches of poor and remote parishes, or simple defensive forts or refuges not intended for permanent human occupation, or the less pretentious examples of railway and canal architecture: canal keepers' cottages, wayside halts, etc. But, since the majority of examples of these other building types were professionally designed and relatively sophisticated, it seems better to confine the study to the three categories of domestic, agricultural, and industrial.

Domestic vernacular architecture comprises the buildings designed for living as normally understood: eating, sitting, sleeping, storage, etc., and also the ancillary buildings which, at certain times, have been quite extensive: brew-house, bake-house, kitchen, sculleries, wash-house, etc. The category includes defensive dwellings in the sense of private houses adapted for occasional defence, as distinct from castles which included some domestic accommodation. It also includes inns, shops, etc., where the domestic activities predominated over the commercial. A distinction is made between the domestic vernacular of the countryside and that of the towns, the one being related mainly to farming and the other mainly to commerce, and both governed until quite recently by the separate lines of development followed by town and country.

The vernacular architecture of agriculture comprises all the buildings of the farmstead apart from the farm-house and its domestic ancillaries. Thus the barn, cow-house, stable, granary, cart shed, shelter shed, pig-sty, etc., would be examples of agricultural architecture, normally in the vernacular range. The isolated field barns and out-farms and the agricultural ancillaries within a village, such as the pound, are also included.

Industrial vernacular is a term intended to include the buildings which housed industrial activities related to the countryside – wind and water-mills, corn and lime kilns, smithies and potteries, etc. – and those manufacturing activities which were related to domestic rather than commercial scale – workshops attached to dwellings or incorporated within them, and the small textile mills based on hand or water power, for example. During the Industrial Revolution, the scale of operations or the unprecedented nature of the processes took the buildings out of the vernacular class, though most operations can be traced to their domestic origin.

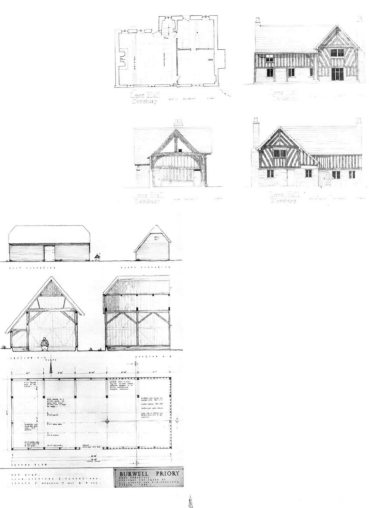

Lees Hall
Dewsbury

Lees Hall
Dewsbury

Lees Hall
Dewsbury

Lees Hall
Dewsbury

BURWELL PRIORY

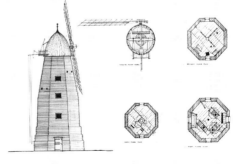

WINDMILL STUDY   soham

23

Size-Types

Before examining an example of domestic vernacular architecture, it is important to try to establish its size-type. Four such categories have been generally accepted: the Great House, the Large House, the Small House and the Cottage, and they correspond to four groups of householders ranging from the top to the bottom of a scale combining wealth and social status. Just as there are graduations within the scale at any period of time, so the boundaries between size-types cannot be precisely determined but the division into four categories has been found to be reasonable in application and convenient in the field.

The Great Houses were occupied by people of national importance. The great residential castles of the Middle Ages, the elaborate mansions and palaces of the 16C. and 17C., the imposing country seats of the 18C., the swollen villas of the 19C., were all Great Houses and were the homes of royalty, the nobility of Church and State, those who occupied high and profitable office at home and abroad, the landowners rich in land through inheritance or trade, the cotton barons, the railway magnates. These people were of national importance through high social status or great wealth, and occupied Great Houses appropriate to their position in society. Such houses are normally excluded from the ranks of vernacular architecture.

People of some local importance lived in Large Houses. The manor house commanding, in partnership with the church, the medieval village street, the house of the unusually successful yeoman, or the highly favoured parson, the small country house of the squire, the imposing farm-house of the wealthy tenant farmer, the house of the clothier or mill-owner, all were Large Houses, and, until the approach of the 19C. normally had qualities which make them a part of the body of vernacular architecture.

For the human backbone of the nation there were the Small Houses. The ordinary yeoman or tenant farmer, the miller, the smith, the minor official, the unfavoured parson, the shopkeeper, the schoolteacher, were people of significance in the village, but of little standing in national or even provincial society. They lived in Small Houses, and their dwellings make up the main body of material which is recognized as domestic vernacular architecture.

But at the bottom of the social scale and only just above the subsistence level were the labourers and artisans who had no wealth apart from the strength of their limbs or the skill of their hands, and the

widows and elderly whose survival depended on the charity of family or community. Undoubtedly many of these lived in the houses of their employers, patrons, or relatives, but many had simple dwellings of their own – the Cottages which eventually were built of materials permanent enough to survive as examples of the most basic domestic vernacular architecture.

The size-type given to an example of vernacular architecture – Large House, Small House, or Cottage – is decided by reference to the sort of person for whom the house was originally intended. The actual buildings tend to pass down the social scale during their lifetime; the manor house becomes a farm-house, then is divided into cottages and finally, abandoned as a dwelling, becomes a farm building or workshop.

The size-type is also decided by reference to regional conditions at a particular time. The Large House of someone of considerable local importance in a poor region might be little bigger than the Small House of a yeoman in a more prosperous region: the armigerous Welshman having a house rather less ostentatious than a contemporary Sussex farmer. Less obviously, the briefly prosperous handloom weaver of early 19C. Lancashire had a cottage which was bigger and better built than that of the depressed agricultural labourer in Norfolk at the same time.

Size-types of a sort were also found among farm buildings. Barns had high status and were given due architectural distinction and constructional thought while at the same time the young cattle, the pigs and the poultry might have scarcely any shelter at all. Even among industrial buildings some, such as the windmills and watermills, housed processes so important that they were properly built from an early date, whereas others, such as the drying sheds in a brickyard, rarely enjoyed the status of permanent buildings.

As in so many aspects of vernacular architecture, a distinction should be made between town and country. The grades of wealth and status in the towns were no doubt reflected in the houses, but the reflection was not a mirror of that in the rural areas.

The Vernacular Zone

From the various origins of the students of the subject there has come a variety of opinions on what constitutes vernacular architecture and which periods and which examples provide the most fruitful study. For some the medieval manor house is most significant, for others the yeoman's farm-house, the weaver's cottage, the squatter's cabin, or even the non-domestic buildings of the farmstead or the factory complex. An attempt is made here to comprehend these varying interests by suggesting a vernacular zone in which examples may be found between the period in which they appear as buildings in relatively permanent materials and the period in which they cease to have the qualities we call vernacular. Where nothing survives of the buildings, study will depend on archaeological methods beyond the scope of this book; where the surviving buildings have more than vernacular quality they may be studied by the ordinary techniques of architectural history.

The polite threshold

It has been assumed for the purpose of this study that the designers of the various buildings have made some attempt, however untutored and however unsuccessful, to make the buildings pleasant to look upon – to make them, in fact, to however slight a degree, examples of architecture rather than building. Many readers will think this rather a wild assumption, but experience does suggest that the designers organized their building elements to produce more than a solely utilitarian result and with far from accidental effects.

Assuming, then, that we are considering architecture rather than mere building, another distinction is made between polite and vernacular architecture. The difference between the two is a matter of degree. The ultimate in polite architecture will have been designed by a professional architect or one who acted as such though under some other title, such as surveyor or master mason; it will have been designed to follow a national or even an international fashion, style, or set of conventions, towards an aesthetically satisfying result; and aesthetic considerations will have dominated the designer's thought rather than functional demands. Aesthetically and, probably, constructionally the designer will have been adventurous, exploring new ways of achieving his conscious wishes; in so doing his materials will have been chosen to help achieve the aesthetic or constructional ends and have been obtained from whatever source could supply such materials. On the other hand, the ultimate in vernacular architecture will have been designed by an amateur, possibly the occupier of the intended building, and one without any training in design; he will have been guided by a series of conventions built up in his locality, paying little attention to what may be fashionable on an international scale. The function of his building would be the dominant factor, aesthetic considerations, though present to some small degree, being quite minimal; tradition would guide constructional as well as aesthetic choice, and local materials would be used as a matter of course, other materials being chosen and imported quite exceptionally. Between the extremes of the wholly vernacular and the completely polite, examples occur which have some vernacular and some polite content. Thus even the most sophisticated design in a provincial town may be carried out entirely in local materials and so include some slight vernacular quality, but a rough distinction can in practice be made between those buildings which have vernacular or polite qualities to a greater or lesser degree. If they are more polite than vernacular they are assumed to have passed over the polite threshold, out of the vernacular zone.

The date at which the polite threshold may be set varies with time, place and size-type. The very earliest examples, even of Great Houses, had mainly vernacular qualities, but most medieval buildings of this size-type were polite rather than vernacular. The Large Houses from the end of the 17C. onwards tended to be designed by architects in the prevailing style and thus moved further and further into the zone of polite architecture. Towards the end of the 18C. and during the 19C. the larger farm-houses were designed by professional designers for effect rather than utility. Even Cottages during the second half of the 19C. came to follow national rules rather than local traditions. Nowadays virtually every house bears the mark of polite architecture and has lost all significant vernacular quality. Thus the polite threshold may be indicated on a graph by a line falling at a steeper and steeper curve down the scale of size-types in approaching the effective end of vernacular architecture.

The vernacular threshold

If in England and Wales, as in the Isle of Man, it had been considered unlucky to demolish a house, we might have surviving examples of all types of house from the earliest times of settlement to the present day. Even without such a helpful tradition one would expect some examples from every period to have escaped demolition so as to give a continuous series diminishing in numbers from the present day back to the most distant past. But in fact when recording the examples of the domestic vernacular of the countryside (the situation is rather different in the towns), one finds that the many surviving buildings provide a continuous thread until a point in time when suddenly all evidence in the form of surviving buildings comes to a stop. This point varies with size-type, but it is so sudden that clearly the emergence, or complete reconstruction of houses in materials permanent enough to survive, is something of great significance. This line on a graph of size-type and time is called here the vernacular threshold. In any locality it tends to curve with an ever increasing gradient; examples high on the social scale surviving from an early period, from the middle of the social scale being more recent and from the bottom of the social scale being more recent still. Or, to put it another way, we can see examples of the vernacular dwellings of medieval knights but generally not of medieval farmers; of 17C. yeomen but not their cottager neighbours; but of 19C. artisans at the humblest level.

Modifications of the vernacular threshold

The absence of examples below the vernacular threshold may indicate either that houses were deliberately destroyed or that they were of such flimsy materials that they were not expected to survive. The strong evidence for the Great Rebuilding, which occurred throughout most of England between 1570 and 1640, explains the deliberate destruction of older sub-standard houses, most being completely replaced even though some were incorporated in improved structures. But it also suggests that for the first time large sections of the rural community had the means available for the erection of relatively expensive buildings of permanent materials and the security of tenure which would make such investment worth while. But the period of Great Rebuilding varied with location as well as social status; it occurred between about 1670 and 1720 in the northern counties of England, and later still in part of Wales, so that any average, national, vernacular threshold requires modification in any specific locality. Furthermore, the later the period of rebuilding, the more likely that it would extend far down the social scale, so that farm-houses and even cottages of medieval date have been identified in advanced parts of England whereas such houses suddenly appear together at quite a late date in more backward parts.

It is interesting that the position of the threshold does not seem to vary with the durability of the available building materials. The hardest stone of Cornwall and Cumberland is associated with a late period for the threshold, the perishable timber of Kent and Sussex may be seen in houses dating from medieval to late 19C., while vulnerable clay and cob continued in use well into the 19C. in parts of the country which were not very far distant from sources of superior building material.

For agricultural and industrial vernacular buildings similar thresholds could be distinguished if only dating criteria were better established for these building types. But it seems that most surviving farm buildings of brick and stone on large, medium and small farms are no older than the 17C. and few built of timber seem to be more than a century older. Those which are clearly ancient are the huge barns of the rich land-owners, clerical and lay.

The vernacular zone

If one accepts the two thresholds, the one representing the extent of conscious architectural effort and the other the sudden emergence of building intentionally in permanent materials, they may be combined to form a vernacular zone. For any size-type this is the period between the emergence of houses in permanent materials but vernacular content, and the abandonment of vernacular design in favour of polite; for any period it represents those size-types for which vernacular examples survive as against those which survive but with the qualities of polite architecture. In fact the size-types and periods within the vernacular zone – medieval manor houses, 17C. yeoman houses, 18C. farm-houses and 19C. cottages – are just those which have already gained the interest of vernacular scholars and for which further field work is likely to be profitable. Beyond one extreme of the vernacular zone, architectural history takes over; beyond the other extreme, field investigation is a matter of archaeology.

Commentary

Research during the past 20 years or so has cast doubt on any theory based on a single Great Rebuilding, no matter at what date and in no matter what locality. Rather it is felt that there were several rebuildings, each one representing a change in house design or methods of construction. Fresh interpretation of evidence from excavation has modified the view that early houses were designed for limited life and so that there was any sudden change from impermanent to permanent building. Historians have suggested that there was a detectable rate of attrition and so replacement of dwelling though great social changes or population explosions would lead to periods of great rebuilding activity, which could be called Great Rebuildings. Nevertheless, the concepts of Vernacular and Polite Thresholds are still tenable for many parts of the country and the Vernacular Zone still defines what students of vernacular architecture may fruitfully study.

a. The 'polite' threshold.
b. The 'vernacular' threshold.

c. Modification of the vernacular threshold between areas of survival from early periods and areas of late survival.
d. Vernacular threshold of farm buildings showing survival of tithe barns from early but superior farmsteads and late construction of farm buildings at lower levels.
e. Modification of vernacular threshold as a result of archaeological or documentary research illuminating a period from which no complete buildings survive.
f. The 'vernacular zone' between the two thresholds with date and assumed size-type of one hundred published dated examples of vernacular architecture superimposed.

THE 'POLITE' THRESHOLD

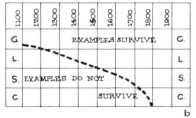

THE 'VERNACULAR' THRESHOLD

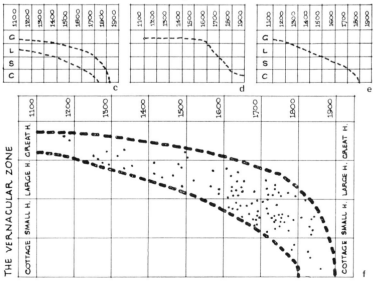

The Organization of the Book

This book has been prepared in order to help those who have little or no previous knowledge of the subject to an understanding and appreciation of the wealth of vernacular architecture in this country. As a handbook it is intended primarily for use in the field as a complement to the several excellent accounts of vernacular architecture, based regionally or nationally, which are now available. It has therefore been designed as a series of opposite pages, one with a photograph and short text on some aspect of the subject and the other with diagrams and explanations of what may be seen in the field. Both text and illustrations are mere tokens of what is already known of the various aspects of vernacular architecture. They may be expanded by reference to the books and articles listed in the notes and bibliography, they should be expanded by further field work, they may well be superseded as research proceeds.

The first five chapters refer mainly to domestic vernacular architecture, though many of the materials and techniques illustrated apply equally to the vernacular of other building types. They are based on the domestic vernacular of the countryside, although much of the comment could be applied to urban vernacular, and they follow the sequence most often adopted in the study of actual examples, both extensively in field surveys and intensively in measured drawing.

Walling materials are divided in the first chapter between mass construction of stone, brick, earth, or combinations and variations of these materials, and frame construction based on timber. Frame construction is further divided between half timber work with exposed framing members and infill panels of wattle and daub or brick, and the various cladding materials, tile, plaster, etc., which have been used to conceal the frame. In the second chapter, roofing problems are shown to vary according to the constructional system adopted, the roofing shape – chosen according to plan shape, sectional form, or the dictates of fashion – and roofing materials, chosen, mainly, according to local availability. In this chapter the projections from the roof – chimneys and dormers – are briefly noted. A chapter on plan and sectional form takes one into the house but also shows how the internal arrangements of these simple buildings are often revealed on the exterior. In spite of the pitfalls which hamper classification, some simple groupings have been suggested and there is a note on the developments in the design of staircases as multistorey construction became normal even at the lower social levels. Then a chapter on architectural details – windows, doors, external and internal ornament – shows how vernacular designs were enlivened by decoration, crude and old fashioned though it so often might be. Some general indications of place and time for the various characteristics have been given.

The next chapter extends the study to the buildings of the farmstead. The domestic vernacular of the countryside was, of course, only one component in the range of buildings which formed the setting for the intricately organized but traditionally-based society of the countryside, and recently some attention has been paid to the range of other buildings which made up the farmstead. In this chapter they have been considered as separate building types and no separate mention has been made of walling, roofing, and architectural detail which usually followed domestic precedent.

A further chapter combines some brief comments on urban vernacular and minor industrial vernacular which eventually coalesced in the terraces of industrial workers' houses which represented the last trace of vernacular architecture and which marked the change from a rural to an urban economy. The domestic vernacular of the towns has suffered more than that of the countryside from the alterations and extensions of the 19C. and it has been comparatively little studied, but redevelopment is revealing many unsuspected remains and the conservation movement is emphasizing their significance so that the balance is being redressed. The effects of early industrial developments on house design, few at first but considerable later, are now being recognized and some examples are illustrated. The developments in design of workers' houses have been ignored as long as we have been obsessed by their ugliness or their lack of those amenities which we now, a hundred years later, consider essential, but now that they are so rapidly being demolished it is suggested that they be recorded before they are forgotten.

In the concluding chapter, some attempt is made to give comparative material in the form of distribution maps and time scales. This is no more than an attempt, for too little information is at present available on a national basis, and while a good deal of material has become available for various regions the lack of standardized procedure means that comparisons cannot be carried very far. The great intricacy of the many factors which have affected vernacular architecture in this country makes the presentation of comparative material as difficult as it is important. A note on American Vernacular may remind the British reader that for a short time some of our vernacular regions were to be found across the Atlantic, and it may inform the American reader of the considerable work which has been done on this side since his standard works were written. Finally, a brief reference to the Vernacular Revival in British domestic architecture around the turn of the 19C. acknowledges the significance of this thread, and, therefore, indirectly, the whole pattern of vernacular architecture in the development of the Modern Movement.

Recent developments in the study of vernacular architecture in Scotland are acknowledged through a note on regional characteristics of this part of Britain.

Appendices suggest three ways in which the further study of vernacular architecture may be conducted. The subject is too extensive, and the rate at which examples are disappearing too rapid, for the very few professionals to cope alone. Most of our information on vernacular architecture has been collected, analysed, compared, and published by amateurs, spending leisure hours in furthering their own understanding of the countryside in which they lived and worked. This little handbook serves only to extend and assist the greater numbers who are now so desperately needed.

Initial Example

This suggests items to be observed in sequence in analysing an example of vernacular architecture.

(*Opposite*)
a. Walling material, shape, coursing, jointing, finish.
b. Roofing shape.
c. Detail at verge.
d. Detail at eaves.
e. Material, method of laying.
f. Ridge.
g. Chimney position.
h. Water tabling, etc.
i. Dormers, position, shape, roofing, walling material.
j. Plan form.
k. Sectional form.
l. Staircase provision.
m. Window shape.
n. Window frames.
o. Door shape.
p. Door details.
q. Relationship between farm buildings and farm-house.
r. Use of farm buildings.

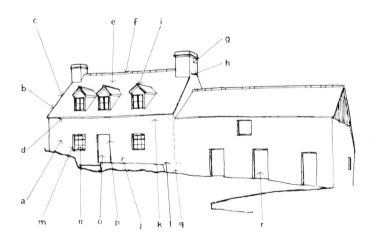

1. WALLING: CONSTRUCTION AND MATERIALS

General

More than any other single component, the choice of walling material establishes the character of an example of vernacular architecture. It is the wide range of walling materials available and the intricacy of their distribution which gives the unique variety to vernacular construction in England and Wales.

With choice of walling material there is related the choice of structural system, though, as we shall see, the two are not necessarily directly related. Broadly speaking there were two structural systems available to the designer: mass construction and frame construction. In the former, the loads of roof and floors were carried to foundations by means of walls which also provided the weather protective envelope to the activities carried on within the building. In the latter, the loads of roofs and floors were carried by a frame which concentrated these loads until they were redistributed by the foundation; the weather protective envelope was non-loadbearing (though it might carry its own weight), and could be independent of the frame (though sometimes it filled spaces between the members of the frame). Both mass walling and frame construction have been used at one time or another over virtually the whole country and, even at the present day, it is not certain that one or the other has become the inevitable choice in domestic construction.

Materials used for mass construction included stone, flint, cobble, brick and earth. Of these, only earth produces a homogeneous mass; all the others are jointed and rely on the skill with which the individual pieces have been put together, and the suitability of the jointing material as well as the quality of the basic material, for stability and weather excluding properties. The succeeding pages examine briefly the characteristics of walling employing these various materials.

The material used for frame construction was almost invariably timber; there are very few examples in which iron has been used in vernacular building. Timber frame construction may follow the box-frame or the cruck-frame schools of carpentry, and the problems of distinction between these two schools will be noted. Buildings of box-frame construction may have panels of wattle and daub, exposing the structural and non-structural timber, or the frame may be entirely concealed behind a cladding of plain tiles, mathematical tiles, weatherboard, or lath and plaster; alternatively the panel may be brick filled. Buildings of cruck-frame construction may have timber framed walls – in which case they are difficult to distinguish externally from box-framed buildings – or they may have walls of some material normally associated with mass construction: stone, brick, flint, cobble, or earth, when they would outwardly be indistinguishable from buildings entirely of mass construction.

As a rule, the walling materials used in vernacular construction were exposed in their natural state, but for reasons of weather protection or fashion they were often concealed. Thus, both wattle and daub panels, lath and plaster cladding and earthen walls were lime-washed, and poor quality masonry was often rendered and lime-washed, while, especially during the early 19C., buildings of any material might be stuccoed and painted in order to meet the demands of the prevailing architectural fashions.

Walling Materials – mass walling

Setting aside for a moment earthen construction, which presented its own special difficulties, the problem of achieving stability in walls made of separate pieces of materials – stone or brick – was one which must have been ever-present in the minds of the vernacular builders, and governed to a large extent their techniques of construction.

Stability of foundations was not usually a serious matter for the quite small low buildings erected by mass constructional methods, but as an aid to foundational stability as well, perhaps, as a survival from a previous form of construction, the use of large rounded boulders, especially in areas of morainic deposit, was common at the base of mass walled buildings.

Collapse by outward buckling of the walls in section was avoided with the aid of heavy floor beams which tied opposite walls together, and this may be one reason why such heavy beams were used. Outward pressure on the top of the wall was countered by the use of heavy tie beams, self-balancing roof members triangulated to transmit loads vertically down the walls, or by transferring roof loads as far down the wall as possible.

There was an equal danger of collapse by outward buckling of the wall on plan. This was countered by introducing cross walls to help divide a long narrow plan into squarish self-buttressing cells and, sometimes, by the use of horizontal timbers bonded into the coursing of the walls as reinforcement. Where brick walling succeeded timber framing this particular danger was not always recognized, and, having the benefit neither of the interaction of a framed structure nor the internal buttressing of a properly organized mass construction, brick walls either bellied out or were tied back with the aid of iron rods and plates.

The strength of a mass-constructed wall being reduced by every opening, there was a limit to the number, size and proportions of window openings. This was in contrast to frame construction where, in theory, every panel could be as conveniently transparent as opaque. Normally, therefore, window openings in mass walls were few and narrow. But where good quality stone, confident masons, and architectural fashion came together, long tall ranges of mullioned and transomed windows might be displayed.

However adequate the general precautions against collapse, the strength of a mass wall depended on the concerted action of its individual members. Good quality stone, which falls naturally into block shapes, presented fewest problems, and walls of, say, millstone grit, permian sandstone or oolitic limestone could be comparatively slender in section. Poorer quality stone, such as clunch, would need reinforcement by use of dressings or lacing courses of better quality material. Large stones, such as Cornish granite, presented such problems in bonding and jointing that a thick wall was unavoidable. Small rounded stones such as cobbles, pebbles and flints were so difficult to bond satisfactorily that they were bedded in deep clay and held together with the aid of frequent horizontal lacing courses and reinforced quoins and jambs. Even if bonding problems could be overcome there was the problem of jointing to be solved. Compact or irregular stones required thick joints and, until lime for mortar became cheap and plentiful, these joints were made simply of earth or clay. In extreme examples one might wonder whether a wall was made of cobbles bedded in earth or of earth mixed with cobbles, or indeed whether a stone wall had been laid with dry joints or whether leaching of clay had led to an effect of dry walling.

Monolithic earthen walls presented their own problems of stability and erection, and generally low height, wide walls, small cubic compartments, and narrow openings are characteristic of this form of mass construction.

Stone: Irregular Types

The following notes refer to walls of the tough, irregular masonry most commonly found in vernacular construction.

At the base of a wall the heaviest stones were used, and these were often boulders of such enormous size that one wonders how they were manoeuvred by hand into position. It seems likely that in many cases these stones acted originally as a plinth to walls of timber or clay and may have survived more than one reconstruction of a building. The main wall would be composed of undressed field stones, quarry faced stones, or straight cut stones, in each case obtained from the ground close by the building under erection. The walls were usually rather less than two feet thick and depended on the bond obtained by overlapping the tails of pieces of irregular depth which backed into the wall from its surfaces; bonding or 'through' stones were placed at intervals to run right through the wall, though in parts of the Northern Pennines they projected beyond the wall face as a series of ledges. The interior of the wall was normally packed with small loose pieces of waste stone. Joints were usually made as horizontal as the nature of the stone permitted, though a 'watershot' technique, in which stones were bedded to slope towards the outer face of the wall, may be found in the Lake District. A somewhat similar technique is found in the Pennines, especially on the western slopes, where the surface is composed of receding facets of each stone, rather like weatherboarding upside down. Drystone walling, in which no bedding or pointing material is used, was very rarely used in buildings, though normal for stone field walls.

While the local stone was used for wall construction as a matter of course, superior stone or brick was often used for bonding purposes, as lacing courses at intervals up the wall, for quoins, and as dressings to doors and windows. Such superior material might be carried for several miles across geological boundaries. Even in the general walling, more than one type of stone might be used if locally available, and sometimes bizarre polychromatic effects were the result.

In many parts of the country, irregular stones were bedded in clay, as revealed when walls of such material fall into ruin. Sometimes the clay was leached away by rain water penetrating the outer skin of the wall even to such an extent that the construction appears to be that of drystone walling. Where available at reasonable cost lime mortar was used for bedding. Such mortar was locally made of limestone or chalk or sea shells crushed and burnt to produce quicklime which was taken, carefully protected from damp or rain water, to the building site where it was slaked and in due course mixed with sand to produce the mortar. Whatever the bedding or jointing mortar, rubble walls were pointed with lime mortar wherever feasible. The pointing was usually finished flush with the surface of the stone; projecting ribbon mortar as often seen in restoration work is not traditional.

(*Opposite*)
SHAPE: Much of the character of a stone wall comes from the shape of the individual pieces of which it is composed. Thus one may contrast the compact, irregular types, e.g. (*a*) Kentish Rag, the elongated irregular types, e.g. (*b*) Mountain Limestone, the hard, thin, slaty types, e.g. (*c*) Lake District Slate, and the quarry faced millstone grit blocks (*d*) of the Yorkshire

Pennines, as well as many others.

COURSING: Irregular 'rubble' may be built entirely uncoursed (e) i.e. without any continuous horizontal joints; built to courses, (g) i.e. brought to a level joint at regular vertical intervals; snecked, (f) i.e. with a regular joint interrupted at intervals; or coursed, (h) i.e. with every horizontal joint continuous.

QUOINS: During the erection process, careful attention was paid to the corners of a building which may be raised by a more skilled craftsman, the general walling between being done by the less skilled. In most masonry techniques the cornerstones, or quoins, are bigger and better finished than the rest, (i) and may be further emphasized (j).

JOINTING: Irregular stones have wide joints which have originally or later been so pointed with lime mortar as to spread over the surface of the wall (k). Sometimes little stones were pushed into the joints as 'galletting' (l). Where a bedding material was unprotected by pointing it would be leached away by rain water to give the effect of a 'dry joint' (m).

RENDERING: To give weather protection or as an improvement to inferior stone, lime-sand rendering was sometimes used (n). This was trowelled to a rough surface or was dashed with pebbles, or was whitewashed. In some districts whitewash applied directly to the stone built up year by year to give an effect of rendering (o).

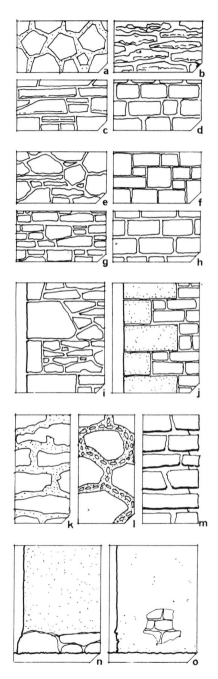

Stone: Regular Types

Although the vast majority of stone-walled vernacular buildings are clearly made of different sorts of rubble, the use of ashlar was not unknown at the vernacular level, and tended to develop from the use of squared coursed rubble for the superior parts of a building.

In ashlar work, regularity and high quality of finish are characteristic, and, where the designers of vernacular buildings wished to present a show to the world, the ashlar might well be used for the front wall of a house. But such a show was confined to the surface. The ashlar itself was backed by rubble or brick, and the end walls, even when exposed to public view, were nearly always in an inferior technique, either rubble masonry or brick. The rear wall of a house was always in the poorest material, and showed the crudest technique of building construction.

As well as in coursing, jointing and selection of stones, ashlar masonry was distinguished by the degree of surface dressing given by the mason in contrast to the natural or crudely hammered surface to rubble used by the waller. The use of mason's tools in vernacular work has not been properly investigated as yet, but it seems plain that the drafted margins, picked, combed, and rubbed work of superior masons were adopted, after an appropriate time lag, at the humbler levels.

Even where the main body of the wall was in rubble, dressed stone was often used for the significant parts of a wall. In millstone grit, red sandstone, and oolitic limestone districts especially, dressings, worked sometimes to a fine finish, were quite normal even in vernacular buildings.

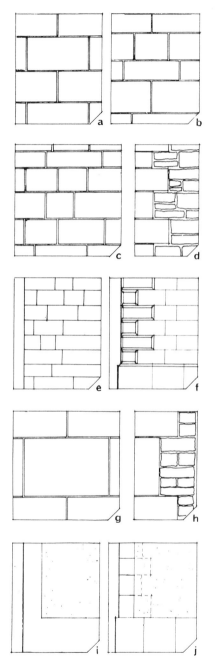

SHAPE: Stone being a natural rather than an artificial material even the ashlar work of vernacular building involved irregularities. Where each course was of uniform height the stones would vary in length (*a*), and both length of stone and height of course could vary without substantially affecting the richness of appearance (*b*).

COURSING: Ashlar work was normally coursed, though snecked walling could be of ashlar quality. Sometimes courses were of an even height but more often they varied in height in such a way as to diminish towards the top of the wall (*c*).

Ashlar dressings to a rubble wall gave a key to the coursing (*d*).

QUOINS, ETC.: As the individual pieces of ashlar masonry were carefully squared it was not always considered necessary to take extra precautions at the corners (*e*). However quoins were stressed where the general walling was of small stones or where architectural fashion demanded. Projections, plinths and string courses were used for similar reasons (*f*).

JOINTING: Fine jointing was customary in ashlar work (*g*), even though the ashlar surface was bonded into a more crudely jointed rubble backing (*h*).

FINISHES: Stucco, a fine smooth faced plaster, was the ashlar equivalent to rendering on rubble masonry. It was, of course, applied to inferior stone, but the intended effect was presumably that of ashlar and, indeed, imitation joint lines were sometimes incised (*i*). Dressings were modelled in stucco or were in superior masonry with stucco applied to the general wall surface (*j*).

43

Cobbles and Pebbles

The following notes refer to the use of cobbles – rounded stones picked from river beds or fields on the Boulder Clay – and pebbles – small rounded stones, sea-worn, and picked up from the shore. Techniques of use are generally similar to those of unworked flint, though the geological origin of the material is quite different.

Both cobbles and pebbles can only be used for building purposes with great difficulty. Cobbled walls are often rendered and whitewashed so as to be almost indistinguishable from similarly finished walls of stone or clay. Pebbled walls, composed of a material so tiny in scale but deep in texture, give quite exotic effects. In both cases some other material is necessary for dressings to door and window, and desirable at the corners.

Both materials tend to be seen on late and humble examples of vernacular building, but cobbled walls were often used at the side and rear of buildings in which the front wall was of brick or unpainted stone, while pebbled walls may be found as an affectation giving character to a cottage ornée.

44

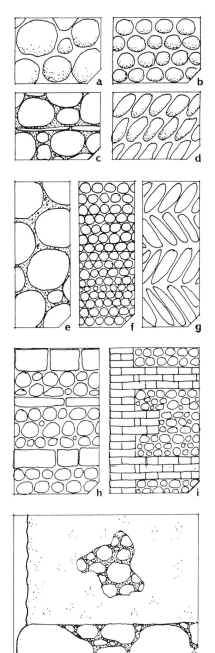

SHAPE: Essentially rounded, the material having been worn by ice action, by water action in the upper reaches of rivers or by sea and tidal action on beaches, including the inland remainders of former beaches. Pebbles are usually less than 3 in. in diameter (b), cobbles between about 3 in. and 9 in. in diameter (a). Generally the materials are globular but they may be flattened (c) and egg-shaped (d).

COURSING AND JOINTING: Cobbles were often laid uncoursed, relying on clay bedding to maintain stability (e). Pebbles, being more uniform in size, were usually laid in courses (f). Elongated pebbles or cobbles may be laid in diagonal or chevron pattern (g).

REINFORCEMENT: Surviving examples of both cobble and pebble walling tend to be late, and reinforcement at quoins, jambs, and by lacing courses will usually be found to be of brick (i). However, cobbles are also found with bands of other stones and walls may be laid in alternate courses of cobble and stone (h).

RENDERING, ETC.: Because of the poor appearance of a cobbled wall, and the difficulty in preventing loss of the jointing material, rendering is quite common (j). Seashore pebbles, both on the Sussex and Norfolk coast, have been tarred as a weather protective measure. The irregular surface modelling and the soft corners of unreinforced cobbles or pebbles help to distinguish such walls when rendered.

Walling Materials: Flint

Flints are irregularly shaped nodules of silica, found in gravel beds, usually from the upper and middle layers of chalk formations. Like pebbles and cobbles they can only be used with great difficulty for building purposes but, nevertheless, in the absence of other walling materials, they have been quite widely used in South and East England.

Taken straight from the ground, the egg-shaped flints were laid precariously in courses, the outer surface of the wall being brought to a reasonably fair face by plentiful use of mortar and with galletting of small chips of flint set in the joints, the inner ends of the flints being allowed to tail into the wall. More commonly the flints were split to give a fairly flat outer surface to the wall, though still with wide joints. Split flints could be further chipped to give a flat, square end, usually about four inches across. In both cases the broken surface of the flint, initially black, developed a white 'rind'.

Although flint can be used without reinforcement to a considerable height – as church towers, both round and square, in East Anglia will bear witness – the material is not really suitable for square corners, e.g. for door and window jambs in small scale vernacular building, and it is most commonly found reinforced with other building materials.

Many people find flint used alone rather drab, but when used in combination with other materials the effect may be highly decorative. At a superior level, as in the well-known Gatehouse of St. Osyth's Priory, Essex, the combination of flint and limestone can be quite spectacular, but even in humble work, the stripes and chequer patterns of flint, brick, and limestone are quite fascinating.

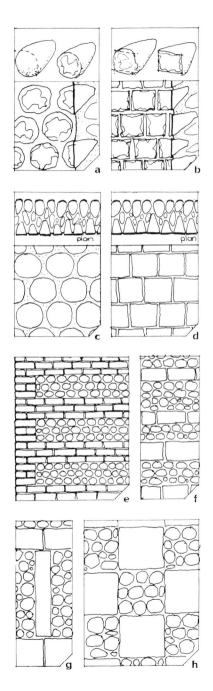

SHAPE: The flints used in walling are rather like a series of flat-topped teeth, each with a root tailing into the wall (*a*). In ordinary flint walling, the exposed ends are round and irregular on surface, in knapped flint work they are square and smooth surfaced (*b*).

JOINTING: This varies between ordinary and knapped flint work. In both varieties the flints are laid in courses, but in the former there are wide joints between the rounded flints (*c*), whereas in the latter, joints are thin, forming a fine net effect over the black wall surface (*d*).

REINFORCEMENT: To help form square corners, brick or stone was used at quoins and at the jambs of door and window. These reinforcing materials were block bonded into the flint (*e*). Horizontal lacing courses of brick or stone ran right through the flint walls at a vertical interval varying from about one to three feet (*e* and *f*).

PATTERN: As well as the overall pattern of flint and joint, and the emphasis given by dressings and lacing courses, a chequer board pattern of alternate panels of stone and flint may sometimes be seen (*h*). In superior work a tracery of thin limestone was combined with the flint (*g*).

47

Brick Walling

Bricks had been used in the Eastern counties as a walling material for superior buildings during the Middle Ages, but came into use for vernacular buildings during the periods of Great Rebuilding in the 16C. and 17C. The use of brick spread throughout the areas formerly dominated by timber frame construction and, in spite of the Brick Taxes which were applied with varying degrees of severity from 1784 until 1850, brick had become the universal building material in England and Wales by the second half of the 19C.

The use of bricks had become fashionable in polite architecture towards the end of the 16C. and this undoubtedly helped to popularize the material at the vernacular level. As well as encouraging new construction in brickwork, fashion led to the use of bricks as false fronts or in total encasement of timber framed buildings. The disastrous fires in towns and villages, culminating in the Great Fire of London, gave a further impetus to the use of this fire-resistant material.

A further advantage of brickwork over other forms of wall construction was the way in which decorative effects could be obtained comparatively cheaply. These included surface patterns, from the use of differently coloured bricks, and surface modelling, as in the imitation of classical details and string courses in brickwork. Moulded bricks and terra-cotta came into use during the 18C. while skilled craftsmen cut, carved, and rubbed bricks to produce delicately modelled forms.

Where stone traditions were strong, bricks were used only for general walling, the dressing to quoins, windows and doors being of masonry. During the first half of the 19C. when exposed brickwork had become less fashionable, the use of stucco in general imitation of stone meant that the decorative qualities of bricks were temporarily neglected. Nevertheless, in the period immediately before the general eclipse of vernacular architecture, brickwork enjoyed a renaissance which has left many charming examples of this building material to be enjoyed.

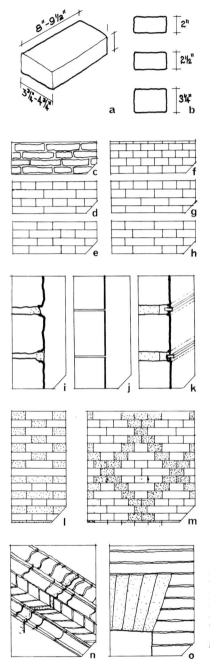

SHAPE: Brickwork shows some variation in size and proportion when used in vernacular buildings. Early and inferior bricks were irregular in shape and size. Even after length and breadth had become standardized (*a*) height varied to reach a maximum during the Brick Tax period and again in the Midlands and North during the 19C. (*b*).

BONDING: Early and inferior brickwork showed no recognizable bond (*c*). Then English Bond (*d*) included variations in which one course of headers matched three or five courses of stretchers (*g*). The later and more decorative Flemish Bond (*e*) was modified to three or five stretchers to each header (*h*). Occasionally header bond (*f*), with each brick exposing its head, was used for display.

JOINTING: As in masonry the more irregular the material the thicker the joint. Thus, early, roughly shaped bricks required wide joints whereas the precise, machine made bricks of the 19C. showed very thin joints (*j*). As a decoration, tuck pointing gave the illusion of fine joints to coarse brickwork (*k*).

PATTERN: Different brick earths and different degrees of firing produced decorative effects. Among the most popular was the use of headers, vitrified by special firing to a metallic purple colour to form chequerboard, geometrical, diaper, or lettered pattern (*l* and *m*).

MOULDED AND GAUGED WORK: Bricks were moulded to crude classical forms (*n*) but the skilful bricklayer preferred rubbed and gauged work (*o*).

49

Brick Walling (continued)

Brickwork Economy

The period of the Brick Taxes coincided with a wave of cottage building and various bonds were used which economized in bricks through the formation of a sort of cavity wall. The most common was Rat Trap Bond, which was like Flemish Bond except that the bricks were laid on edge rather than on bed. A wall 9 in. thick had a cavity 3 in. wide between outer and inner leaves of brickwork, each 3 in. thick. Fewer bricks were needed than in a solid wall of similar height; stability was adequate for the relatively low walls and minimal loads of a cottage; some benefit in heat insulation may have been obtained; but as the cavity was bridged by each header the walls were just as vulnerable to rising damp and driving rain as solid 9 in. walls.

Brickwork Openings

The problem of spanning door and window openings exercised the bricklayer as well as the mason and solutions were generally similar except that the standard-sized bricks made arches of large radius fairly easy to construct. The simplest and crudest was the rough brick segmental arch in which the bricks were uncut and the taper was confined to the joints. Segmental arches of rubbed or purpose-made voussoirs were also fairly easy to produce. The cambered arch which was curved at the bottom but flat at the top required much more skill and usually involved rubbed and gauged work with special bricks of a different colour from those of the main wall. Alternatively, in many vernacular buildings, windows and door openings had no outer arch or lintel, the wall being carried over a stout window frame.

Brickwork Decoration

The skilled bricklayer working on polite architecture could perform the wonders of his craft but at the vernacular level quite simple devices were effective enough.

Brick Ties

It is clear from bulging or leaning walls in old brick buildings that some bricklayers were not clear on the need for adequate buttressing of external walls by internal partitions, and tie rods were often used in order to keep the most vulnerable parts of brick walls in position. Tie rods usually ran from gable to gable and when tightened held the walls against wrought-iron tie plates.

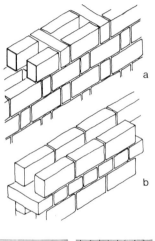

a. Rat Trap Bond showing outer and inner leaves of bricks laid on edge and with cavity in between. The header bricks, also laid on edge, run right through the wall and bond the two leaves together.
b. Dearne's Bond: a variation of English Bond in which the stretcher courses are laid on edge, producing a cavity are laid on edge, producing a cavity and economizing in bricks. *c*. Rough brick segmental arch with tapered mortar joints. *d*. Segmental arch of tapered bricks; a timber lintel behind would carry most of the loads on the wall. *e*. Cambered arch of rubbed bricks. *f*. Opening spanned by a wooden lintel.

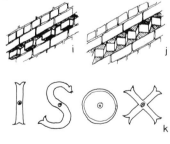

g. Soldier 'arch' of bricks on edge: a crude device in which the bricks carry little of the load on the wall. *h*. Soldier arch of bricks on end: rather less crude and gaining some structural benefit from the friction of bricks and their joints. *i*. Dentilation in which header bricks project about 2 in. *j*. Dog-tooth brickwork: bricks laid diagonally and projecting to carry brick courses above. *k*. Four examples of tie plates such as may be seen on the gables of brick buildings. The S shape was sometimes given the head and tail of a snake.

Walling Materials: Earth, Clay, etc.

The use of turf, clay, mud, cob, wychert and other earthen materials available on the surface of a building site was formerly a good deal more widespread than is sometimes imagined, while the evidence of place and occupation names suggests that the practice may well have been even more widespread than surviving examples would indicate – by the nature of the material, archaeological evidence is likely to be scarce.

Materials and processes of erection varied with locality, but all gave walls which were capable, on proper consolidation, of supporting the loads imposed by vernacular buildings. However, a cruck-frame was usually used with the quick process. The following techniques may be distinguished:

1. *Sods or turf* – surface close cropped, sods cut two to six inches depth, three feet by two feet size, laid in courses on plinth of stones, single storey height, sometimes loose stones on top to take roof timbers. Reinforcement of timber posts at corners, and along walls, sometimes those related to roof construction. Finish by paring with hay knife.

2. *Clay and straw mix, used without moulds* – clay, incorporating pebbles, chalk, etc., as available locally was moistened, mixed with chopped straw, and kneaded to a glue-like consistency. Walls were raised by either (a) *slow process* (an interval between each lift); or (b) *quick process* (a wall of thin courses raised in one operation).

3. *Earth or clay used with moulds* – timber or wattle shuttering filled either with (a) loose dry earth, poured and rammed; or (b) wet clay.

4. *Clay blocks* (cf. adobe) – large blocks of clay (e.g. 6 in. by 18 in. by 9 in.) were moulded, left to dry naturally, then laid with clay mortar. At first sight it is difficult to distinguish earth-walled buildings from those built of other materials and then rendered or whitewashed.

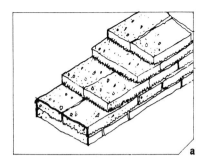

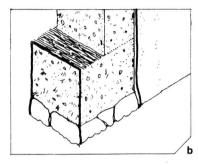

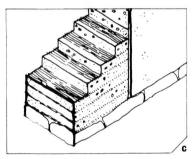

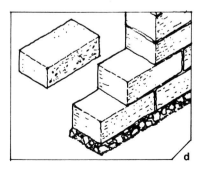

SODS OR TURF: There is little trace of this technique in England or Wales, though it was formerly widespread in parts of Scotland and Ireland. Walls were thick, irregular, and required protection unless used for purely temporary shelters (a).

SLOW PROCESS: Where the weather-protective coating of plaster has fallen away, the joint lines between each 'lift' can clearly be seen. Usually the earth includes plenty of pebbles, and chopped straw was used as horizontal reinforcement and to reduce cracking on drying out. The diagram (b) shows a boulder plinth and straw used as a thin layer between each lift as well as mixed with the clay.

QUICK PROCESS: This is distinguished by the use of thin layers of clay-like material interspersed with straw. Although originally laid horizontally the layers have usually drooped and deformed on drying out (c).

CLAY LUMP: This technique has not been widely used in England and Wales, though examples survive in parts of Norfolk, Suffolk, and Cambridgeshire. The blocks were bonded and laid in courses exactly like bricks even though considerably larger in size (d).

Timber Frame Walling

There are three main types of timber-based wall construction which have been commonly used in Europe: horizontal log, in which the wall was composed of solid timbers laid one on top of the other and jointed at the corners; post and plank, in which the wall consisted of a series of heavy planks slotted between even heavier posts; and timber frame, in which the structural frame was separate from the weather protective part of the wall. As far as is known, there are no examples of the first two techniques in Great Britain.

The structural distinction between cruck- and box-frame timber construction has already been mentioned; in the former, roof loads were transmitted by means of inclined crucks to the ground, in the latter they were taken on framed walls. The existence of hybrid forms of construction, and the problems which arise when a timber roof is carried on a wall of some other material, tend to obscure detailed differences in the technique, but for most purposes the difference is clear enough.

It appears that the process of erection was radically different in the two versions of timber frame. In cruck construction the A-frames were assembled on the ground, then 'reared' one by one into a vertical position so that the ridge purlin, side purlins, and wall plates could be dropped into their sockets, and tie the frames together. In box-frame construction it appears that in most cases the posts were erected separately, being propped into position either by temporary stays or by permanent diagonal braces; next, the wall plates were dropped onto the top of each post, and finally the tie beam was dropped into position, simultaneously locking post and wall plates. The intermediate studs were placed piece by piece at the same time. There were some variations in this practice as, for instance, where a 'bent' of posts and tie beams was reared, cruck fashion, or where a whole wall was framed on the ground and then reared, but these were not common.

As an aid to identification of joints, carpenters' marks were used. These appear to have varied with time and place, but were based either on a series of Roman numerals made with a chisel, or a series of symbols made with a gouge and scratched with the point of a chisel. Sometimes all the joints on each truss were separately marked; alternatively each joint was given a number in sequence from one end of the building to the other. Presumably, both types of marking related to the erection process.

Oak was the timber predominantly used for structural purposes, though elm and imported softwoods came into increasing use. There was a general tendency to use lighter timbers as carpentry techniques improved and supplies of suitable timber diminished. In the cruck-frame tradition, this led to the use of very poor and spindly members, especially in remote areas where cruck trusses were ancillary to other load bearing construction. In the box-frame tradition, technical improvement led to the eventual elimination of the distinction between load bearing posts and non-load bearing studs so that a whole wall of members of approximately the same section acted as one. This development appears to have occurred first in the use of trussed partitions and party walls, but later spread to the external walls of small buildings. The availability of softwood timber, in uniform sections, and cheap machine-made nails meant that the elaborate joints of earlier timber framing techniques were no longer required. Two variations, platform framing and balloon framing, came into universal use in North America in the second half of the 19C., but platform framing, at least, remains in common use in this country for humble buildings such as garages and garden sheds.

One problem in the study of timber frame construction is the re-use of timber. Redundant joints and peg holes, often useful as a guide to lost members, may equally often refer to former use of a piece of timber in quite a different structural context.

Cruck-Truss and Box-Frame Construction

The distinction between cruck- and box-frame construction is not universally accepted, and the essential characteristics of cruck construction, its geographical spread, and the social status of this carpentry technique give cause for argument amongst the scholars of vernacular architecture. The problems are most acute in the cruck variants like the base-cruck (which seems like a pair of posts inclined at the top to take a collar), and the jointed cruck in which vertical post and inclined blade were joined together, sometimes with very little curve on post or blade.

Although they differ in detail, distribution maps on surviving cruck trusses show that the technique is not found in East or South-East England but is normal in Central and Northern England and most of Wales. If jointed crucks are excluded, then the West of England and the south-western counties of Wales are also excluded from the cruck province. Box-frame construction, unchallenged in the Eastern counties, is also found alongside cruck construction in the Midlands; even in the Northern and Western counties, box-frame construction was often chosen in preference to cruck for buildings in the town and buildings for superior uses, such as the tithe barn of a great religious house. Hybrid forms of construction are found alongside the two pure techniques in the Midland Belt.

We have seen that the development of box-frame construction has continued almost to the present day. Cruck construction, once assumed to be exclusively a medieval technique, is now seen to have a continuous development, in raised crucks and upper crucks until well into the 19C.

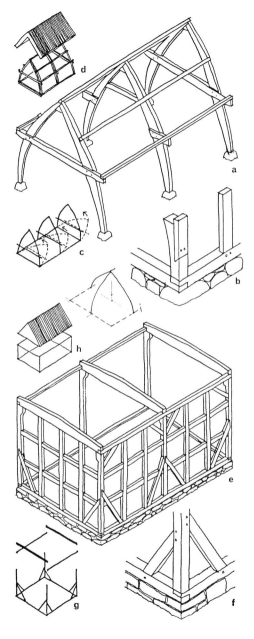

a. Diagram of cruck frame with two closed and one open truss.

b. Typical detail at corner showing cruck blade and wall post rising from a timber sill and stone plinth.

c. Rearing cruck trusses after assembly on the ground.

d. Roof covering in relation to cruck frame.

e. Diagram of box-frame two bays in length with posts and wall plates connected by tie beams and with a stud and rail infill wall.

f. Typical detail at corner showing post rising from a timber sill and supported by angle braces.

g. Diagram showing sequence of assembly.

h. Roof covering in relation to box-frame.

i. Half-cruck (end-cruck).

Timber Walling

We have seen that, with reservations, a general structural distinction between cruck- and box-frame carpentry may be made. But timber external walls of cruck based, box-frame based, or hybrid construction, concealing the pure structural form of the building, appear to have characteristics of their own, according to recent research.

A distinction has been made between three schools of timber frame wall carpentry: a western school, characterized by squarish panels, short straight braces between post and wall plate, and the development of decorative timber around the panels; an eastern school, characterized by tall narrow panels and the use of curved braces between sill and post; and a less precisely defined northern school, characterized mainly by the omission of a sill between wall posts. The explanation of the difference in technique is, as yet, as obscure as the explanation for choice between cruck and other forms of timber construction.

Multi-storey construction in timber presented its own problems. When long straight timbers of substantial section were available, the constructional problems could be overcome, though at the cost of considerable waste of timber. But on restricted urban sites, and making use of shorter lengths of timber, jettied construction was adopted and spread as a fashion throughout most of the country. In jettied construction, floor beams were cantilevered to provide a base for the wall of each upper storey; with the use of dragon beams at the corners, jettied walls could be carried around adjacent sides of a building. The many-storied, multi-jettied half-timbered building represented the greatest flourish of heavy timber-framed wall construction but its origin and thorough explanation is still one of the greatest conundrums of the subject.

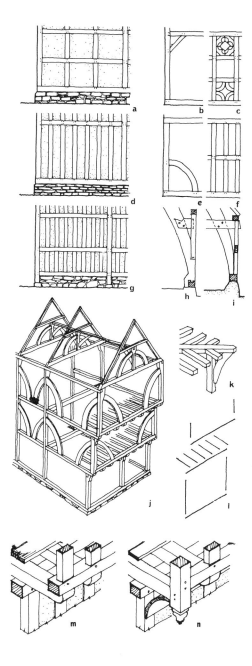

Western School
a. Square panels
b. Angle brace from post to wall plate.
c. Decorative members at corners.

Eastern School
d. Vertical panels.
e. Curved brace between post and sill.
f. Vertical panels with middle rail.

Northern School
g. Interrupted sill (*a* to *g*) after J. T. Smith) See also distribution map.
h. Wall post and cruck blade (after F. W. B. Charles).
i. Wall post and cruck blade (after Fox and Raglan).
j. Jettied construction, eastern England (after T. L. Marsden).
k. Dragon beam allowing heavy floor joists to project on two sides of a building.
l. Diagram showing sequence of erection of members of a jettied storey.
m, n. details of jetties.

Timber Walling: Wattle and Daub Infill

The material most commonly found as an infilling to the panels between the members of a timber frame wall was wattle and daub. In square panels, it was usual first to spring pointed staves between auger holes in an upper member and a slot in a lower to provide vertical bars, rather like the mullions of a window. These formed the warp between which a weft of pliable withies was woven in a basket weave pattern. On this wooden fabric a mixture of clay, dung, horsehair, etc., was daubed, and this was finished, inside and out, by a coat of plaster. As there might be decorative cusping or other patterns formed in the timber work, the shape of the panel would vary, but the technique was still followed.

Where, as in a barn, ventilation was more important than complete weather exclusion, then the daub and finish would be omitted. Where good quality timber was scarce the panels might be so large as to stretch like hurdles from post to post; then the daubing would be so thick as to make the technique more akin to a reinforced mud wall. It is possible, though evidence is as yet inadequate, that this form of infill preceded the division of timber walls into panels by means of studs and rails.

Other infill materials, such as thin stone slabs, tiles, and slate have been used, and when rendered are hard to distinguish from wattle and daub.

The contrasting black and white of pitch-coated timber and white-washed plaster gives the most spectacular results when this technique is used, but, except in the North Midlands, Cheshire, and Lancashire, a softer effect from naturally weathered oak and colour washed panels was more common.

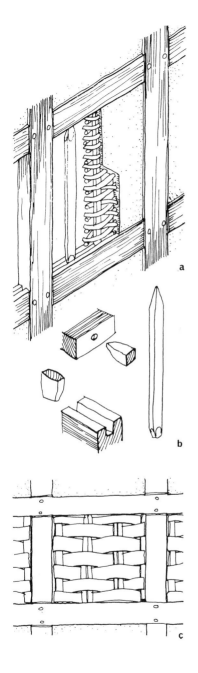

a. The cutaway isometric shows, diagrammatically, the vertical studs and horizontal rails joined to make a square panel. Staves sprung into the underside of one rail and slotted into the top of another form a base for woven wattles. The daub on both sides is finished with a thin plaster coating.

b. Here the shape of the staves, and details at top and bottom are indicated.

c. An undaubed panel is illustrated, typical of the ventilator panels used in the wall of timber-framed barns in Hereford and Shropshire. There are many local variations of size and weave used in such panels.

d. For tall narrow panels laths may be sprung into grooves in studs and daubed.

e. Alternative for tall panels; laths woven around short staves sprung between auger holes and short grooves in the studs.

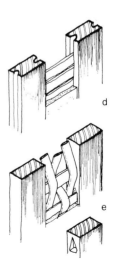

61

Timber Walling: Plain Tile Cladding

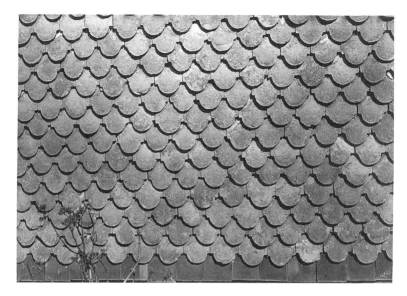

However pretty a half-timbered building might be, the thin panels of fragile wattle and daub were a poor weather protection, especially in exposed situations. When clay roofing tiles became cheap and easily available they were adopted as a cladding material over timber-framed walls.

The plain roofing tiles were hung on laths nailed to the wall timbers and other special tiles were moulded to cover the corners and jambs, or wooden cover moulds and architraves were used. Although the ordinary $10\frac{1}{2}$ in. by $6\frac{1}{2}$ in. roofing tile was most commonly used, other tiles with a shaped bottom edge were used to give decorative effects, and patterns were also derived from the use of differently coloured tiles. When tile cladding was added to existing buildings which had jettied upper floors, the opportunity was usually taken to build a new brick wall outside the lower framing timbers and in line with the tile hanging above.

Where tile hanging is carried down the face of a building this is usually an indication that the cladding was intended from the first. Indeed the material was an appropriate finish for the lightweight timber framing techniques which were being developed in South-Eastern England during the early 19C. It has recently enjoyed a renaissance through use as a cladding for timber-framed industrialized housing and as an alternative cladding to give variety in school construction.

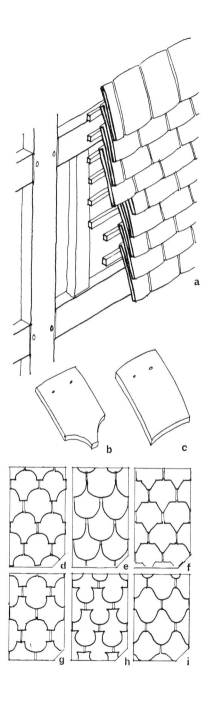

a. In the cutaway isometric, plain tiles are shown as a cladding to a heavy timber-framed wall. The tiles are hung on laths so as to give a triple lap, each tile covering two others. Where the members of the heavy frame were far apart intermediate studs are needed to help carry the laths. In light timber frame construction the closely spaced studs need no duplication.

b., c. Here shaped and plain tiles are illustrated. Hand-made tiles usually had a camber in both directions; this helped to cover irregularities in the wooden wall.

d., e., f., g., h., i. Various shaped tiles are illustrated. They could be combined together, as in *g*, or with plain tiles, or in alternating colours to give an almost infinite series of variations.

63

Timber Walling: Mathematical Tile Cladding

Mathematical tiles (otherwise known as brick tiles or wall tiles) are like vertically hung roofing tiles but are shaped in section to imitate the header or stretcher face of a brick. They were nailed to timber boarding or hung on laths nailed to a timber-framed wall, like plain tiles, but had joints pointed in mortar like bricks. They gave a convincing imitation of a brick wall, especially when appropriately moulded tiles were used at corners and jambs.

Introduced towards the middle of the 18C., mathematical tiles were used in towns and villages throughout the South Eastern counties of England until well into the 19C. They provided a cheap means of giving a fashionable appearance to a timber-framed building though were subject to the Brick Taxes. Usually the tiles were confined to the front elevation and, with plain tiles at the side and half timber at the rear of a building, the deception was not very serious. But when, in a town, only the front elevation was visible, the mathematical tiles were difficult to detect. At door and window openings, the usual details were replaced by imitations of stone dressings in painted wood or plaster or, not very convincingly, by scratching imitation voussoirs on the tiles. The natural red brick colour was usual, but greys, yellows, and even black, were also used.

Like plain tiles, mathematical tiles also served as the cladding for light timber-framed walls newly constructed in the early 19C., and they were used as a decorative covering to inferior materials such as flint or cobble.

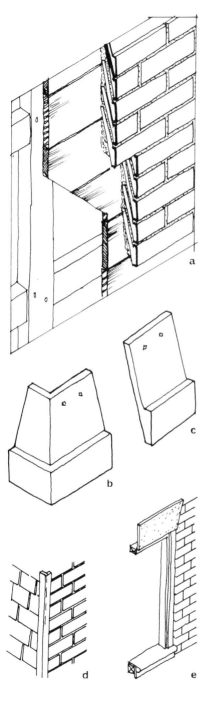

a. In the cutaway isometric, mathematical tiles are shown as a cladding to a heavy timber-framed wall. The section shows how each tile was moulded to present a brick-like face, the body of the tile being fitted behind the other tiles which provided the lap. The tiles were hung or nailed to laths spanning between frame and studs. Alternatively (and perhaps more commonly) butt-edged boarding was nailed to the timber frame and the tiles were bedded in mortar and nailed to the boarding.

b. Specially shaped tiles were sometimes used at corners to help maintain the bond, and so preserve the illusion of brickwork.

c. Narrow tiles used as 'closers' in bonding were also used.

d. Timber cover strips were used to conceal joints between the tiles and other materials.

e. The detail around windows usually shows the shallow depth of a wall clad with mathematical tiles. Here the imitation brick arched head is really of painted plaster and the architraves are of wood.

f. Alternative sections of tiles.

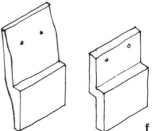

Timber Walling: Weatherboard Cladding

The earliest adaptation of English building practices to American conditions made by the East Anglian settlers in New England was the use of clapboard or weatherboard as a cladding to their timber-framed buildings. The technique was not unknown in this country, and surviving examples suggest that weatherboards had been pegged to the framed walls of barns and other farm buildings at least from the late 16C., and to timber-framed church towers earlier still. But the technique never seems to have been popular for domestic buildings until weatherboarding was adopted as one of the cladding materials for lightweight timber-framed construction in South-Eastern England towards the end of the 18C. Even then, use was practically confined to Cottages, and a few Small Houses, in domestic architecture, though the technique was popular for the timber-framed buildings for agriculture, transport and commerce.

Early weatherboarding was of oak or elm and was pegged to the timbers, but deal, nailed to studs, was used in the later phases. In this country, horizontal weatherboarding was customary, though vertical boarding with a cover strip was sometimes used and vertical boarding had been used for the church towers.

There are a few examples in this country of the use of planed and painted timber in imitation of ashlar masonry, a technique used on the front elevation of a house with weatherboarding elsewhere. It is a technique which was widely used in North America, and George Washington's house at Mount Vernon is a famous example.

66

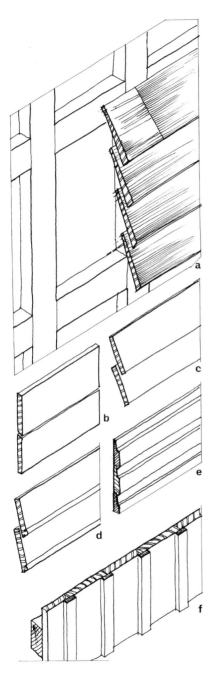

a. Weatherboards are shown here as a cladding to a timber-framed wall of fairly heavy section. The boards are shown as 'feather-edged' and with a single lap, each board covering one below. Usually it was not necessary to provide battens as the boards could span between posts or studs.

b. Butt-edged boarding.

c. Parallel-faced boards.

d. As a. but with beaded edges.

e. Lapped boards.

f. Vertical boards, nailed to rails and with cover strips to the vertical joints.

Timber Walling: Plaster and Pargetting as Cladding

An unbroken weather protective cladding has several potential advantages over the wattle and daub or tile claddings normally used with timber walled buildings. This became available with the widespread use of lime plaster on wooden lath. The lath and plaster could be plain, decorated only with a white or colour wash, or it could be moulded in one of the various forms known collectively as pargetting. Examples of decorative pargetting may be as early as the late 16C., though the technique was most popular in the second half of the 17C. and it fell out of favour after the middle of the 18C. At this time plain plaster cladding renewed its following and it continued to be associated with new and refurbished timber frame construction except in the North and the West Midlands, where 'magpie' or black and white work remained in favour.

Given adequate maintenance, properly applied lath and plaster will remain perfectly waterproof, but penetration of dampness from behind or through cracks will quickly lead to deterioration of the plaster and its key to the laths. Heavily moulded pargetting is vulnerable to the weather and soon loses its crisp outline; the simpler combed or incised panels are better preserved. Both techniques were more commonly used in the towns and larger villages than in hamlets or on isolated farm-houses. The period of greatest use of plain plaster cladding corresponds with the greatest popularity of smooth stucco renderings to rubble or brick walls, and, except for the general flatness which comes from the shallow window reveals of a timber-framed building it is difficult to distinguish the one form of construction from the other.

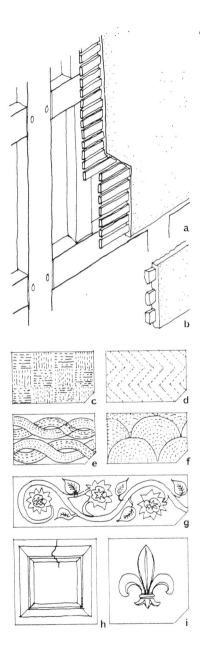

a. In the cutaway isometric the use of plaster on riven timber laths is illustrated. The laths were nailed, closely spaced, to the studs and any necessary intermediate members of a frame. Plaster, in two coats was then applied to the outside. There would be a separate lath and plaster interior lining. The illustration shows plaster cladding to an existing heavy timbered building, but the technique was also used with lightweight timber frame.

b. Detail of plaster and laths.

c. Basket weave combed pattern.

d. Herring-bone combed pattern.

e. Cable moulded and combed pattern.

f. Fan combed pattern.

g. Moulded pargetting, debased medieval pattern.

h. Moulded panel pargetting.

i. Fleur-de-lis motif in pargetting.

69

Other Cladding Materials

Occasionally roofing slates were used as a cladding to timber-framed buildings. They were cut as small slates then nailed to laths and so to the timber frame, and they often included decorative patterns. The technique was found in towns and villages of the South-West of England and is quite common across the Channel in Brittany. Slates were also used in North Wales and the Lake District as a weather-protective skin to stone walled buildings, especially to exposed gables.

A curious example, possibly unique, of a cladding to timber frame occurs in Kendal, Westmorland, where cast-iron plates appear to have been hung on to a timber frame. One of the plates carries the date 1853. The technique is related to the widespread practice in North America of the same period when cast-iron mouldings were used to give an imitation of Italianate masonry to timber-framed buildings.

Mud and Stud

A technique akin to conventional timber framing was used on humble buildings such as cottages and cowsheds at a fairly late date. A slender frame of rough timbers had walls made of staves thickly plastered with mud. Unlike half-timbering, the storey-height and bay-width panels were not divided by exposed studs and rails; unlike clay walling, the panels were only about 4 in. thick and reinforced by the staves; but sometimes, like plaster cladding the covering was carried over the structural frame. Examples are known in Lincolnshire and coastal Lancashire but the technique may have been more widely used.

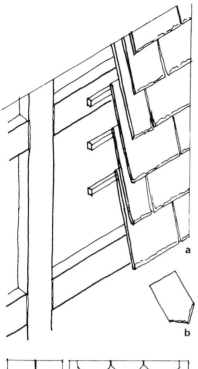

a. The isometric sketch shows the use of slates hung by nails on to laths spanning from post to post. The slates may have a single or double lap, according to the exposure of the situation.

b. Detail of a slate shaped at the bottom for use in decorative patterns.

c. Simple lozenge type pattern.

d. Composite pattern of slates.

e. Cast-iron panels applied to timber frame.

f. Framing for a two-bay mud and stud building.

g. Detail to show stave reinforcement for daubed mud.

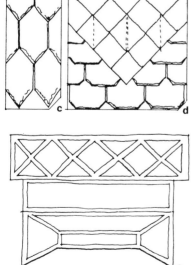

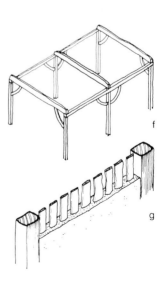

71

Timber Walling With Brick Nogging

Many black and white timber houses prove on closer inspection to have the panels between their timbers infilled not with wattle and daub but with whitewashed brickwork. It is difficult at first view to decide whether this was an original filling or a later replacement. If closer examination shows that the auger holes and slots for staves were included in the timber then obviously the bricks have replaced wattle and daub, but brick nogging is in fact quite an old established practice. Apart from its possible use in medieval town houses, examples are beginning to come to light in the villages. In two timber-framed houses near Lutterworth, for example, one has the date 1695 scratched into one of the infill bricks, the other has the initials I B D and the date 1712 picked out in patterned bricks. In both examples the dates are consistent with the general character of the house and its construction; earlier dates in Essex.

Brick nogging is most appropriate to square panels, but other materials, such as tiles, slate, and thin stone slabs, have been used in tall narrow panels. Bricks were arranged in herring-bone fashion, diagonally and vertically as well as in the more customary fashion.

The understanding that brick panels could help to carry some of the loads in a wall must surely have helped to change the attitude among carpenters towards thinking of the wall acting as a whole, rather than as a separate series of posts. It certainly accompanied a reduction in the amount of timber used in the walls.

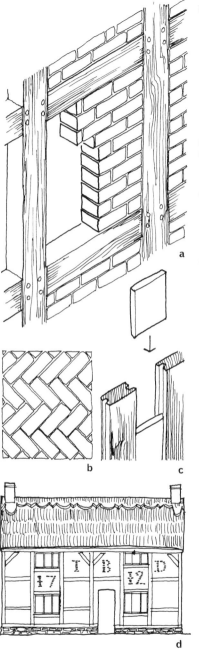

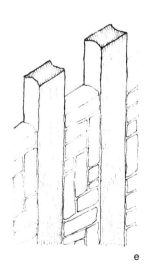

a. The isometric shows brickwork conventionally laid in courses as the infill to a heavy timber frame. Herring-bone brickwork was sometimes easier to fit into the panels as well as being more decorative. Brick-on-edge was used with lighter timber sections.

b. Herring-bone brick infill.

c. Stone or slate pieces in narrow panels between closely-spaced studs.

d. Elevation of an early 18C. timber-framed Small House with brick nogging infill, including initials and date picked out in coloured bricks.

e. Sketch of shaped studs for 16C. brick nogging (after J. McCann).

2. ROOFING: SHAPE, CONSTRUCTION AND MATERIALS

The intimate connection between roof and wall construction has already been discussed. Vernacular designers were constantly faced with the problem of choosing a sufficiently weatherproof covering and an appropriate form of roof construction to take it. Their choice was affected by the difficulty of relating suitable roof shapes to desired plan shapes and the increasing difficulty of achieving roof spans which were either greater than the length of available timber or which had to be constructed without obstructing the headroom in the rooms below. The record of their choice of roof covering is on external display. The history of roof construction is on view in open halls or repays exploration over plastered ceilings.

There are several basic distinctions which should be made, at the outset, before discussion of roof construction. In the first place, a roof may be *single*, i.e. consisting only of rafters (with various bracing members), or it may be *double*, i.e. consisting of rafters and purlins. Secondly, a roof may be divided into *bays* by *trusses*, or it may run uninterruptedly from end to end. (A double roof, for instance may consist of purlins spanning from wall to wall without intermediate support, or those purlins may be supported along their length by framed trusses of heavier timber. In such a case the purlin would normally be divided into separate lengths joined at the truss.) Thirdly, a roof may be considered as a *rafter roof*, a *butt purlin roof*, or a *through purlin roof*. In a rafter single roof each pair of rafters is either without triangulation or is triangulated separately from every other pair of rafters; in a rafter double roof each pair of rafters is supported by purlins, either directly or indirectly, as when a purlin supports the collar of each individually triangulated set of rafters. A butt purlin roof consists of a series of trusses between which span purlins which are butted (or, more correctly, tenoned) into the principal rafters of the truss. A through purlin roof – and most crucks have through purlins – consists of a series of trusses supporting purlins which either rest simply on top of the blades of the truss, or are trenched into those blades. Fourthly, there are some roofs which incorporate parts of various of these categories.

The exact basis of roof construction, especially during the medieval period, has still not been satisfactorily revealed in spite of the best efforts of both architects and historians.

There is obvious relevance in the separate cruck- and box-frame traditions of timber frame construction, but recent research has tended to blur rather than clarify distinction between the two, while also suggesting that techniques of wall construction seem to be distinct from those of roof construction. However, a fair understanding of what the carpenters thought they were doing may be gained by applying the observation that all members were thought to be acting in compression or were purely decorative, and that the medieval carpenters seemed to be preoccupied with the task of reducing unsupported spans.

The restrictions imposed by the various types of roof construction on plan shapes were only removed with the recent adoption of the flat roof. The simplest roof was that covering a rectangular plan, and the picturesque and irregular plans of some surviving buildings are the result of additions and subtraction rather than original intention. Roofs were, therefore, combinations of double pitch against double pitch. Roof construction also had some effect on sectional form. One obvious example is the use of the 'catslide' extension of the main roof over an outshut at side or end; another is the modification of roofs to light loft spaces. The choice of roof covering affected roof construction in that each material had its appropriate pitch, and the weight of a roofing material affected the required dimensions of roof timbers. The choice of roof covering also affected roof shape in that thatch and plain tiles, for instance, were easy to form into hips, whereas slate and pantiles were more appropriate to gabled roofs. Finally it is clear that, even at the vernacular level, fashion played its part, both locally in variations in decorative thatching (probably competitive) and nationally in the desire sometimes to hide a low-pitched slated roof behind a parapet in order to give the illusion of a flat roof.

Since the roof covering is especially vulnerable it will have been changed at least once in the lifetime of very many houses. Often the opportunity was taken to alter the roof construction or sectional form at the same time.

Roofing: Shape, Gable and Eaves Details

The actual shape of a roof varies basically according to membership of the hipped roof family or the gabled roof family. In the former the roof slopes in from all sides of the building; in the latter a pair of opposite walls continues up, above the eaves. There are several variations within the families; roofs begin as hips and end as gables and vice versa. Because of the special weather protection problems of a gable wall, various special details, e.g. 'tumbling-in' of brickwork, have been developed.

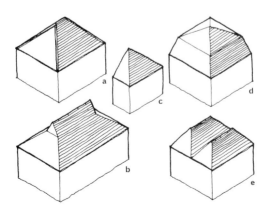

Hipped roof family
a. Hipped roof.
b. Gablet roof.
c. Hipped roof on a projection.
d. Hipped gambrel (mansard) roof.
e. Hipped M-shaped roof.

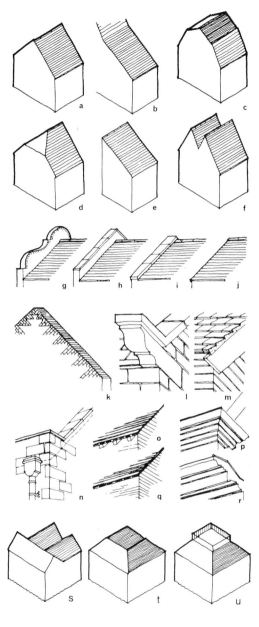

Gabled roof family
a. Gabled roof.
b. Gabled roof on a projection.
c. Gabled gambrel (mansard) roof.
d. Half-hipped roof.
e. Gabled single pitch roof.
f. Gabled M-shaped roof.

Some variations at the gable
g. 'Dutch' gable.
h. Parapet at gable.
i. Coping at gable.
j. Plain close verge.
k. 'Tumbling' in at gable.
l. 'Kneeler' forming a termination at the eaves of a parapet or coping.
m. Barge board.

Some variations at the eaves
n. Parapet at the eaves with rainwater head serving a concealed gutter.
o. Exposed rafters at eaves.
p. Cornice returned at gable.
q. Plain close eaves.
r. Wooden cornice serving as a gutter.

Roofing the double-pile plan
s. Two gables at rear.
t. Two hips at rear.
u. Hips with flat centre section (M-shaped, gambrel and gabled roofs were also commonly used).

Single- and Double-Rafter Roofs

Some of the common forms of single- and double-rafter roofs are illustrated. In this type of roof construction a ridge is uncommon; pairs of rafters were usually halved and pegged at the apex of the roof. Where the roof was carried on a thick wall, each rafter was usually triangulated at the foot by short members in the detail known as ashlaring. In rafter single roofs, the forest of rafters, collars, and braces often acted as studding for a ceiling of boards or plaster. In rafter double roofs such a ceiling is not often found, instead the exposed tie beam or arch braces may be decorated.

The most characteristic rafter double roof is the crown post roof in which a short post rises from the centre of a tie beam and carries a horizontal purlin or plate which in turn supports the collars of each individual set of rafters. The collar purlin was usually braced back to the crown post, and sometimes struts rise from the crown post to a collar.

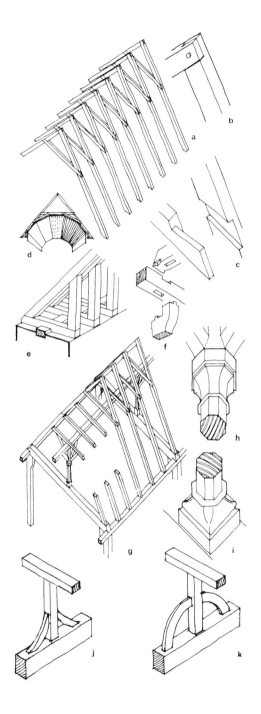

a. *Collar rafter single roof* showing each pair of rafters separately triangulated and the absence of ridge and side purlins.

b. Rafters halved and pegged together at the ridge.

c. Dovetail halved joint between collar and rafter.

d. Boarded ceiling giving the effect of a barrel vault.

e. Ashlaring at junction of rafters.

f. Junction between post, wall plate, and tie beam.

g. *Crown post rafter double roof* showing crown post rising from tie beam to support a collar purlin which in turn supports collars and rafters.

h. Crown post seen from below and showing the spread of the post to provide a seating for braces.

i. Crown post seen from above to show the base swelling to meet a tie beam.

j. Concave braces.

k. Convex braces.

79

Aisled Buildings

One way of increasing the useful floor area of a hall or barn was to add aisles on one or both sides and on one or both ends. Similarly, one way of spanning economically a given width of building was to introduce one or two sets of posts in order to reduce the unsupported span of roof beams. Some aisled cruck-framed buildings may be found, though aisles do not fit happily in the cruck tradition, but many aisled box-frame or post and truss buildings survive and evidence for the former existence of aisles may be seen in many more. Aisled halls appear to have been commonplace during the Middle Ages while aisled barns were still being erected well into the 18C. and possibly even into the 19C.

The essential feature of the aisled building is the arcade plate, a horizontal member running from post to post in the position of a wall plate but within the building. Arcade plates supported common rafters as they ran from the main roof to cover the aisles and were usually linked to the aisle posts both by the action of the joint at the end of each tie beam, and by the triangulation of straight or curved braces. In the earlier aisled buildings, transverse rigidity was given to the structure by means of passing braces: light timber members running along the surface of each main structural member.

Of necessity an arcade plate running from end to end of a building had to be assembled from several lengths of timber jointed end to end and carpenters used much ingenuity in devising various methods of joining or 'scarfing' the parts of the arcade plate – and other horizontal members.

Most aisled buildings are examples of 'normal assembly' in box-frame or post and truss construction, i.e. the head of the post carries both wall plate or arcade plate and tie beam, ingenious joints linking post, plate and beam as they run in three dimensions. Some aisled buildings, however, show 'reversed assembly', i.e. the wall plate is carried on the end of the tie beam which in turn is carried on the post.

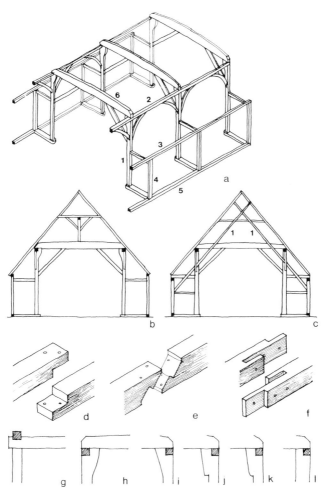

a. Isometric view of part of an aisled hall showing aisle post (1), arcade plate (2), wall plate (3), wall post (4) and cill (5), both the tie beam (6) and the arcade plate have braces running back to the aisle posts. The rafters which run from the ridge across the arcade plates to the wall plates, have been omitted in order to show the main structural members. *b*. Cross section through an aisled hall showing a rafter roof with a collar purlin supported by a crown post rising from the tie beam. *c*. Cross section to show the use of passing braces (1) running along the face of a series of members from wall post to rafter. *d*. Scarf joint halved. *e*. Scarf joint splayed and tabled. *f*. Scarf joint lipped and halved. *g*. Reversed assembly in which the wall plate is carried by the tie beam. *h*. Normal assembly in which the tie beam is above the wall plate. *i*. Flared jowl. *j*. Jowl with taper and square-cut return. *k*. Jowl with taper and curved return. *l*. No jowl at head of post.

Roof Construction: Butt Purlin Families

Where a roof includes rafters which are supported by purlins which in turn are supported by roof trusses, the form of the joint between purlin and truss is significant, and has been used as the key to the difference between two of the three main schools of roof carpentry. In the butt purlin roof, the purlins run between principal rafters in such a way that the top of the common rafters is in line with the top of the principal rafters; in other words the principal rafter acts also as a common rafter. In order to permit this combination, the purlin either passes right through the principal, or, more commonly, it is joined to the principal by a mortise and tenon joint. Sometimes the section of the principal is reduced at this point so that it continues to the ridge as a common rafter.

Butt purlin roofs are usually associated with box-frame timber construction, for the tie beam of the box-frame could act also as the tie beam of the roof truss. But often the tie beam was in an unsightly or inconvenient position, and various devices were adopted, both with timber and mass walls, to eliminate it. One popular device was to provide a collar at a higher level and use deep arch braces to help transfer roof loads well down the wall. Another was to eliminate the central portion of the tie beam, leaving the remainder as hammer beams, using short posts and arch braces to transmit loads from principal and collar respectively. A further, and rather confusing device, was to provide posts which curved inwards, like crucks, but which were topped by a collar or did not continue to a ridge; these base crucks seem to have been adopted sometimes to deal with erection problems. It was usual, though by no means universal, to halve the common rafters together rather than provide a ridge. Wind braces were sometimes provided, though whether the original purpose was lateral stability, decoration, or reduction of purlin span is not clear.

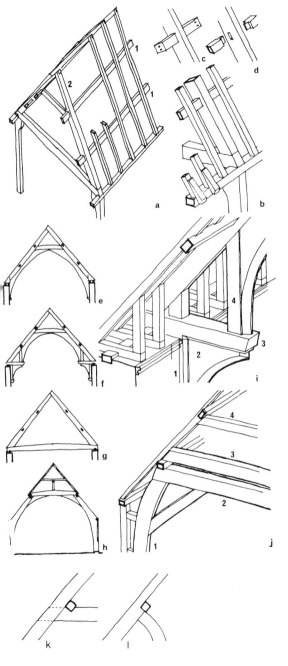

a. Cutaway isometric showing butt-purlins (1) and a principal rafter reduced in section to terminate as a common rafter (2).

b. Isometric showing butt-purlin, and sprocketed eaves.

c. Butt-purlin passing through principal and scarfed between trusses.

d. Butt-purlins tenoned into principal.

e. Butt-purlin arch-braced collar truss.

f. Butt-purlin hammer beams collar truss.

g. Butt-purlin tie beam truss.

h. Butt-purlin base cruck truss.

i. Isometric showing the formation of the hammer beam (3) with the aid of the hammer post (4), wall piece (1), and an arch brace (2).

j. Carrier butt purlin base cruck truss with inclined post in the form of a cruck blade (1), lower main collar (2), upper main collar (3), and subsidiary collar (4).

k. Purlin clasped between collar and principal rafter.

l. Purlin clasped as principal rafter is reduced to become a common rafter.

83

Roof Construction: Through Purlin Families

In contrast to the butt purlin roof, the purlins of a 'through purlin' roof are carried on the backs of the blades of the roof truss. The blade cannot act as a common rafter and indeed there is a space roughly corresponding to the depth of the purlin between the underside of the common rafter and the top of the blade. The side purlins may be carried on the top of a blade, kept in position by a block, or, more securely, they may be trenched into the top of the blade. In relatively crude construction, lengths of side purlin are lapped over each other at the blades, but, in superior work, scarfed joints link the lengths of purlin between trusses.

Though purlins are usually associated with cruck construction, the side purlins give intermediate support to common rafters which are also supported by a ridge purlin and wall plates. Because of the 'rearing' process involved in erecting a cruck truss, the joint at the head of the cruck blades was difficult to maintain, and several ways of dealing with the problem were devised. Again, because of the rearing process, the wall plate was most conveniently carried on top of the ends of a tie beam. Where, e.g. for reasons of headroom, the tie beam had been replaced by a collar at a higher level, then short cantilevered cruck spurs carried the wall plate. Where a wall of, e.g., stone or clay was considered capable of carrying the loads of a wall plate, the cruck spur might be entirely eliminated or a much more slender cruck tie used to maintain some link between wall plate and blade. Because the pitch of the roof was usually more shallow than the slope of the cruck blades, lower purlins were supported on separate blocking pieces or duplicate blades. So called 'wind braces' or 'sway braces' were often, though by no means invariably, provided to run diagonally between purlin and blade.

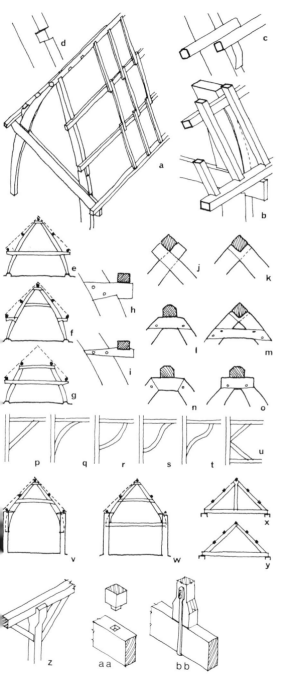

a. Diagram showing the relationship between through purlins and cruck construction.
b. Detail showing the relationship between through purlin, blade, and common rafters.
c. Block carrying side purlin.
d. Trenching for purlin.
e. Closed cruck truss.
f. Open cruck truss.
g. Truncated cruck truss.
h. Cruck spur.
i. Cruck tie.
j. Blades crossed at ridge.
k. Blades halved at ridge.
l. Plated yoke.
m. Collar yoke.
n. Link yoke.
o. Saddle.
p. Straight wind brace.
q. Concave.
r. Convex.
s. Ogee.
t. Reversed ogee.
u. Double straight wind braces.
v. Raised cruck truss.
w. Upper cruck truss.
x. Through purlin king post truss.
y. Through purlin tie beam truss.
z. Longitudinal support to ridge purlin.
aa. Early king post (with stub tenon) resting on tie beam.
bb. Late king post with strap tying post to tie beam.

85

Roofing Materials: Thatch

Thatch was formerly so universal a roofing material that the dialect word 'thack' is still applied to any roof covering. Although a great deal of thatch still remains – about 50,000 thatched buildings in England according to a recent estimate – replacement of thatch by Welsh slate, plain tile, and corrugated asbestos conceals the former use of the material over virtually the whole country.

The principal materials used were reed, straw, and heather, though other materials including turf and ling have been used at times. The best reed came from beds specially cultivated in Norfolk. Straw was usually wheaten, and combed wheat straw has similarities in use with reed, but rye straw was sometimes used. Heather was available in moorland areas where straw long enough for thatching was scarce. Threshing machines ruined straw for thatching purposes and there was presumably some relation between the spread of threshing machines in the north and west where other roofing materials were available, and their slow adoption in the east and south.

Thatch is a relatively light material, does not need a particularly massive roof construction, and can be used with poor walling materials such as mud or chalk. Often two courses of stone tiles were used at the wall head as a damp proof course over the most vulnerable part of the construction. The ridge was given extra protection by a further thickness of straw, often scalloped at the edge, and brought to a decorative peak at the apex. Hazel spars were used to give a great variety of decorative patterns at ridge, verge and eaves.

The nature of the material allowed valleys and dormers to be incorporated in the roof, and the soft, all-embracing lines of a thatched roof cannot be equalled in any other material.

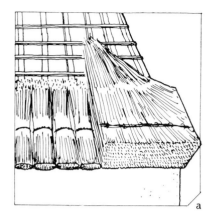

a. The diagram shows various stages in thatching a roof with Norfolk reed. The basis having been formed with rafters and laths, a bunch is laid at the corner of the verge at 45°, other bunches are placed along the eaves, butt down, and, after tying, fixed with hazel sways. The brow course is neatly dressed into position.

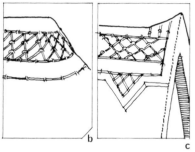

b. A detail at the apex of a hipped roof in long straw.

c. A detail at the apex of a gabled roof in Norfolk reed with a scalloped edge and pattern of sways.

d. A thatched roof trapped between brick parapets.

e. A thatched roof over a cob building showing the easily swept shapes over a complex plan.

f. In a few humble cottages or farm buildings the thatch was carried not on rafters but on a pile of twigs or straw heaped on wattles and joists to make a roof shape (after D. M. Smith).

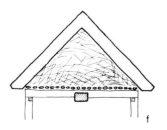

Roofing Materials: Slate

True slate is found in restricted areas of north and west Wales, Cornwall and Devon, Leicestershire, the Lake District, and the Isle of Man. The weight of the material and the difficulty of transport restricted its use to the vicinity of the quarries, or for exceptionally expensive buildings elsewhere. Improvements in water transport, both by coastal shipping and canals, during the second half of the 18C., led to increasing use, especially of the slate from the Lake District. The material was sought in towns as a substitute for inflammable thatch. However, rail transport during the second half of the 19C. led to the widespread use of Welsh slate for all building types and in all districts.

Welsh slate is usually used in thin slabs of uniform thickness and uniform size; courses are regular, and a roof slated with this material appears thin, smooth, and precise. The other slates are used in random widths and thicknesses, giving irregular courses, diminishing in depth from eaves to ridge. Both types are hung by nails on riven or sawn battens, and can be satisfactorily laid at pitches of 30° to 35°, though large Welsh slates have been laid at an even lower pitch.

Slate is best used on gabled roofs with few valleys. Hips must either be covered by moulded hip tiles or hewn stone sections or they must be mitred in a flimsy and vulnerable fashion. Valleys require substantial and equally vulnerable lead gutters.

There seems little doubt that in the majority of roofs covered with Welsh slates in English country districts – and in most Welsh country districts also – the material is a replacement for an earlier covering of thatch. The opportunity was often taken to raise the eaves and give greater height to upper floor bedrooms.

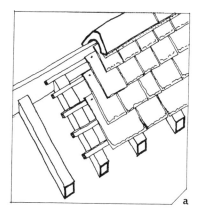

a

a. The cutaway diagram shows rafters, ridge piece, laths laid at an interval diminishing towards the ridge, and the slates, random in width and reducing in length to form diminishing courses. The ridge is covered by sections of stone cut to shape and bedded in mortar.

b. Lake District type slates, rough in section, random width, diminishing courses.

c. Welsh slate, smooth in section, uniform width, even courses.

d. Ridge of 'wrestler' slates.

e. Stone ridge.

f. Lead ridge.

g. Tiled hip.

h. Mitred slate hip with concealed lead soakers.

i. Rough slate, head nailed.

j. Smooth, precisely cut slate, centre nailed.

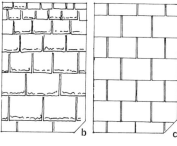

b

c

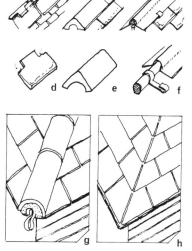

d   e   f

g   h

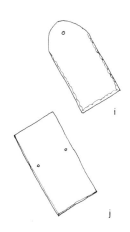

i

j

89

Roofing Materials: Stone Flags and Stone Tiles

Based to some extent on local terminology, a distinction is made here between stone flags – thick, heavy, roofing slabs found chiefly in the Pennines, and stone tiles – the thinner, lighter, stone roofing material of the Cotswolds and elsewhere in England and Wales. Most stone flags are basically sandstone in origin, and they include the products of the Kerridge quarries which roofed much of north-east Cheshire; most stone tiles are basically limestone in formation and include the well-known Clipsham tiles of Rutland.

The method of laying the roofing material was similar in both versions: each tile of flag was pegged by an oaken peg (or a sheep's bone peg in the Lake District) to a stout lath, pegged or nailed in turn to the rafters; diminishing courses were used, and the top of each tile was usually rounded off, presumably to help reduce weight. The underside of the roof covering was often 'torched' with a mixture of clay and hair in order to reduce draughts and the penetration of snow.

Stone flags were usually laid to a low pitch of about 30°. They were graduated in size from slabs as much as four feet wide and three inches thick at the eaves to quite tiny, thin slabs at the ridge. They were used only on simple broad surfaces of roof. Stone tiles, however, were usually laid to a much steeper pitch, 50° or even more, their graduation was less marked, and the smaller tiles, swept around valleys, gave intricate roof shapes of quite a delicate effect.

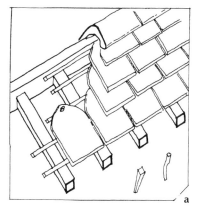

a. The diagram shows a roof of rafters, ridge purlin, and laths laid in diminishing courses with stone flags held in position by wooden pegs (or sheep's bones)
b. Stone tile with lap over.
c. Stone flag with lap over.
d. Stone tile showing rough texture.
e. Stone flag showing smooth but bold texture.
f. Stone flags laid, at the eaves, beneath a thatched roof.
g. Stone flags laid at the eaves of a tiled or slated roof.
h. Stone tiles swept round a valley.
i. Stone tiles laced up a valley.

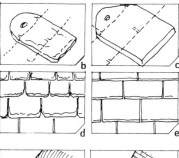

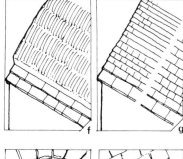

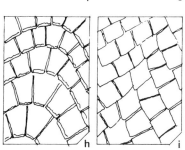

Roofing Materials: Plain Tiles

The manufacture and use of clay plain tiles has marched along with the development of brick making. The size of the plain tile, $10\frac{1}{2}$ in. by $6\frac{1}{2}$ in. by $\frac{1}{2}$ in. was standardized in 1477 and its use, like that of brick for walling, was at first confined to the Eastern and South-Eastern counties. Like brick, tiles were favoured in the towns as a fire-resistant material, and their use spread wherever slate or stone was not available.

Plain tiles were nailed, or were hung by means of nibs, moulded into the tile, from light battens. They were laid in regular courses but, in order to protect the joints between tiles, each tile lapped two others, leaving only about four inches exposed and the tiles were usually laid at a pitch of more than $45°$. By means of specially moulded hip and valley tiles it was quite satisfactory to cover intricate roof shapes with plain tiles.

Early plain tiles were hand-made and the exaggerated camber in both the length and breadth of the tile gave an intricate character to an old tiled roof which a modern roof in the same material entirely lacks. Later developments included the use of multi-coloured tiles in order to display pattern, dates, and initials in the roof, as well as the use of specially shaped tiles to give varying textures and patterns.

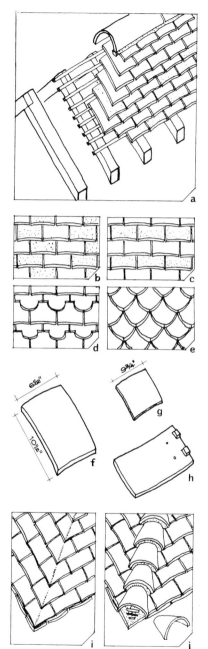

a. The cutaway diagram shows rafters halved at the ridge, laths laid at a regular interval from eaves to ridge, and plain tiles, each one overlapping two others so that there is a thickness of three tiles at each joint. The ridge is a half-round tile.

b. Decorative tiling in alternate colours.

c. Decorative tiling in alternate courses of different colours.

d. Alternate courses of plain and shaped tiles.

e. Fishscale tiles.

f. Size of tile.

g. Tile and a half for closing at eaves.

h. Underside of tile showing nibs and nail holes.

i. Hips formed of shaped hip tiles.

j. Hips formed of bonnet hip tiles.

Roofing Materials: Pantiles

The pantile resembles the plain tile in material and manufacture but differs in form and use. The size of a pantile, $13\frac{1}{2}$ in. by $9\frac{1}{2}$ in. by $\frac{1}{2}$ in., was fixed during the reign of George I, pantiles having been imported from Holland, certainly towards the end of the 17C., probably before, and local manufacture having started at the beginning of the 18C. They quickly spread over the whole of the Eastern counties north of London right up to the Scottish border. Except for a strong tradition in Bridgwater, Somerset, pantiles are virtually unknown in the western half of the country.

Pantiles are single lap tiles in the sense that each tile laps over only one tile beneath, but the side joints, so vulnerable in plain tiles, are protected by a sideways lap, permitted by the flat S section of the tile. They could be laid to a low pitch of $30°-35°$, provided a lightweight roof and required a relatively insubstantial roof structure. The underside of the pantiles was usually torched with clay to reduce snow penetration.

The bold form of a pantiled roof is best used in simple shapes as hips and valleys and small roof sections generally are difficult to form; the verge of a pantiled roof is often protected by a low parapet.

Other forms of single lap tile, such as Roman and Spanish tiles, have not formed any significant part of the British vernacular tradition.

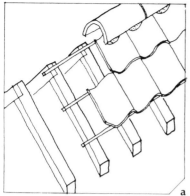

a. The cutaway diagram shows rafters halved at the ridge, widely spaced laths, and pantiles lapping sideways and at each course, together with half-round ridge tile.

b. Detail of the pantile and the sideways lap.

c. Detail showing gable carried up as a parapet and half-round ridge tiles with galletting of small pieces of plain tile.

d. Hip with half-round ridge tiles.

e. Detail of torching.

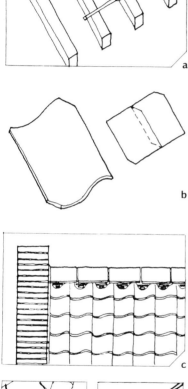

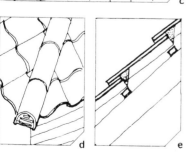

95

Roofing: Chimneys

Just as the relationship between fireplace and entrance is one of the two major factors governing plan arrangement in vernacular houses, so is the relationship between chimney and roof a major determinant in the external appearance of such a building.

A chimney can be located so as to pass through the ridge, at a gable, at the eaves on side or end of a hipped roof, or through some point part way along the slope of a roof. Each location has a meaning on plan and created problems in construction.

A chimney passing through the ridge meant that little of the chimney stack need be exposed to the weather, and weather proofing problems were minimized; early chimneys projected from the gable wall and were kept clear of inflammable thatch; at the eaves chimneys were clear of thatch, but the joint with the roof material collected rainwater unless protected by a tiny roof pitched opposite to the main roof; part way up the pitch meant waterproofing problems and yet was often unavoidable because of planning requirements.

Chimney stacks were made of brick or stone according to the material available locally. Brick was the most satisfactory material, and gave the opportunity for splendid displays of craftsmanship. Dressed stone suffered from the heat and water penetration but provided good opportunities for decoration; undressed stone was difficult to use for chimney stacks, and the circular stacks of Pembroke and parts of the Lake District were an attempt to avoid the jointing problems at corners.

Although chimney pots have been used for superior houses from the early medieval period they were rarely used at the vernacular level. Most chimney pots now seen are 19C. work and it is doubtful if devices like the inclined slates of the Lake District are much older.

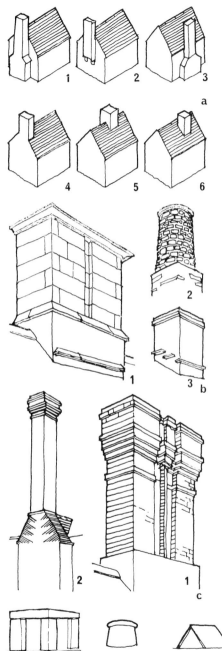

a. Positions for chimneys.
  1. Projecting from gable.
  2. Projecting at first floor from gable.
  3. Projecting from side wall.
  4. In gable wall.
  5. Within the house, passing through the ridge.
  6. Within the house, avoiding the ridge.
b. Stone chimney stacks.
  1. Panelled stack, on a base.
  2. Circular stack of small stones.
  3. Square stack with water tabling to protect the joint between stack and roof.
c. Brick chimney stacks.
  1. Two flues with decorative shape on plan and use of oversailing brick courses.
  2. Separate stack projecting from side wall, tumbled-in brickwork, small gabled roof masking joint with main roof.
d. Various chimney pots.
  1. Slate or stone on short pillars; found in Devon.
  2. Common tapered tile pot.
  3. Inclined slates as in the Lake District.
  4. Medieval tile pot.

Roofing: Dormers

Dormer windows may be contained entirely in the roof slope or may include some vertical continuation of the house wall. In either variety they serve to provide light to rooms contained partly in the roof space.

The gradual development of the loft into a full height first floor will later be noted. Light could be provided to the end rooms by means of windows in the gables; for the centre rooms and in hipped roofs light was obtained from dormer windows. Where loft space was the result of inserting a floor into a room originally open to the roof, dormers would be inserted at the same time. Where architectural fashion required the roof slope to be hidden behind a parapet, or a strong horizontal cornice to be included at eaves level in order to complete the architectural composition of an elevation, then, again, dormer windows would serve the top floor.

Generally, in vernacular work, the main roofing material was continued over dormers. In thatched roofs this was conveniently and agreeably done by sweeping the thatch over 'eyebrow' windows or around full dormers; in stone tiled roofs, swept or laced valleys continued the coursing of tiles neatly over dormers. In plain tiled roofs, specially shaped valley tiles linked major and minor roofs, but pantiles, slates, and stone flags required lead valleys to separate the roof of the dormer from the main roof. At the same time the roof of the dormer tends to follow that of the main roof, hips with hips and gables with gables.

One alternative way of providing light to a loft was by means of a roof-light, following the slope of the main roof, and this was often associated with top floor workshops in the early 19C.

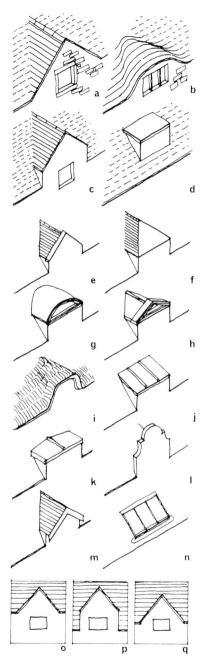

a. Gabled dormer, window above eaves.
b. Eyebrow dormer at eaves.
c. Gabled dormer window partly below eaves.
d. Dormer wholly in roof space.
e. Gabled dormer with plain coping.
f. Hipped dormer.
g. Segmental pediment to dormer.
h. Triangular pediment to dormer.
i. Thatched hood to dormer.
j. Sloping lead roof to dormer.
k. Flat lead roof to dormer.
l. 'Dutch' gable to dormer.
m. Bargeboards to dormer gable.
n. Sloping rooflight.
o., p., q. Distinguish between dormer windows below, above, and across the eaves line.

99

3. PLAN AND SECTION

In this chapter the different forms of plan and section commonly found in vernacular houses are examined, together with the forms of staircase which usually relate plan to section. The three items are considered together as, even in such simple buildings, they are inextricably linked, any designer of a multi-storey structure having to think simultaneously of plan, section, and staircases, and to acknowledge that modification of one element has its repercussions on the other two.

Consideration of plan form occupies the major part of this chapter as it so often represents the culminating phase in any study of vernacular architecture. Those students who are especially concerned with the way of life enshrined in an example of minor domestic architecture will be primarily interested in plans and will consider architectural details, building materials, and forms of construction, as ways of establishing and explaining the plan form at various periods. Recently, attempts have been made to set up a classification of vernacular plan forms, and we are approaching the time when such a classification, capable of national application, can be accepted. Against this, individual examples may be set and regional and local variations established. It is possible that in so doing we will find rather less local variation in plan form than was once expected.

The elements of plan and sectional form at the vernacular level are very few. Whatever the local variations, the permutations of these few elements adopted nationally from time to time are surprisingly numerous.

While some examples of a single build may illustrate the plan and sectional form appropriate to a particular family in a particular place and at a particular time, many examples show the development from one plan or cross-section to another. By examining changes in material and structure one may determine how simple or archaic plans were extended at side and rear to form new plans while single-storey buildings were extended upwards to provide extra levels of accommodation. In addition, of course, houses were 'modernized' through alterations to window shape or door position without alterations to plan and section, and this process still continues.

Plan Forms: Introduction

It has already been suggested that plan and sectional form are inextricably linked and yet some attempt should be made to distinguish at least the ground floor plans to be commonly found.

The variations in plan form in domestic vernacular depend on the inter-relationship between the positions of the main hearth or fireplace, the main staircase, the main entrance, and the overall plan shape. Some of these components can be fairly reliably detected from outside the house: the front door and the general plan shape can be distinguished, the main chimney (which is not always the biggest) will usually still be in use, and a small 'fire window' may be present to confirm the position of the principal fireplace. The position of the staircase is usually less obvious unless it is contained in a projection or lit by a window at a half landing. Often, however, a house will show two or more phases of construction and these can usually be distinguished through changes of material on the exterior.

Apart from the plans which relate to first floor living, eight plan form families are here proposed. These families each contain many members, though there are also a few orphans to add to the numbers of individual plan variations. The classification, such as it is, will seem coarse when set against some of the other published classifications related to different regions of the country, but it is presented as a simple basis on which more detailed classifications may be established for each different locality.

Generally, projections or outshuts from the main plan shape have been ignored, but sometimes they are shown as essential to the organization of the plan.

Conventionally the 'upper' end of a house includes the more private rooms – parlours, etc. – while the 'lower' end is closest to the cooking, cleaning, and dirty operations of the household, and closest to the farm buildings; in fact, where a house is built across a slope, the upper and lower in status usually correspond to the slope of the ground.

For each plan form a diagram has been prepared to show position of fireplace, door, and staircase in relation to the ground floor plan shape; other elements such as windows and subsidiary doors have been ignored. Smaller, even more diagrammatic, plans have been added to show the common variations. Generally the first floor plan has been ignored.

Although most of the diagrams are based on stone walled buildings, the plans were equally appropriate to other materials.

Plan Form Families:
The First-Floor Family

First-floor living may be either patrician or defensive in origin. Two versions appear at the vernacular level: the tower house and the upper-floor hall house.

In the basic *tower house*, the main living-room occupies the first floor, private rooms and bedrooms occupy the second and any higher floors, while the ground floor contains service or storage space. Usually the living-room was heated by a mural fireplace. Connection between the floors was by a spiral staircase in one corner of the tower, entrance was normally at first-floor level, though it could be from the ground floor, and staircases were alternatively placed in a projecting turret or were fitted as straight flights into the thickness of the wall.

In the basic *upper-floor hall house*, the first floor was occupied by a larger, general living-room, and a smaller private room. Above were subsidiary bedrooms in a full storey or garret space. It is generally assumed that the ground floor was used for storage, though in the bastel house version it is believed to have accommodated cattle. It is, however, possible that the ground floor was used for subsidiary living accommodation. The principal fireplace was located in the first-floor hall, either on a side or an end wall, and sometimes there was a small fireplace in the private room. Entrance was normally by means of an outside staircase on the front wall.

Tower houses were common on the Scottish border but several examples have recently come to light on both sides of the Welsh border. Upper-floor hall houses remain in small numbers from Norman times, but most of the surviving examples in Northumberland and Cumberland and, again, in parts of Wales, appear to date from the mid-14C. and mid-16C.

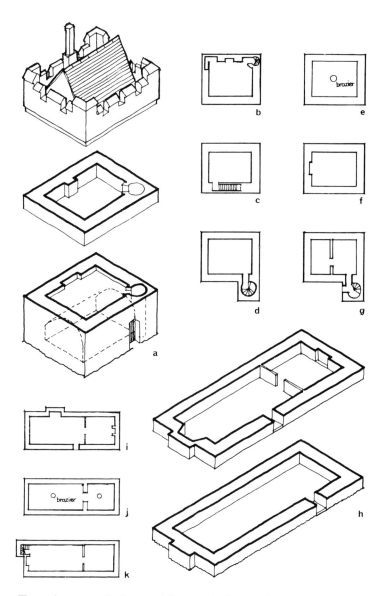

a. Tower house, vaulted ground floor, typical upper floor, and battlemented roof. *b*. Corner staircase. *c*. Mural straight flight staircase. *d*. Staircase in projecting turret. *e*., *f*. Alternative fireplace positions. *g*. Alternative ground floor. *h*. Upper-floor hall house (bastel house if defensible), ground floor and first floor. *i*., *j*. Alternative fireplace positions. *k*. Alternative staircase position.

Plan Form Families: The Hall Family

The hall family comprises all those house plans in which the principal ground-floor living-room is open to the roof, together with such plans as retain a room similar in position and function but ceiled. There are two main versions: the single-ended and the double-ended halls.

In the *single-ended hall* plan, a two-storey wing is attached to one end of an open hall. This wing usually projects beyond the side wall of the hall but may only project in one direction or even have no projection at all apart, possibly, from a jettied upper story. There is usually a cross-passage between hall and wing, but this may be found to have been blocked by the insertion of a later fireplace. Alternative fireplace positions include the long wall, against the cross-passage, or at the exposed end of the hall. The staircase is usually contained entirely in the wing.

In the *double-ended hall* plan, an open hall is flanked by two multi-storey wings. These may be marked externally by no more than jettied upper floors as in the so-called Wealden plan, may have a bold gabled projection, as in the clothiers' houses of the West Riding, or may be extended to give a U-shape, as in some late examples in Cambridgeshire. There is usually a cross-passage, the 'screens passage', at one end of the hall, off which open buttery and pantry and a passage leading to an outside kitchen. At the other end a staircase gives access to a first-floor private chamber. Early examples have an open hearth in the hall but this has usually been replaced by a side- or end-wall fireplace.

Both single-ended and double-ended halls may be found in all parts of the country and the plan form, originating at the highest levels of society, passed eventually to the lower ranges of the social scale.

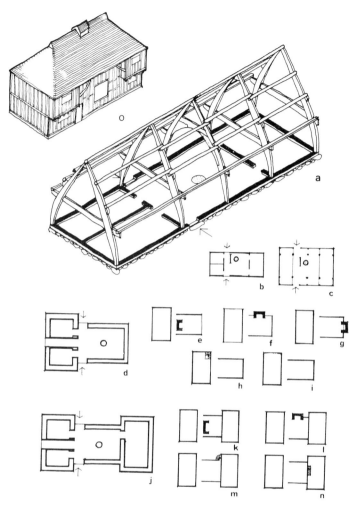

a. A house with open hall; the version illustrated has two rooms and a cross-passage at the lower end, an open hall, and one room at the upper end; the cruck trusses include an open truss over the hall. b. Example of a small hall house with open hearth near the cross-passage. c. Aisled hall. d. Single-ended hall, the open hall and cross-passage is shown attached to a wing with buttery, pantry, and kitchen passage on the ground floor and a solar above. e., f., g. Alternative fireplace positions. h., i. Alternative staircase positions. j. A double-ended hall, the open hall and cross-passage are flanked at the lower end by a wing with buttery, pantry, and kitchen passage and a room above, and, at the upper end, by a store or private room with a solar above. k., l. Alternative fireplace positions. m., n. Alternative staircase positions. o. Wealden house.

Plan Form Families: The Two-Unit Family

This family comprises two groups of house plan – those consisting essentially of one structural cell divided by a partition into a larger and a smaller room and those in which a further unit is added at one end though with the interruption of a cross-passage.

In the first group the larger room performed the function of the hall but was never open to the roof, having a bedroom or loft above; the smaller room acted as a private space and was itself often partitioned to give a small pantry separately entered from the living-room. Usually only the larger room was heated and this by a fireplace in an end wall. Sometimes the smaller room had a fireplace, though this was more likely to be a later addition than an original feature. The main entrance might be in the end wall, alongside the fireplace, at the fireplace end of the front wall, or about the centre of the front wall, near the partition (though in this last version of the plan there would not usually be a contemporary cross-passage). The staircase was usually tucked into a recess alongside the fireplace on the end wall, although it might be set in a turret projecting from about the centre of the rear wall or even be taken out of a corner of the private end.

In the second group, the plan forms are similar except that an extension incorporating a cross-passage was added to the lower end. Many examples of the first group have undoubtedly been extended to form the second, but it must be acknowledged that many more seem to have been so built from the beginning. The extra room was a service room (sometimes agricultural rather than domestic) and it might have a fireplace in the exposed gable wall. Sometimes the private room at the upper end of the basic plan was replaced by a wing at the rear.

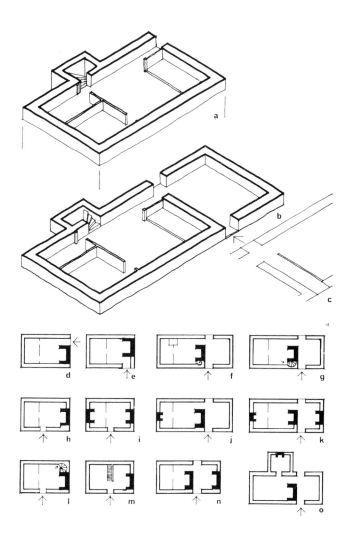

a. The basic two-unit plan, with living-room, pantry, and parlour on the ground floor and bedrooms or a loft above. b. The two-unit plan with cross-passage and service room added at the lower end. c. A modification of b with a cross-passage and farm buildings added at the lower end, 'longhouse' style. d., e., h. Alternative fireplace positions. i. Two fireplaces. l., m., Alternative staircase positions. f. g. Alternative staircase positions to plan b. j. An additional fireplace at the upper end. k., n. Additional fireplaces at the lower end. o. A parlour and fireplace projecting from the rear.

Plan Form Families:
Central Fireplaces Family

In the *central fireplace* family the basic plan consists of an upper room, a living-room and a service room, with living and service rooms heated by two fireplaces back to back, and with the main entrance at the junction of these rooms where fireplace jambs and outer wall form a little lobby. Although having some superficial similarities to the two-unit plan family there is the important distinction that the fireplaces are set back to back and there is no cross-passage. Variations from the basic plan depend, again, on the position of the staircase and other fireplaces. In some versions the upper room may be eliminated, its functions performed by upper floor rooms; in others the two main fireplaces heat living and private rooms while the service room projects from the rear. This family appears to be confined to Lowland England, especially the Eastern counties, but was popular among 17C. New England colonists.

The most compact version, having only two rooms on the ground floor, could also be the most cramped and some examples were made more convenient and imposing through the use of a multi-storey porch at the front and a staircase projection at the rear.

While most examples of the central fireplace family have the two fireplaces built at one time, in some instances only one was provided initially and the other added later. This sequence may show on the outside of the building when the front door lies to one side of a line running from chimney stack to ground instead of in the middle of it.

The family is sometimes called *lobby entry* or *baffle entry*.

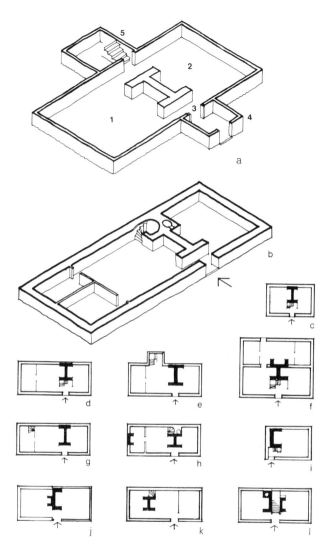

a. The basic plan with only two rooms on the ground floor: hall (1) and parlour (2) with lobby entrance (3) and, in this instance, a porch (4) and staircase projection (5). b. The basic plan with central fireplaces back-to-back, one serving the living-room which has unheated pantry and parlour opening off it, the other serving a service room. c. Variation with living and service rooms and a central staircase. d., e., g., h. Alternative staircase positions. f. Additional service rooms in an outshut at the rear. i. Single unit. j. Single unit extended. k. Back-to-back fireplaces without lobby entrance. l. Staircase between fireplaces (flues join over).

Plan Form Families:
Inside Cross-Passage Family

There is a plan form family which is characterized by a *passage* which runs *across the structural cell*. Partitioned off the passage, there are on one side unheated storage rooms (e.g. buttery and pantry) and, on the other side a passage which runs across the end of the principal living-room and opposite the main fireplace; private rooms and bedrooms are confined to the upper floors. Although the main fireplace is usually in the end wall of the living-room, it may be in the side wall in which case there may be a parlour at one end of the house. The staircase is usually to be found alongside the main fireplace but it may, in late examples, back on to the cross-passage. The plan form is not as common as some others, though many examples are to be seen in North Wales.

While the standard arrangement has a fireplace only at one end of the ground floor the principal chamber on the first floor at the opposite end is often provided with a fireplace. This projects slightly from the wall, the chimney breast being corbelled out at first floor level.

Plan Form Families: Central Service Room

Generally, unheated service rooms are placed at one end of the house: below a cross-passage, alongside a small parlour for instance, but there are some houses in which this room is placed in the middle of the house, between the two principal heated living rooms. It is rather as if a two-unit house had been stretched by the insertion of such a room. Where the entrance was at the centre of the main elevation, a compact lobby gave access to the two rooms and the service room, an arrangement which may well have appeared odd at a time when one room usually opened off another.

Examples of this plan are not especially numerous or widespread but they may be seen in the southern half of Wales and in the South-West of England.

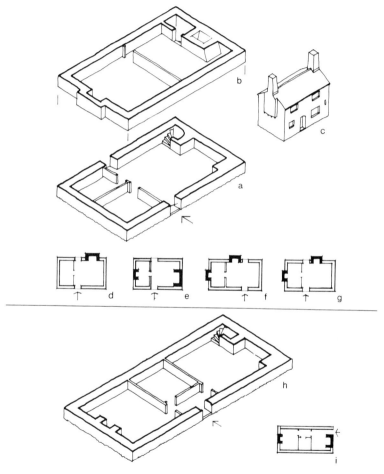

a. The basic inside cross-passage plan ground floor. b. First floor of the basic plan showing projecting chimney breast. c. Isometric sketch of an example of this plan. d. Alternative fireplace position. e. Alternative with two gable ground floor fireplaces. f. Two fireplaces and the passage across the main room. g. Two fireplaces and the passage in the normal position. h. The basic central service room plan. i. Alternative with gable entry.

Plan Form Families:
Side-Wall Fireplace Plans

When the open hearth fell out of favour and was replaced by a fireplace, there were two positions in which that fireplace could be located: on an end wall facing along the length of the hall, or on a side wall facing across the hall. In the majority of smaller houses the former position was chosen; in the majority of larger houses the choice fell on the latter position. In the small houses the fireplace could be conveniently located to back on to a cross-passage (if this were to be retained) or could be so located in a redundant cross-passage as to give the greatest possible useful floor space to the hall. In the larger houses, with correspondingly larger rooms, the best distribution of heat came from a position at the middle of a side wall. Usually the rear side wall was chosen for the fireplace and this gave the best impression to the visitor entering through the front door and between the screens. In a number of small houses, concentrated mainly in certain areas on each side of the Bristol Channel, the side wall was chosen but at the front of the house where, no doubt, the best possible impression was given to the visitor as the chimney breast and stack were the most prominent objects on the front elevation.

The plan whose distinguishing feature was the fireplace on the front side wall, alongside the entrance doorway, is associated with the longhouse arrangement occasionally, with other two-unit plans, but mainly with houses of three units. Welsh examples may either have the service room beyond the cross-passage or a heated parlour, and the latter arrangement has been found to be the most common. In Wales, especially, the front chimney is given even greater emphasis by the tall chimney stack.

Houses of this type appear to date from the late 16C. and the plan was used throughout the 17C. and into the 18C. These are the dates of transformation of older houses as well as new construction on the same plan. There is a heavy concentration in Pembrokeshire, but the plan is also used in other parts of the Welsh side of the Bristol Channel; there are also numerous examples in North Devon stretching both into Somerset and Cornwall, and also down into South Devon near Exeter.

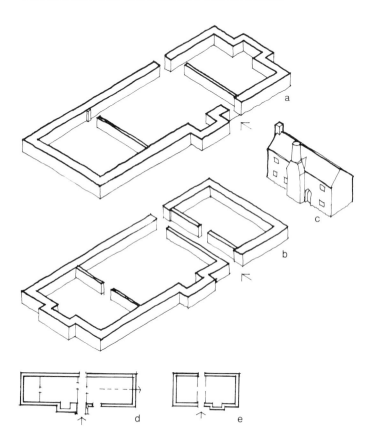

a. Front fireplace serving hall which incorporates cross-passage; parlour beyond the passage. b. Front fireplace serving hall, true cross-passage, parlour beyond hall, service room beyond passage. c. Sketch to show front side-wall fireplace, chimney breast and stack. d. Front side-wall fireplace as part of longhouse (animals beyond cross-passage) (cf. Alcock, Sanders, Lettaford). e. Two units with inside cross-passage and front fireplace (cf. Williams, Poltimore, Farway).

Plan Form Families: The Double Pile Plans

The essential characteristic of the double pile plan is that it is entirely two rooms in depth. In all other plans the principal room has run through from front to back walls, even though subsidiary rooms may only have occupied part of the depth of the building.

The basic version of the double pile plan consists of four rooms, a principal living-room, a private room, a kitchen, and another service room (e.g. a dairy or a pantry). A staircase at the rear between the two subsidiary rooms rises to the upper floors. Fireplaces, which are usually provided to all rooms except the service room, are built into the end walls. The front door is placed close to the centre of the main elevation, and a lobby serving the entrance, the staircase and all four rooms was, in the larger and later examples, partitioned off the main living-room. As an alternative, especially in Eastern England, the fireplaces may be found placed back-to-back on partition walls. In another example the staircase rises between the two principal rooms. Where further accommodation was needed, then a sideways extension was provided, with its own fireplaces and even, sometimes, its own staircase.

While the basic version of the double pile plan gave the effect known to house agents as 'double-fronted', half the plan gave the 'single-fronted' elevation commonly found in urban terraces and rural cottages. In this variation there are two rooms on each floor, not four, and extensions could be made at the rear, as in the 'tunnel back' town houses.

The double pile plan was introduced high in the social scale towards the beginning of the 17C., by the middle of the 18C. it had spread to all parts of the country and all levels of society.

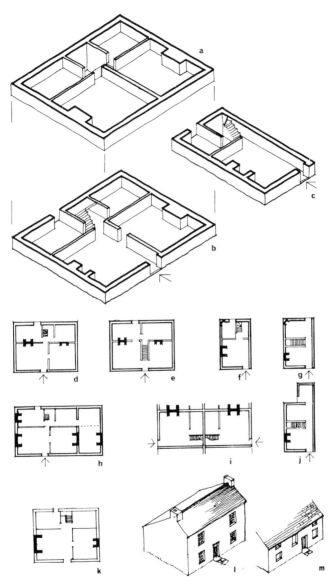

a. First floor and *b*. Ground floor, double-fronted. *c*. Ground floor, single-fronted. *d*., *e*. Alternative fireplace and staircase positions. *f*., *g*. Alternative staircase positions, single-fronted. *h*. Double-fronted extended by an additional unit. *i*. Back-to-back single-fronted. *j*. Extension at the rear of a single-fronted cottage, the 'tunnel back'. *k*., *l*., *m*. Plan, front and rear view of continuous outshut predecessor to double pile plans.

Cottages

The cottage family comprises those dwellings which gave the minimal accommodation to the members of the cottager class – those who had no stake in the land, apart from a garden-sized plot and rights on the common, and who depended on the strength of their arms as labourers, the skill of their fingers as craftsmen or the charity of their neighbours or family. The basic cottage consists of one room only, about 12ft. to 14ft. square and containing a door, a window and a hearth or fireplace. In this room the family lived, cooked, dined and slept. Most surviving cottages have rather more accommodation, being extended upwards, to the side, to the rear or built as two full storeys.

The simplest extension was into the roof space above the basic shell and this loft was lit by a window just below the eaves or in the gable or by a dormer window. Often the extension was to one side, giving a plan of one larger and one smaller room, a miniature version of the hall and parlour plan of the two-unit Small House. Sometimes there was a loft over the smaller room as in the Welsh 'croglofft' cottage. Alternatively, the extension was to the rear, especially if only a narrow frontage was available. In later versions there was bedroom space over the whole of the ground floor.

Construction was similar to that of the smaller houses of the locality – timber-frame, stone, brick or clay and thatch of inferior quality. Many cottages, however, were built of insubstantial construction such as mud and stud, and even fewer of these survive than those of standard construction.

Few surviving rural cottages were built before the middle of the 18C., and after the middle of the 19C. they tended to be built as 'estate cottages' to the designs of the landlord's professional adviser or to pattern-book designs.

Almshouses are a special type of cottage, usually with minimal accommodation though often built with style.

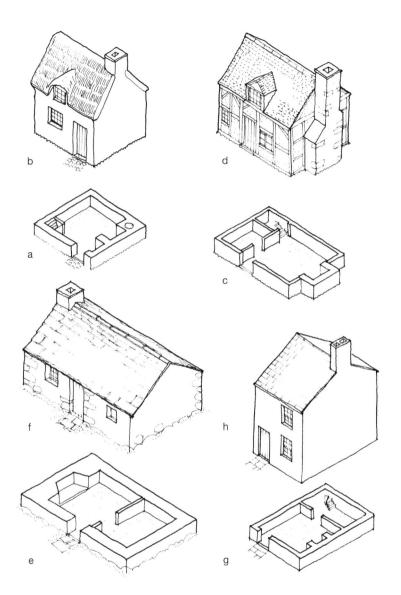

a. One-room cottage, ground-floor plan. *b*. Sketch of one-room cottage. *c*. One-and-a-half-room cottage, ground-floor plan. *d*. Sketch of one-and-a-half-room cottage. *e*. Two-room single-storey cottage plan. *f*. Sketch of two-room single-storey cottage. *g*. One-room and scullery cottage, ground-floor plan, narrow-fronted. *h*. sketch of a single-room and scullery cottage, narrow-fronted.

Sectional Form: Introduction

Some of the earliest surviving examples of minor domestic architecture were designed for first-floor living. These might be tower houses, with the main living-room on the first floor, private rooms above, and service rooms below – for such houses continued to be built at the vernacular level until the early 17C. – or they might be houses with a living-room and private rooms on the first floor and service rooms beneath, having a long history stretching from Norman times until Elizabethan. But with these exceptions the story of vernacular architecture is one of modification and adaptation based on ground-floor living.

The open hall, a ground-floor room open to the roof timbers, seems to be the vernacular counterpart of the Saxon communal hall. The evidence from excavations as well as examination of surviving fragments suggests that the aisled open hall was once in common use, at least in the eastern half of the country, to accommodate all living quarters, but the earliest surviving examples of the open hall, aisled or not, are combined with a two-storey wing. In such a wing the room on the upper floor was normally the most important and might itself be open to a roof of decorated timbers. The open hall remained in use at a steadily decreasing social level until the 19C., when the principal living-room of a quarryman's cottage might be open to its roof.

However fine the architectural qualities of an open hall, the physical discomforts were considerable and, percolating gradually down the social scale, it became customary to insert an intermediate floor over the whole house. At the inferior social levels the principal bedroom remained on the ground floor and the upper storey was an ill-lit loft, cramped and with inadequate headroom. However, by using dormer windows or by raising the eaves and altering the roof construction, a more commodious upper floor was made possible and eventually became the bedroom floor.

Even the two-storey house usually had a garret space available for storage, for servants' accommodation, or for other service functions.

Open Hall

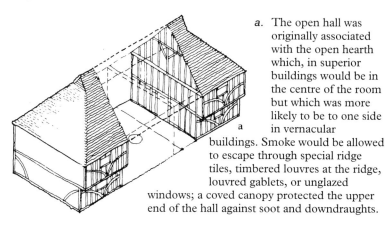

a. The open hall was originally associated with the open hearth which, in superior buildings would be in the centre of the room but which was more likely to be to one side in vernacular buildings. Smoke would be allowed to escape through special ridge tiles, timbered louvres at the ridge, louvred gablets, or unglazed windows; a coved canopy protected the upper end of the hall against soot and downdraughts.

b. The most common type of open hall had a cross-passage at the lower end with doors to buttery, pantry and kitchen. The hall was screened by a partition or 'spere' with two doors leading in to the cross-passage. In the North and West there was often a spere truss with fixed partitions at each end and a moveable screen between.

c. Even after the central hearth had been abandoned the open hall remained in use with the fire either contained in a conventional fireplace with flue and chimney or set against a wall and with smoke collected in a hood usually of studs and thick daub though sometimes of stone. In some districts platforms on each side of the hood provided storage space or even beds.

d. The 'croglofft' cottage had a single room open to a low roof. At the 'upper' end, opposite the hearth, a cubicle was partitioned off, partly with furniture, above this was a low loft reached by a ladder. This is probably a late and rude survival of the process by which the hall was eventually floored.

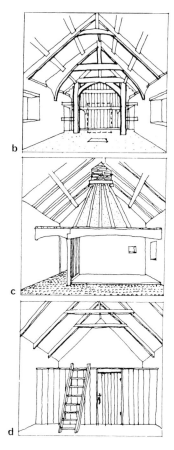

One and a Half Storey

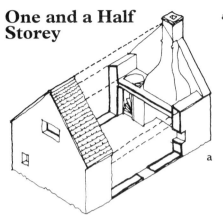

a. The two obstacles to full use of the loft space over a rectangular house were difficulties in lighting and lack of headroom. In a house with a gabled or half-hipped roof, light could be fairly easily obtained from the end walls. Light from side walls could only be obtained with the use of dormer windows or by raising eaves to allow for low level window.

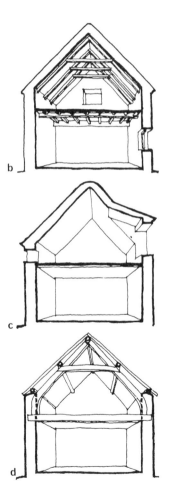

b. In the example illustrated the ground floor has full height but the loft space above is low and cramped. The collar rafter roof eliminates obstructive beams and the gable window provides some light but the eaves are too low to enable the centre of the loft to be daylit.

c. Here, one of the many types of dormer window is illustrated in half the section. In this type the main wall has been carried up to provide the window and the dormer has been roofed in a flatter continuation of the main roof. The many other varieties of dormer are illustrated in another chapter. The other half of the section shows side windows down at floor level.

d. The upper cruck truss was one of the devices adopted to improve headroom. Others included the use of purlins carried on cross walls avoiding the need for trusses, and use of the double pitch or gambrel roof. Improved lighting and adequate headroom made possible the full use of an upper floor.

Multi-Storey

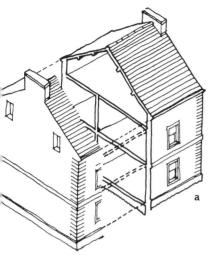

a. The use of two full storeys allowed the principal bedroom to move from the ground to the first floor. Consequently the two floors became comparable in importance and therefore similar in height. The prevailing fashion for lofty rooms and tall windows emphasized the change.

b. In many parts of the country, the adoption of a full-height first floor was accompanied by an extension of the ground floor by means of an 'outshut' at the rear. Some parts of such an outshut would be open to the roof, others would be ceiled to give small cramped storage places or bedroom lofts. These gradually passed through the same process of improving lighting and headroom as the main part of the house but quite often the rear part was rather lower than the front even when both had adequate height.

c. Use of the upper floors for storage and service functions continued after two full floors were in domestic use. The garret space was usually lit by small gable or dormer windows. Once cross-walls instead of trusses were used to carry purlins, the problems of headroom were reduced. In the example illustrated, such purlins permitted the unbroken floor space required by some types of cottage industry. Here light was obtained by a dormer window and by a rooflight of glass in a timber frame and following the roof slope.

d. Cellars were not often used in vernacular buildings unless the slope of the land or the pattern book examples called for them. Even in quite small and remote villages the influence of such books led to the occasional use of the 'piano nobile' and the more common use of an attic storey hidden behind a parapet.

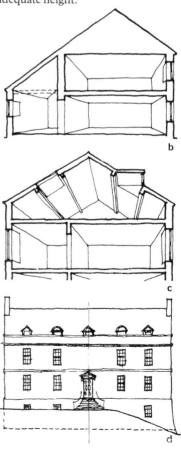

Hearths, Smoke Bays and Fireplaces

Recent investigations, especially in Surrey, have shown that there were three distinct stages in the development of heating for Small Houses: use of the open hall, provision of a smoke bay or hood, and insertion of a fireplace.

In Wealden Houses, where a hall open to the roof was flanked by two-storey bays, smoke from an open fire collected in the roof space before emerging through a louvre, through gablets, or through the chinks in a tiled roof. As the partitions between hall and flanking bays were usually carried up to the ridge, smoke-blackening was present but confined to rafters over the hall. In some such houses, the chamber on the first floor of the socially superior end of the house was jettied into the hall rather than out to the front or the side. This idea was developed by introducing a chamber over the main part of the hall. A portion was left, however, to channel smoke into the roof and this 'smoke bay' confined blackening to certain rafters over the hearth and, usually, over the cross-passage. In some instances the smoke bay was also confined on one or both sides. Later the use of a brick fireplace, chimney breast, flue and chimney stack gave relatively efficient combustion, concentrated the fire and its attendant implements in one place, and allowed the chamber to be heated by an extra flue in the same stack. In existing houses it proved convenient to insert the fireplace in the cross-passage, using space no longer needed for control of draught to an open hearth. In new construction of the same period two fireplaces back to back serving the two principal ground-floor rooms produced the central fireplaces (lobby entrance) plan.

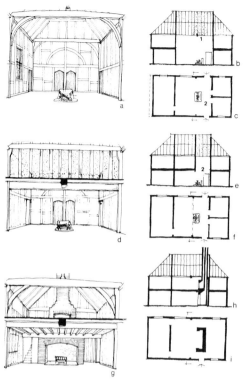

a. Cross-section through an open hall showing that smoke could ascend freely from the hearth to the roof. *b.* Longitudinal section with smoke blackening on rafters above the hall (1). *c.* Plan showing the hearth and the opposed door which gave the effect of a cross-passage. (In this and other plans the position of the staircase is not indicated.) *d.* Cross-section showing the smoke bay rising beyond the partition wall of the chamber over the hall. *e.* Longitudinal section with smoke confined within the smoke bay (2). *f.* Plan showing the smoke bay accommodating hearth and passage.

g. Cross-section to show an intermediate floor over the whole of the hall and the provision of ground- and first-floor fireplaces. The sketch indicates a chamber open to the roof but ceilings were usually introduced to improve the comfort of the room. *h.* Longitudinal section showing fireplaces and flues. *i.* Plan illustrating a large brick fireplace in the cross-passage; only one door is retained; the space between the fireplace and the rear wall was available for a staircase.

In the South and East there was usually nothing more than a timber framed partition between the hall and the rooms beyond until the complete fireplace had been introduced; elsewhere, the open hearth was normally succeeded by a smoke hood projecting from a solid wall which was usually of stone.

The dates of the various improvements varied with the size-type of the house and, to some extent, with its location. In Surrey, smoke bays were being introduced in Small Houses during the second half of the 16C. and the early 17C. Fireplaces were introduced shortly afterwards but mainly in the early and mid-17C. In the North and West most surviving Small Houses, which are often no earlier than the late 17C., had smoke hoods, and fireplaces were not introduced into the main living room until the late 18C. or early 19C.

123

Staircases

Until the late 18C. the means of communication between the various floors of a multi-storey vernacular dwelling-house was virtually confined to variations of the straight flight ladder or the spiral staircase. Both were inconvenient in their separate ways but became gradually less cramped and awkward.

No doubt the simple ladder was once an essential ancillary to life in the simplest vernacular buildings, but, apart from the primitive 'croglofft' type cottages of Wales and Ireland, the form survives only in the straight flight stone staircases of some of the superior medieval houses and in the steep companion way framed up of treads and strings, or cut from roughly shaped timber baulks found in the inferior houses of the late 17C. and early 18C.

The vernacular counterpart of the stone spiral staircase of the medieval castle is usually found alongside a fireplace where its steeply tapered steps describe one half revolution in rising from one floor to the other. Quite often, and especially in the North-West, such a staircase was fitted into a projecting turret and, following an earlier architectural fashion, developed into a series of straight flights of solid stone or timber steps around a solid core.

From the late 17C. onwards, and gradually passing down the social scale, the framed timber staircase appeared in vernacular houses and was a prominent part of the 'double pile' plan. Such a staircase could be framed with 'newels', each newel post helping to make the transition between the various angles turned by the staircase as it rose, or it could be 'geometrical', employing even more skilful joinery to eliminate the heavy newels. However, the so-called 'dog-leg' staircase of stone or heavy timber, remained popular in Small Houses until well into the 19C.

Most vernacular houses had only one staircase, except that when an open hall separated two wings, each would have its own staircase and, especially in farm-houses of the late 18C. and early 19C., a separate service staircase was sometimes provided to help isolate family from servants.

Except when needed for defensive purposes, external staircases were rarely used to give access to upper storeys. When found in farm-houses, they usually served a granary or other storeroom rather than the domestic quarters.

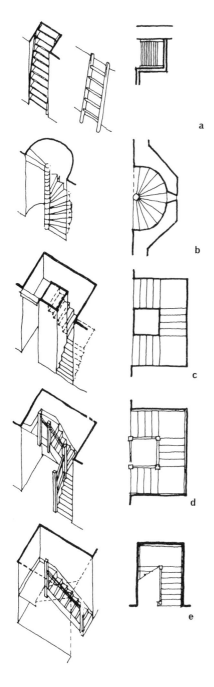

a. The simple ladder and the slightly more elaborate companion way are illustrated. The latter was often fitted into a shallow cupboard at one end of the partition which separated the private rooms from the living-room.

b. The spiral staircase could be made either of separate stone steps cantilevered from the walls and meeting in a central vertical newel, or they could be of solid timber steps spanning between a timber wall and a mast-like newel.

c. Towards the end of the 16C., Large Houses began to have staircases consisting of straight flights of solid stone or timber steps rising around a solid stone or brick core. These were more convenient than the spiral staircase but gave no opportunity for display.

d. The framed newel staircase came into common use about the middle of the 17C. and both the newel posts, and the balusters encouraged elaborate carving well displayed in the open well.

e. In the smaller houses the dog-leg staircase had many of the advantages of the newel staircase but was easier to construct and more compact. In the double pile plan the half-landing encouraged invention in window design.

Staircase Details

As an alternative to rising round a solid stone or brick core (diagram *c* on preceding page), the flights of stairs sometimes rose around a timber 'cage' left open or with panels filled with plaster. Where the posts of an open timber cage were cut at each flight the newel staircase was created. This developed to give a spacious stairwell without structural posts taking up floor space or interrupting the rising view of the staircase. The newel posts were often decorated with mouldings at the top and pendants at the bottom.

Generally, wooden staircases were designed to have treads and risers framed into inclined strings but a later fashion cut the strings to follow the outline of tread and riser relying on an inclined bearer beneath the middle of the tread to help carry the load. Strings were usually moulded.

The most decorative elements of a staircase were the balusters. These could be either turned from the solid or cut as splats from a plank-like section. Turned balusters were preferred, splat balusters being confined to attic or cellar or used in the more modest houses. Among turned balusters designs were based on the classical column with the equivalent of an abacus block, a shaft and a pedestal base all elongated and exaggerated in the turned work with the shaft sometimes turned as a barley-sugar shape. Alternatively the balusters were double-ended to make a design symmetrical about a central moulding. Splat balusters either gave a silhouette of the design of a turned baluster or had a more fanciful design of their own.

Handrails were heavily moulded in the 17C. but became simpler in shape as wooden staircases became lighter in the Regency period. Modest and late staircases had simple square section light wooden or iron balusters and simple moulded handrails.

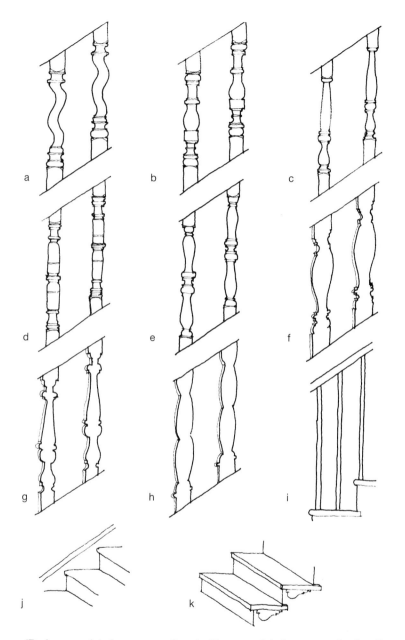

a. 'Barley-sugar' balusters, c. 1670. *b*. Fat turned balusters, end of 17C. *c*. Slender turned balusters, mid-18C. *d*. Double-ended balusters, early-mid 18C. *e*. Double-ended slender balusters, late 18C. *f*. Splat balusters, early 18C., late 17C. *g*. Splat balusters, early 18C. *h*. Splat balusters, c. 1800. *i*. Slender square balusters, late 18C. – early 19C. *j*. Riser and tread housed into string. *k*. Cut string.

4. ARCHITECTURAL DETAILS

Few vernacular buildings and very few examples of domestic vernacular are entirely without architectural adornment. The architectural details chosen may be inappropriate, the proportions unhappy, and the execution crude, but the intention – to extend the process of architectural design to the level of detail – was patently there.

To judge from surviving examples, the aim was to follow national fashion, and each change in fashion displayed on the supra-vernacular buildings of the capital or the great provincial centres was eventually followed at the vernacular level. But as a result of the time lag caused by slow communications and the natural caution and conservatism of vernacular designers, an innovation would often be introduced into a remote village long after it had passed out of use in fashionable society. The time lag diminished as communications improved, but it was never entirely eliminated. As a result of the varying characteristics of different building materials, the national fashions tended to develop regional variations. Thus, in a region of half-timbered building, nationally developed stone mouldings would be modified for use in timber and so help to develop a sub-style, or, in a region of hard, intractable stone, the mouldings developed nationally by skilled masons working in selected materials were adapted locally to the materials and skills available. Only in those regions where the available materials could permit absolutely no adornment, or poverty was so complete that only the barest essentials of buildings could be financed, would architectural details be absent.

Even in a single house there was a gradation in the quality of materials and details from the front, to the sides, and then to the rear of the building. Thus the windows on the front of an 18C. Lancashire farm-house might have double hung sashes in moulded stone architraves, the sides having horizontally sliding sashes in the jambs of a squared rubble wall, while on the rear wall re-used stone mullioned windows with timber casements would be set in random rubble. Similarly in a farmstead of one build, stable, barn, and granary would normally have the type of window and mouldings which had recently been abandoned for domestic use, while the cow-house, pig-sty, etc., having lower status, would have unglazed openings following an even earlier pattern.

Towards the end of the vernacular period the resources of the local designer were extended by use of the newly available pattern books. With the aid of such a primer an up-to-date elevation could be designed and given appropriate details even if the sides and rear of a house followed the vernacular version of earlier architectural fashions. The pattern books usually indicated windows and doors as shaded voids; these were often provided in the vernacular elevation and glazed or not as internal arrangements suggested; the Window Taxes have been unjustly blamed for careless application of the rules from a pattern book.

There is no doubt that a good deal of local imitation took place, building contracts sometimes refer to one house which was being used as a model for another, and equally, there is little doubt that a craftsman, having adopted or devised a particular detail used it at every opportunity within the radius of his operations.

The evidence of architectural details ranks with documentary evidence in dating vernacular buildings. Reference to the authoritative architectural textbooks will help in using this evidence for dating, but one must always remember that these books have established dating criteria based on the use of architectural details in the most advanced and expensive buildings in the country and when making use of these criteria the time lag, itself varying with period and location, between initial appearance at national level, and final use in the remotest vernacular building was a very long one, measured in centuries rather than years in extreme instances. It is to be hoped that before long enough research will have been done with the aid of dated vernacular buildings for a full series of corrected time scales to be available for use in various parts of the country.

Windows and Doors Generally

Three stages in the continuous development of the window are distinguished here; they have been given the convenient, though only partially appropriate, names of medieval, sub-medieval, and renaissance. In each phase a distinction has been made between the overall shape of the window opening, the mouldings associated with it, and the provision for glazing and ventilation.

The three stages relate to the changes in sectional form of the domestic interiors which the windows were intended to serve. In the medieval hall house, tall windows with a few narrow lights were needed for the main hall or the solar, both rooms being open to the roof. But in the storied late medieval house, and in the Small Houses which were coming into the vernacular zone, rooms were low and often ceiled and so horizontal runs of mullioned windows became the most appropriate type. By the early part of the 17C. the tall windows of the Italian Renaissance had begun their long period of influence. At first, rooms remained low in vernacular buildings and so the long horizontal run of the medieval window was replaced by two or three short square windows, but gradually tall rooms came into use and with them the tall renaissance window shape.

In most stone-bearing districts, some attempt was made to employ fashionable mouldings around the window openings. Where brick or an inferior stone was used for walling, superior stone was often carried from a quarry in an adjacent district in order to permit these mouldings.

The earliest surviving vernacular buildings appear to make no provision for glazing, and, indeed, it seems unlikely that glazed windows became common before the late 16C. in Large Houses or the late 17C. in Small Houses. But, as the early lattices of glass quarries in a network of lead cames required no structural preparation other than the provision of a few bars to which the lattices could be tied, it is difficult to decide if any specific example of a window of such a period was actually glazed. Early glass was cut from blown discs and is usually very thin and heavily marked. Later glass, from disc or cylinder was set in thick wooden glazing bars; these were gradually reduced in thickness until the early 19C., when, becoming almost too thin for stability, they were sometimes replaced by glazing bars of iron. Cheap but good quality sheet glass, available after about 1840, meant that most glazing bars could be omitted, and many earlier window frames were adapted for these large panes with unfortunate results for the scale of the building.

Three stages in the continuous development of the doorway have also been distinguished and they compare roughly in period with those suggested for the window. In each stage the shape of the door, the nature of any associated mouldings, and the form of the door itself have been separately considered.

As the doorway in a vernacular building was almost invariably related directly to human size and rarely depended on the needs of extravagant display there was little variation in the basic size and shape. However there were variations in width which are not easy to explain and the basic shape permitted a wide variety in the form of the head of the doorway.

In most stone-bearing districts the doorway was the point of concentration for such carving as the nature of the material, the wealth of the owner, and the skill of the mason would permit. This detail included the mouldings of the door jambs and the various embellishments – drip courses, shields, carved mottoes, pediments, swags, etc. – which were demanded by changing architectural fashion. In districts of timber frame construction, and in those stone-bearing districts where the material was unsuitable for carving, the doorway was often framed out of heavy timber sections displaying an adaptation of the mason's mouldings.

There was a continuous improvement in the construction of the door and its method of hanging. Early doors were made of heavy vertical planks, battened at the rear and harr-hung on vertical wooden pins or hung by heavy strap hinges from brackets set in the jambs of the doorway. Later the door construction became lighter, and the door might be hung or hinged to a frame. Eventually the panelled door became available and this was hung on concealed hinges in the type of slender frame with which we are now familiar.

Some token acknowledgement is made of the wealth of fashionable architectural adornment displayed both on the exterior and the interior of quite humble dwelling-houses. These range from bays, porches, and other projections from the face of the building, to the simple panelling and ingeniously stopped mouldings which so often decorate the living-room of the most severe looking farm-house.

Windows: The Medieval Phase

Illustrated here are window forms originating in the medieval period but continuing, at the vernacular levels, almost until the 18C. There appear to be two main variations: the horizontal which was based on a series of vertical lancet type lights, and the horizontal which was based on a series of diamond-mullioned divisions of a wooden window frame. But both probably derive from the more commonly accepted medieval window shape of a vertical in stone or timber.

The stone-mullioned versions may run from between two and sixteen lights in one horizontal range, but the long runs are usually subdivided by king mullions into groups of three or four lights. In later examples, the windows were made taller with mullions steadied by transoms to give a rectangular shape more appropriate to the sub-medieval phase.

Mouldings in stone-mullioned windows followed the fashions set earlier at higher architectural levels. Wood-mullioned windows were normally square-cut bars set diagonally with narrow intermediate bars, but they could also be more or less direct copies of stone forms in the cheaper material. Windows were linked and protected by horizontal label or drip moulds.

During the earlier part of the phase, glazing was unusual, even for quite superior houses. Some examples survive of the hinged or sliding shutters which provided security and draught protection. A few examples also survive of the early lattices wired to the bars of wood-mullioned windows or to iron bars in stone-mullioned windows, but most have been replaced by later sashes.

Windows in half-timbered buildings followed these same general lines but usually with flimsier sections and more spindly details.

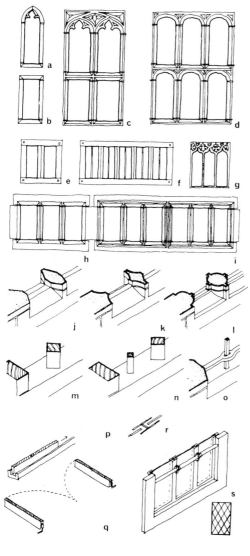

a. Lancet with cusped head.

b. Lancet with square head.

c. Transomed window with cusped lights and spandrel at the head; designed for a rectangular opening; would normally have a 'drip' or 'label' mould above.

d. A squarish opening mullioned and transomed to give six lights each with three-centred arched heads.

e. Wooden window frame with single diamond mullion.

f. Range of five lights in a wooden frame with diamond mullion and intermediate vertical bars.

g. Three-light window with ogee-arched heads and cusped spandrels, all of slender section appropriate to a timber-framed wall.

h. Three-light window, square headed, and with splayed stone mullions.

i. Six-light window, square headed, and with a king mullion and depressed beyond a separate splayed moulding.

j. Splayed mullion and jamb. k. Cavetto mullion and jamb. l. Ovolo-moulded mullion and jamb. m. Diamond mullion, square cut jamb. n. As before but with intermediate vertical bar. o. Iron barred window (no glazing). p. Horizontally sliding internal shutter. q. Side hung internal shutters. r. Glass quarries in lead came. s. Lattice wired to horizontal iron bar; square and diamond panes shown.

Windows: The Sub-Medieval Phase

The sub-medieval phase was a transition between the earlier period of long horizontal runs of narrow mullioned lights and the later period of tall balanced sash widows. It lasted in minor domestic work certainly until the mid-18C. and for workshops, etc., until the mid-19C.

The characteristic window shape in this period was square. In stone districts the square shape was divided into two by a mullion, but often this has been removed to allow a new window frame to be inserted; where it survives the mullion may be thin, square-cut, set-back, and unrelated to any mouldings which surround the window. In brick districts the square or slightly elongated window would be set beneath a shallow arch and either divided by thin wooden mullions within the window frame into two or three lights, or filled with an overall network of horizontal and vertical glazing bars. In timber framed work, the window frames were of fairly heavy sections, often flush with, or even projecting slightly from the various cladding materials, tiles, plaster, etc., which had come into use.

At this stage some form of ventilation by opening lights had become normal. In stone districts this took the form either of side hung opening casements in wrought iron or wood, or of horizontally sliding sashes. This latter form, the so-called Yorkshire sliding sash, was the inferior equivalent of the superior vertically sliding sash, but with its one fixed and one sliding portion, was particularly appropriate to the square window shape. In brick and timber frame districts, side hung casements were more common. In all districts at this period, the humbler buildings might be ventilated by no more than a single small opening light in a window of otherwise entirely fixed glazing.

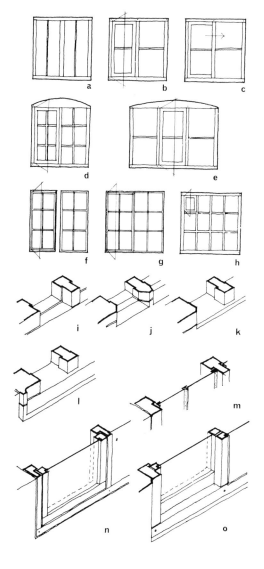

a. Square opening of two lights with vertical bars.

b. Square two-light opening, one side-hung wooden casement, single horizontal wooden glazing bars.

c. As *b.* but with 'Yorkshire' horizontally sliding sash.

d. As *b.* but small panes under brick arch.

e. Three-light window, wooden frames, centre light a side-hung casement, all under a shallow brick arch.

f. Two-light window with square-cut stone mullion, wrought-iron frames, one side-hung one fixed, small panes.

g. As *f.* but in one square opening.

h. Fixed window of small panes in wooden frame and with one small opening pane.

i. Square-cut mullion and jamb adapted for glazing by lattices applied from the outside.

j. Chamfered mullion and jamb adapted for inside glazing. *k.* square-cut mullion set back from chamfered window opening. *l.* As *k.* but window has simple architrave surround. *m.* Wrought-iron side-hung casement. *n.* Wooden side-hung casement. *o.* Wooden horizontally sliding sash.

Windows: The Renaissance Phase

The period characterized by the vertical window shape began at the higher vernacular levels towards the end of the 17C. and continued until the end of the vernacular tradition 200 years later. It included the Georgian window as normally understood together with the detailed variations introduced as part of the Greek and Gothic Revivals.

Although the basic shape was that of a vertical rectangle, lighting requirements sometimes led to variations. The most decorative of these was the Palladian or Gibbs window which was very popular for staircase landings; to provide more light into a living-room the basic window was widened, two hollow mullions containing counter balances for the sashes; in the North of England, where the mullioned tradition was never entirely lost, two vertical windows were added together to give a square shape. For Gothic Revival purposes the head of the vertical window was rounded or pointed, or two windows were collected beneath a label mould.

Mouldings were dominated by the standard renaissance forms, except in brick buildings. There, interest was concentrated on head and sill. At the window head the lintels were based on flat arches of gauged brickwork or had Gibbs-type details in stone, sometimes a single stone lintel being cut in imitation of separate voussoirs.

Early examples of the renaissance type window had stone or wood mullions and transomes with side hung opening casements, but few of these survive as they were soon superseded by the vertically sliding sash window developed in the late 17C. and early 18C. In vernacular examples the upper sash was originally fixed, the lower sliding in grooves and held by wedges or balanced by weights. Later in the 18C., the familiar balanced sash came into universal use.

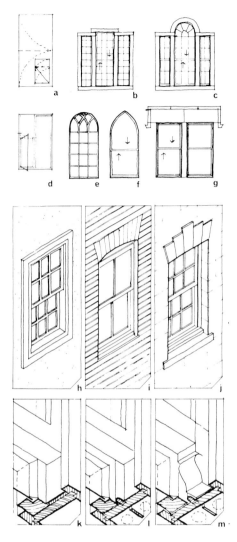

a. Window proportions: double square for window opening and 'side and diagonal' for individual panes.

b. Hybrid with stone mullions and raised head to central light, quite commonly found in the Pennines.

c. 'Palladian' or 'Gibbs' window, central arched light and narrower square-headed lights at each side.

d. Late 17C. type with mullion and transome of stone or timber and with side-hung opening light, wooden or of wrought iron.

e. 'Gothick' tracery in semi-circular head, a common staircase window.

f. Gothic Revival arched head.

g. Two-light square-headed Gothic Revival window under label mould, vertically sliding sashes without glazing bars.

h. Upper sash fixed, shown with heavy wooden glazing bars and with shallow reveals and wooden architrave as in timber framed wall.

i. Balanced sashes in brick wall.

j. Balanced sashes in deep reveal in stone wall.

k. Detail of fixed upper sash, note absence of parting bead and weights.

l. Balanced sashes.

m. Details of Victorian modification with drooping 'horns'.

Doors and Doorways: The Medieval Phase

During this period the most characteristic doorway at the vernacular level included the frameless door; the actual door being hinged direct to the structure of stone or wood rather than being hung on a door frame. Nevertheless in some parts, e.g. the West Country and Wales, a heavy door frame set into a stone opening was used.

The characteristic shape of the doorway depends on the width and the form of the head. Usually the doorway was the 2 ft. 10 in. or 3 ft. width we would expect at the present day, but there are a number of examples, especially in the West of England, where the door is much wider than normal; these may possibly be related to use of the doors by wide-horned cattle as well as humans, or, it has been suggested, even designed for milk maids carrying two pails on a yoke! The form of the head includes variations on the arch, two-centred, three-centred, four-centred, etc., following, with appropriate time lag, the general architectural fashion.

Mouldings on doors resembled those on windows except that the termination of a moulding at the base of a door jamb gave opportunity for variations in the design of a stop similar to the stopped mouldings of ceiling beams. Moulded drip courses, following the line of arched heads, or horizontal with dropped and returned ends, were used towards the end of the phase, but decorated lintels were uncommon.

Some examples of the original door survive. These are usually massive, consist of heavy ledges and planks or two layers of battens placed alternately, are usually studded with the ends of iron or wooden pegs, and are usually strong enough to give a defensive capability enhanced by a heavy drawbar. But carved and applied Gothic decoration is equally characteristic of the phase. In earlier examples, or in remote parts of the country an additional wrought iron grille was provided.

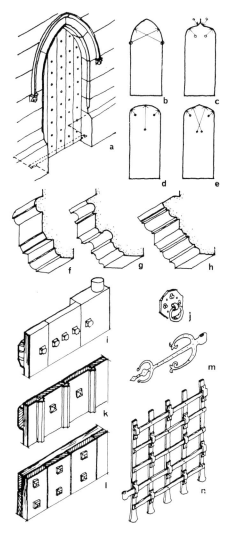

a. Arched doorway in stone wall, splayed moulding to jamb and arch, drip mould terminating in carved corbels, wooden vertically planked door with studs, set in rebate in stone.

b. Two-centred arch.

c. Ogee arch.

d. Three-centred arch.

e. Four-centred arch.

f. Moulded jamb and label, early 14C. type.

g. As *f.* but early 16C. type.

h. as *f.* but early 17C. type.

i. Door of vertical planks and horizontal battens connected with wooden pegs, the innermost plank has been thickened and shaped to provide pegs for 'harr' hanging into a wooden socket at the top and an iron shoe at the bottom.

j. Door knocker.

k. Plank and batten door, iron pegs and moulded cover strips.

l. Alternate plank and batten door, closely spaced wooden pegs.

m. Wrought iron hinge used to hang the door on iron brackets built into the stone door jamb.

n. Wrought iron gate used as inner defence, like a portcullis but side hung.

139

Doors and Doorways:
The Sub-Medieval Phase

Roughly corresponding with the period of vernacular window design here called sub-medieval, there was a phase of doorway design which was neither medieval nor renaissance in substance but which included elements of both phases. In many parts of the country most of the surviving vernacular houses have doorways with the characteristics of this phase, including at one extreme, crude developments of Gothic precedent, and at the other, untutored introductions to the Renaissance.

In the stone bearing districts of the Pennines and extending westwards into the Lake District the most characteristic detail is the decorated lintel. No two examples are exactly alike, but one common form has a single lintel shaped at the base into a flat suggestion of a four-centred arch, decorated on the face with various combinations of initials and dates, and set below a simple dropped label mould; another, equally common, has the splayed or moulded jamb of the doorway carried up into the lintel to give a battlemented or false arched effect. Towards the end of the phase the mouldings took on a crude classical form and the label mould was simplified into a cornice-like shape. Where a heavy wooden door frame was provided, this was sometimes quite heavily moulded, or had a shaped head, presenting an exotic, almost oriental, combination of curves and angles.

Heavy wooden doors continued to be hung from brackets in the door jamb and secured by a drawbar, but in later examples, simple framed doors came into use, hinged to the door frame, and equipped with clumsy, though sometimes well-decorated, locks.

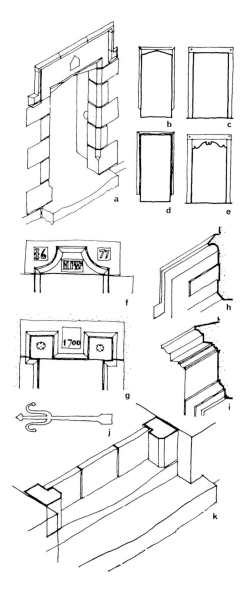

a. Doorway with a false four-centred arched head (straight sides to pointed head) in a splayed jamb, deep lintel with carved device, label mould with dropped and returned ends, the door is shown open to reveal a drawbar socket.

b. False four-centred arch.

c. Heavy wooden frame.

d. Moulded square-headed opening.

e. Carved head framed into heavy wooden door frame.

f., g. Two examples of decorated lintel.

h. Chamfered jamb and label mould late 17C. type.

i. Moulded jamb and cornice early 18C. type.

j. Wrought iron strap hinge.

k. Door of planks and battens with concealed hinges in heavy wooden frame.

Doors and Doorways:
Renaissance and Revival Phase

During this phase the emphasis of the doorway as the point of concentration of interest and decoration in the centre of an elevation reached its culmination. Even in the plain, utilitarian design of a terraced cottage, few doorways were without some form of pediment or canopy.

As well as the normal square head, semi-circular and elliptical heads were adopted, and, during the revival phase, the arched head returned to fashion. These variations depended to some extent on the development of the fanlight to introduce daylight into the lobby or 'hall' into which the front door now opened in all but the poorest houses. The square head, however, was modified by the use of voussoirs, or a flat brick arch, or a decorated keystone, to provide a decorative effect.

The conventional door surround in this phase included a pediment, triangular or segmental, together with moulded architraves, and a good deal of detailed variation was made even within the standardized form. Where the type of stone permitted, initials, date and a motto were sometimes incised.

With the improvement in joinery techniques the doors during this phase usually had four or six raised and fielded panels and bolection moulds. The panels could move within the grooves of their frames, the raised and fielded effect gave shape and substance to the panel, while the bolection moulding embraced the joint between the body of the door and the panels but concealed movement between them.

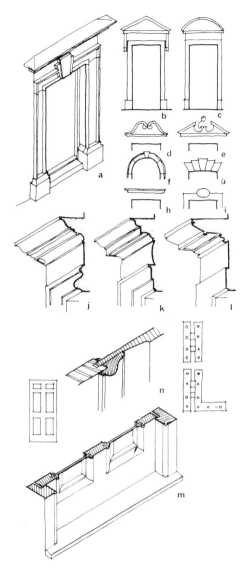

a. A type of door and doorway found at the vernacular level from the middle of the 18C. onwards. The stone architrave and head with heavily emphasized but quite false keystone show reasonably faithful imitation of classical precedent. The door is framed and panelled and set in a separate light timber frame or casing.

b. Triangular pediment.

c. Segmental pediment.

d. Scroll type pediment.

e. Broken pediment.

f. Semi-circular arch with keystone.

g. Stepped voussoirs (usually carved out of a single stone lintel).

h. Flat hood or cornice.

i. simple architraves with date panel.

j. Bolection moulded architrave, late 17C. to mid-18C.

k. Architrave and cornice with pulvinated frieze, mid- to late 18C.

l. Simple chamfered architrave with Greek Revival cornice, early 19C.

m. Framed wooden door of six panels showing mouldings and raised panel.

n. Details of bolection moulding and the H and L type hinges used especially on internal doors.

Architectural Details:
Other External Ornament

It is quite impossible to give more than a token representation to the minor architectural details in which the vernacular designers displayed their ingenuity, and since so many buildings of this class present no more than the bare bones of peasant building techniques for inspection it would, perhaps, be inappropriate to emphasize the few which came closest to the conventions of polite architecture. Nevertheless three categories of ornament are mentioned here: bay windows, porches, and decorative details.

Bay windows, popular in the superior buildings of the medieval period, returned to favour, in both bold and shallow projection, during the Regency. Oriels had no comparable successors except in the seaside towns where such projecting windows could give a view of the sea and ships. Galleries of various sorts were occasionally found in vernacular buildings, especially when the lie of the land entailed building on several levels. Balconies and verandahs were found towards the end of the period of vernacular building and were an unusual feature adopted for development by the clever designers of the Vernacular Revival movement.

At the vernacular level, porches seem to have come into favour towards the end of the 16C., possibly as a last token of the former dignity of a defensive tower, or possibly as a remote acknowledgement of the form of the classical portico. Apart from its use as a means of reducing draughts through the main doorway, the porch also gave an opportunity for display of the limited extravagance of vernacular detail. Smaller, single-storey porches were surprisingly uncommon, even in exposed upland situations.

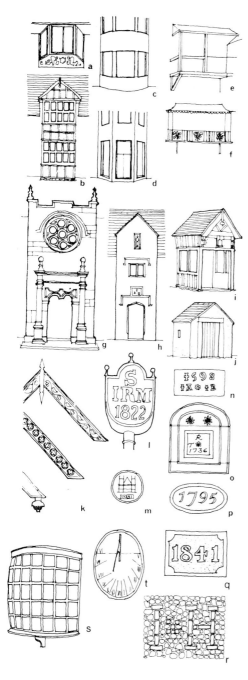

a. Oriel window from timber framed building, carved solid bracket (late 16C.).
b. Square-cut bay window (early 17C.).
c. Bow window (early 19C.).
d. Splayed bay window (late 18C.).
e. Spinning gallery (late 17C.).
f. Balcony of wrought iron (late 18C. – early 19C.).
g. Two-storey porch with rose window (mid-17C.).
h. Multi-storey porch with carved plaque and niche for statue (late 16C.).
i. Open single-storey porch (late 16C.).
j. Closed single-storey porch (mid-18C.).
k. Barge boards with finials, pierced decoration and pendants.
l. Lead rain water head with initials and date.
m. Fire mark.
n. Date plaque, raised lettering.
o. Date plaque, incised lettering.
p. Date plaque, deeply incised lettering.
q. Date plaque, recessed base leaving bold raised lettering.
r. Lettering in stone set in flint.
s. Bow window used in shops in early 19C.
t. Sundial.

Architectural Details: Internal Ornament

In spite of the many modifications which most vernacular buildings have suffered in order to make them more comfortable or, more recently, to help them match the suburban image of the ideal home of the women's magazine, there is a quite substantial survival of internal architectural details. Of the wealth of regional variation over the course of time, three groups of detail have been selected for comment: partitions, built-in cupboards, and moulded ceiling beams.

Many of the common plan forms adopted by the vernacular house designers made use of a partition to separate private rooms from the main living-room. These were usually non-structural and could conveniently be made of timber, whatever the material of the main walls of the house. The most common type of partition has been given the name of 'muntin and plank'. It consisted of alternate thick and thin planks, the latter set in grooves running vertically along the edges of the former. The muntins, in superior examples were moulded on the living-room side, while the planks might be given some simplified version of the linenfold pattern. Later these and other internal partitions were framed of studs and rails with square panels between and with light renaissance mouldings for decoration.

During the later 17C., built-in cupboards were popular in farm-houses. The larger cupboards were sometimes built into the timber partitions, while the smaller cupboards included the so-called spice cupboard, set into the fireplace wall, and generally assumed to be the dry depository of valuable salt and spices.

When the open hall passed out of favour, the architectural invention which had been devoted to the cusping and other ornament of roof timbers was diverted in part to the moulding of the heavy beams which carried the intermediate floor. The simple chamfered beam was the basis of many varieties of moulding and stop.

146

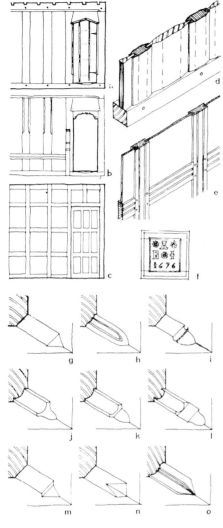

a. Part of a partition between living-room and private rooms showing muntin and plank partition framed between beam and cill and incorporating a doorway. Many examples survive dating from late 15C. to late 17C.

b. These partitions sometimes incorporated a built-in bench with shaped pew-like ends.

c. From about the middle of the 17C. framed partitions were used in vernacular buildings; the example incorporates a framed door.

d. Detail of a muntin and plank partition; there were several variations, the one illustrated has thick planks chamfered to slide into grooves in the muntins.

e. Detail of early framed partitioning; later examples used mitred, or scribed joints to allow the mouldings to run around the panels.

f. Detail of a built-in 'spice cupboard'. g. Basic chamfer and stop. h. Early 17C. moulding to a beam, ovolo flanked by cavettoes. i. Flat chamfer stopped by a quirk and a tongue, early 17C. j. Ovolo stopped by tongue, late 16C. or early 17C. k. Variation of j. with ovolo stopped before the tongue. l. Bead type mould stopped by flat and tongue, mid 17C. m. Flat chamfer with fillet and stop, mid-17C. n. Flat chamfer with half pyramid stop, mid-17C. o. Ovolo, fillet, and cavetto tapered stop, late 17C.

147

5. FARM BUILDINGS

Introduction

The association of the farm-house with roses round the door and ivy on the wall compares favourably with the manure underfoot and dust up above which are more commonly associated with the other buildings of the farmstead. Perhaps for this reason, as well as others more academic, the design and construction of farm buildings has received even less attention from scholars than the planning, choice of materials and architectural detailing of farm-houses. And yet the sheer volume of space enclosed, quite apart from the constructional problems presented by farm buildings should remind us that the expense and effort devoted to farm buildings has, for the past three centuries been greater than that devoted to farm-houses, while the architectural qualities of cathedral-like barns and elegant granaries are often superior to those of the farm-houses they served. No apology, therefore is made, for devoting a reasonable proportion of this handbook to farm buildings.

As the study of farm buildings is even further extended into infancy than the study of other branches of vernacular architecture, this chapter is even less well-founded on published research than the others. But comprehensive national studies of the history of farm buildings have now been published and regional studies have also appeared, together with more and more articles devoted to selected farmsteads or typical farm buildings. The subject is now becoming much better covered. This chapter attempts to list briefly the characteristics of the farm buildings normally found in England and Wales, to note the arrangements commonly adopted in the layout of the farmstead, and to illustrate the effects of different farming practices and improved farming technology on the development of farm building design.

The surviving evidence from which the vernacular architecture of farm buildings can be studied covers an even shorter period than that relating to domestic vernacular architecture. Apart from the great medieval barns such as Bredon or Great Coxwell which are scarcely in the vernacular zone, few surviving agricultural buildings, stone or brick walled, appear to have been erected before the middle of the 17C. or, if timber framed, before the 16C., and the majority appear to be of late 18C. and early 19C. date. However, the vernacular content of farm buildings remained considerable until late in the 19C. and a terminal date of 1880 encompasses most of the examples worth study.

While the farming pattern of England and Wales gives a variety almost as complex as that of geology, for the present purposes there appear to have been three main types of farming practice which were significant: the predominantly arable cultivation of the eastern counties of England, the predominantly pastoral farming of the hilliest regions of Northern England, Central Wales and South-Western England, and the large area of mixed farming of the remainder of the country. Pastoral farming required virtually no buildings, arable farming required little more than capacious barns and sheds for the few loose cattle, but mixed farming required a considerable and increasing variety of buildings for the closely interrelated farming processes.

It is hard for the present day farmer, let alone the layman, to appreciate the importance of home-grown corn until late in the 19C. Oats, wheat and barley were essential for consumption by the farmer and his family, while oats at least were a vital part of the diet of his animals. Straw was essential for bedding and the conversion of manure into fertilizer for return to the land, while in most parts of the country it was the normal roofing material. But as yields were low harvesting difficult and the proportion to be retained for seed was high, much cultivable land had to be devoted to cereals. For the temporary storage and conversion of the cereal crop, one or more barns were required on every farmstead, and this building is the one most commonly found, and usually the one most ancient on the typical farmstead. However, changes in animal husbandry, the greater use of root crops and vegetables both to improve the diet of the animals and maintain the fertility of the soil, and improvements in the method of threshing and winnowing meant that after the middle of the 19C. the barn as commonly understood had become obsolete, and the large scale imports first of prairie-grown corn and later of frozen meat has led to the elimination of the barn as a building type.

Because the arable land was so vital to farming operations over most of the country, the power source which permitted cultivation of this land was equally vital. Until comparatively recent times the power for plough, harrow, and cart was provided by the ox, and as not all farmers could field a complete team, systems of common cultivation depended on the contribution of one or two healthy members from each participant. Similarly, the milking cow and her butter and cheese were so important, especially during the winter months that a house for the accommodation of cow and ox is found on most farmsteads. Where associated with the dwelling house in the 'long house' and similar arrangements, the significance of the cow-house as a building type becomes even more clear.

The horse has often been considered second only to man in the kingdom of mammals, and his accommodation has been given almost as much attention in early times. But in most parts of the country use of the horse was restricted to carriage, pack, and riding, it being considered too valuable an animal, and too expensive to keep, to replace the ox for general farm purposes. Even when the horse became, during the later 18C., the principal draught animal, the farm horses were separately housed from the carriage and riding horses. Both, however, required stables and this building type was commonly found on the farmstead from about 1750 onwards.

With the virtual elimination of the horse by the tractor since about 1950 few stables remain in use, but conversion to other uses has rarely obliterated all evidence of their original design.

The edible or marketable produce so dearly won from the land was for a long time carefully guarded within the dwelling house. But improvements in farming methods and increased productivity generally from the middle of the 18C. onwards meant that a specific building in the form of a granary was designed for the accommodation of threshed grain and, perhaps, ground flour and bran. At the same time the increasing range of wheeled implements and carts available to the farmer and required for improved cultivation led to the demand for a cart and implement shed. As the cart shed had to be at ground level, while the granary was best placed at the upper level, the combined granary/cart shed was provided on most farmsteads in mixed farming areas from the late 18C. onwards.

While the especially valuable and particularly vulnerable cattle were kept in a cow house, in most parts of the country the young stock were folded in the farmyard during the winter. There they were contained and protected by other farm buildings, but the shelter shed was developed as a building type to provide some shelter from the weather when feeding. In some parts of the South West, this was combined with hay storage to form the two-storeyed linhay. The open sided haybarn was developed in other parts of the country for the accommodation of such of the hay crop as could not be housed in the lofts over cow-house and stable. In districts with a more severe climate, hay was enclosed in a barn similar in form to the corn barn, and this was often located in the fields distant from the farm-house where combined accommodation for hay and young cattle took the form of the field-barn. Amongst the other minor buildings of the farmyard may be mentioned the pig-sty and the dovecot, the one sometimes incorporating a hen-house and the other, occasionally surviving from more aristocratic days as an independent structure but more commonly incorporated with barn or even granary.

Some farmsteads also incorporate minor industrial buildings in the form of various kilns. The best known is the oast-house of South Eastern

England, but corn-drying kilns were formerly equally common in the wet high-lying districts of England and Wales, where late and poor cereal crops had to be harvested damp or not at all. In barley growing districts, a malting kiln is sometimes found, while in districts with limestone outcrop, lime kilns dating from the late 18C. may be seen, usually in the fields, rather than as part of the farmstead.

Thus the barn, cow-house, stable, granary, cart shed and other minor buildings combined with the farmyard to form the working part of the farmstead as a whole. These buildings were, of course, lower in status than those of the domestic part of the economy and within this lower rank had their own grades of quality. Pride of place was normally granted to the great corn barn, though the stable might be given more careful architectural adornment, while pig-sty and kiln were the most utilitarian. In construction they followed, normally, the local patterns set by domestic buildings, though with an appreciably longer time lag for the adoption of new materials: many a set of timber framed and thatch-roofed farm buildings, for instance, lies alongside a brick and tiled farm-house. In architectural detailing, similarly, they lag behind: the granary for instance being provided with wood mullioned and shuttered unglazed windows at a time when even the humblest part of the farm-house had glazed casements.

The need for recording and study of farm buildings is even more urgent than the need for study of houses. Most houses can be adapted or extended to meet a changing way of domestic life; the drift of permanent settlement from the countryside is to some extent counteracted by the enthusiasm for weekend cottages. But there is scarcely a single traditional farm building type which can be employed or even adapted to contemporary farming methods. The barn has been obsolete for a century, the traditional cow-house is unhygienic for milk production and unsuitable for labour-saving methods of feeding and care. The stable has been obsolete since the tractor superseded the horse. Neither granary nor cart shed are needed. The silage pit has replaced the Dutch Barn; the pig fattening factory has replaced the pig-sty. Farmers and landowners have, in many cases, maintained obsolete farm buildings which they know to be uneconomical; but stone tile will not be replaced much longer and stone walls will eventually crumble; the multi-purpose steel and asbestos shed will replace the farmyard and its attendant buildings. The process is in its early stages, but before long the evidence will disappear; before it does so, it is imperative that the buildings be recorded, their story unravelled and forgotten farming processes recalled, and significant examples defined for preservation.

Farm Buildings: Location and Layout

Before examination of the individual building of the farmstead, the location and layout may be of interest.

Most farmsteads will be located either in nucleated settlements (villages), in groups of two or three (hamlets), or will be isolated. The nucleated settlements survive from periods of common cultivation on the open field or related systems of agriculture. Farms located in villages will be the few survivors of the many, large and small, which made up the community. Farmsteads located in hamlets or as part of very tiny groups are normally associated with pastoral farming, or mixed farming with a high pastoral element – there are few villages but many hamlets in mountainous Wales. But such farmsteads in other districts may be the survivors of a former nucleated village which has become otherwise deserted and decayed. Isolated farmsteads usually represent occupation of waste land which may have occurred at any time: medieval clearance of wooded land, or occupation of uncultivated moor; Elizabethan colonization of the upper slopes of valley sides, or 19C. enclosure of common land with new farmsteads established in the centre of a compact group of square fields. Other evidence is essential before the full implication of farmstead location may be understood.

The layout or pattern of the farmstead has been a source of fascination; between the extremes of the scattered building of the hill farming peasant and the carefully marshalled ranks of the 'model farmery' various attempts at classification have been made. A simple broad distinction is suggested here, but a great deal of work remains to be done before we understand such meaning as there may be in the shape of the farmstead.

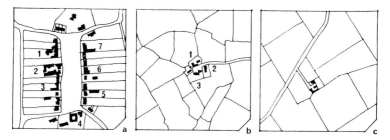

Some farmstead locations: *a.* nucleated village, surviving farmsteads numbered; *b.* hamlet in fields of ancient enclosure, three farmsteads indicated; *c.* isolated farmstead in fields of recent enclosure.

Some farmstead layouts (the hatched portion represents the farm-house).

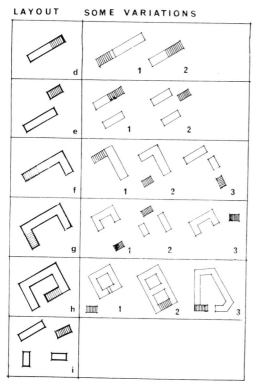

LAYOUT   SOME VARIATIONS

d. Elongated – variation (1) indicates a 'longhouse' house and cow-house interconnected, (2) indicates a laithe house of one build but not interconnected.

e. Parallel – variation (1) has a connected and (2) a separated farm-house.

f. L-shaped – the three variations differ mainly in the position of the farm-house.

g. U-shaped – among variations (1) shows a separate farmhouse axially related to the farm buildings, (3) a farm-house quite detached and distinct.

h. Courtyard – (1) has a detached farm-house, (2) a farm-house incorporated in one of the yards, (3) an irregular courtyard resulting from amalgamation of buildings. *i.* Scattered – especially in mountain farmsteads, different periods of build as well as difficult sites lead to disorderly development.

Farm Buildings:
Combination Arrangements

One of the devices employed in design of farm buildings at the present day is the combination of all or most of the activities of the farmstead under one roof. Like so many of the inspirations of modern designers it is, in fact a resurrection of a former practice. Two examples of the practice are illustrated here.

The huge steeply pitched roof enfolding house and farm buildings is still a dominant feature of the rural landscape in Denmark and North Germany. It is more than likely that such combined buildings were erected in those parts of England which came under Danish influence after the Dark Ages, and the medieval domestic aisled hall may be a remnant of such a traditional form. No such combined dwelling and set of farm buildings survives intact and on such a scale, but there is an echo of the arrangement in some of the larger 18C. barns in which cowhouses, loose boxes, and shelter sheds are enclosed between the projecting porches and covered by the extended roof of a threshing barn.

An extremely compact combination farm building is the Bank Barn of the English Lake District. Here a natural or artificial slope is essential; from the lower level there is access to a cart shed flanked by cow-houses and stable, while at the upper level, a ramp, on the opposite side of the building, leads to a conventional barn. Hatches enable fodder to be dropped from barn to manger, and an economical building form was equally economical in labour. Most Cumbrian bank barns range in date from the early 18C. to the early 20C. but there are notable examples from the late 17C. on a few of the larger farmsteads and one barn at least may be earlier than that, according to the research of Dr Tyson.

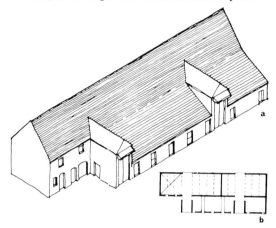

a. Combination barn, cow-house, and stable, isometric. *b*. Plan.

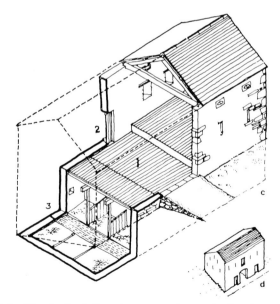

c. Typical Lake District Bank Barn in cutaway isometric showing threshing floor (1), winnowing door (2), cow-house (3).
d. View from the lower slope showing the doors to cart shed and stable.

Bank Barns (continued)

Although the majority of bank barns in Cumbria are sited along the slope, a significant minority – between 20% and 25% – are sited across the slope. This allows for entry to the cow-houses through the gable wall rather than one of the side walls but restricts the amount of lower ground level space available for stable and cart shed. Such an arrangement has been called a 'variant bank barn'. In the south-east of Cumbria on the border with Lancashire there may be found a farm building type which combines the variant bank barn with the three doors in the gable wall (serving feeding passage and two manure passages) of the 'Lancashire barn' with the other characteristic of a plan widened to accommodate the three passages at the cow-house end. Although bank barns are numerous in Cumbria they are also quite plentiful in Cornwall, Devon and probably in parts of Somerset too. In Cornwall the bank barn is known as the 'chall barn'. The arrangement is generally similar with a barn for storage and processing of grain crops at the upper level and a cow-house, an ox-house or stable and sometimes a cart shed at the lower level. There are detailed differences in that the winnowing door is often double width and protected by a pentise canopy and the feeding passage may be double width and reached through double doors; also, many of the barns have two threshing floors with the corresponding two winnowing doors. Like the Cumbrian bank barns they are built of stone with slated roofs but usually with a hipped or half-hipped roof rather than a gabled one.

Some bank barns have been noted in the highlands of Scotland but none in Wales or the English Pennines (outside Cumbria) even though the traditional farming methods and the topography are similar to Cumbria and the South-West of England.

Combination farm buildings with some of the characteristics of the bank barn are well known in the mountainous parts of France, southern Germany, Austria and Switzerland but none of them is more than superficially similar to the English bank barn. In Norway, however, a similar pattern but with a timber-framed barn over a stone-walled set of buildings for animals is widespread.

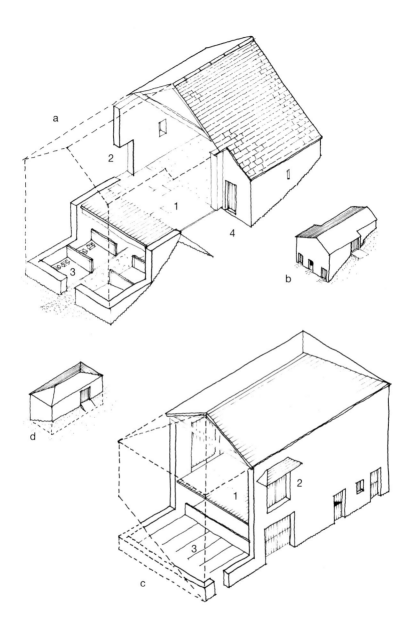

a. Cutaway isometric of variant bank barn showing threshing floor (1), winnowing door (2), cow-house (3) corn hole (4). *b*. Lancashire-type variant bank barn. *c*. Cutaway isometric of chall barn with threshing floor (1), winnowing door (2), cow-house (3). *d*. Sketch of upper level of chall barn.

Farm Buildings:
The Barn for Hand Threshing

The barn is normally considered as a warehouse; a place in which crops were stored; but most surviving barns are more properly considered as factories where raw materials were processed into finished products and stored only temporarily.

The process of hand threshing with flail, which was universal until the mid-19C., and which has only recently passed finally out of use, required that the sheaves of unthreshed corn be stacked on one side of the threshing floor, while threshed straw was stacked on the other side. Day by day throughout the winter, sheaves were opened onto the floor, beaten by the flails of the two-man threshing team, the straw residue lifted to one side, and the ears winnowed by natural draught between two doors. The process was necessarily a slow and laborious one, but it provided fodder and litter as it was needed by the animals, and it provided employment for the labourers when they could not work in the fields.

The process of hand threshing governed the basic design of the barn which is illustrated here.

Variations on the basic design arose through different farming practices and improved farming methods and several of the common variations are also illustrated.

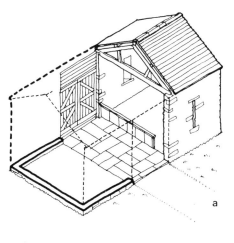

a. Cutaway isometric showing threshing floor, storage bays for sheaves and straw, opposite doors for light and draught, low partition.
b. Single barn, one threshing floor.
c. Double barn, two floors.
d. Asymmetrical barn, unequal bays.

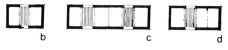

b   c   d

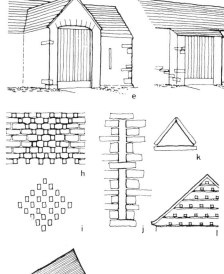

e. Projecting porch extending threshing floor.
f. Cheeks protecting floor.
g. Canopy protecting floor and doors.
h., i. Ventilation patterns in brick.
j., k. Ventilators in stone.
l. Dovecot in gable of barn.
m. Weatherboarded single aisled barn.
n. Barn aisled on all four sides.

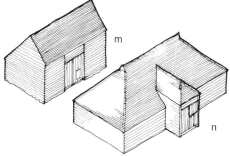

Farm Buildings:
The Barn for Machine Threshing

Many attempts were made to improve upon the slow and costly process of hand threshing, especially as improved farming methods increased the yield of cereal crops. But it was not until 1786 that the invention by Andrew Meikle of a threshing machine began the elimination of the hand process. Simple hand-operated winnowing fans had been used, but from the early years of the 19C. improvements in the threshing machine enabled threshing, winnowing, and grading to be done in one operation.

The threshing machine required a lot of power and several sources were used: occasionally windmills provided power, more frequently water-mills, either from continuous supply or using water from a pond. On the largest farms a stationary steam engine provided ample power. But the most frequently used power source for threshing, and for the cutting and mixing machines which were simultaneously developed, was the horse engine. This could take two forms, the sweep, in which the horses stepped over the drive shaft, and the overhead gearing, in which the horses trod a circular route underneath a crown wheel and pinion gear serving a horizontal drive shaft. The former type was usually in the open air, and only a circular sinking or embankment will now show its position; the latter type was usually housed in a building, of which many still survive.

Later in the 19C., the portable steam engine taken, with the threshing machine, from farm to farm converted a slow daily process into a quick two or three day operation. The remaining stationary threshing machines were eventually converted to drive by oil or gas engine, but horse engines remained in use for the lighter cutting and mixing machinery.

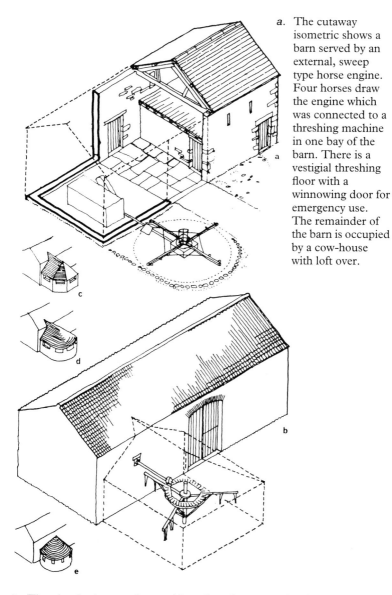

a. The cutaway isometric shows a barn served by an external, sweep type horse engine. Four horses draw the engine which was connected to a threshing machine in one bay of the barn. There is a vestigial threshing floor with a winnowing door for emergency use. The remainder of the barn is occupied by a cow-house with loft over.

b. The sketch shows a barn with a three-horse overhead type threshing machine. This was housed in a square-ended projection from the barn. c., d., e. Alternative forms of horse engine house; all show the ventilation openings needed; e. is the type found in Northumberland and in Devon.

Farm Buildings: The Cow-House

The cow-house was required on most farms to accommodate the more valuable oxen and cattle in safety and protected from the worst of the weather. Variations appear to be mainly in provision for feeding and tying and development lay mainly in the improvement but eventual elimination of the loft as a store for fodder.

There appears to have been a difference in feeding practice within the country: in some parts a wide feeding passage ran across the cow-house and cattle were tethered nose on to the passage and tail on to the manure passages; in others cows were tethered nose towards the cross wall and tail on to a single manure passage, the fodder being brought to individual feeding boxes from behind. Similarly there were variations in tying: in some parts cows were tethered in pairs, a low timber, slate, or stone partition separating each pair; in other parts, they were tethered singly between light posts. There is insufficient information available at present to define the areas of each different practice.

It was usual for hay and sometimes straw to be stored in a loft over the cow-house, with a trap door and ladder giving access between the two levels. During the 18C. and early 19C. this loft space tended to increase in height until it became a full upper storey with a regular series of pitching eyes facing the yard.

Early cow-houses were low and dark with the little ventilation provided by the open upper part of a feeding passage door. Light and ventilation were considered detrimental. During the 19C. there was a change in practice, and cow-houses became larger, well lit and ventilated, open to the roof without loft and with separate feeding and manure passages running along the building.

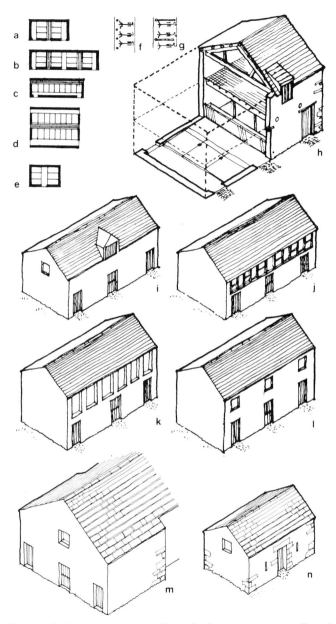

a. Central feeding passage. *b.* Two feeding passages. *c.* Longitudinal feeding passage. *d.* Central longitudinal feeding passage. *e.* No feeding passage. *f.* Single tethering, no partitions. *g.* Double tethering, partitions. *h.* Cutaway isometric shows relationship between feeding passage, stalls, and loft. *i.* Low loft mainly in roof space. *j.* Timber framed loft wall. *k.* Tall loft with open side. *l.* Tall loft with pitching eyes. *m.* Cow-house with central longitudinal feeding passage and flanking manure passages added to one end of a barn. *n.* Small cow-house intended for cattle fed from behind.

Farm Buildings: Stables

Probably for reasons of status as much as anatomy, the horse was given taller, more spacious, and better lit accommodation than the cow or humble ox.

Each horse was given a separate stall with a substantial wooden partition long enough to prevent horses kicking each other and tall enough to prevent them biting each other. Often there would be a separate manger and feeding trough. On the smaller farms the stalls ran along the building, three horses being accommodated in the width of the building, but on the larger farms there were usually ranks of horses with stalls running across the building. In both cases a loose box for sick horse or foaling mare would be included.

Over the stable there was normally a loft containing hay. Access was by trap door and ladder from within the stable, and often a gap in the floor or a series of trap doors enabled hay to be dropped direct into each manger. Sometimes, the loft acted as a granary, hence the legends of carters piercing the floor to obtain extra oats for their horses. Sometimes also the loft acted as a barrack room for the carters, the horses serving as a source of heat.

Within the walls of the stable there were usually 'keeping holes' for grooming equipment while tackle was hung on the wall. On the larger farms, however, a separate but adjacent harness room was provided.

Since so few stables remain in use on farms it is sometimes difficult to distinguish the former stable. Usually the height and shape of the room, the height and width of the door, and the provision of windows act as clues, while a horse's shoe over the door should clinch the matter.

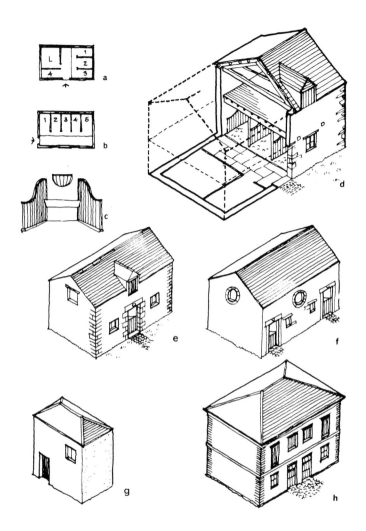

a. Stable with four stalls and a loose box. b. Stable with five stalls and longitudinal manure passage. c. Diagram showing a stall with its manger, trough, and partitions. d. Cutaway isometric showing the stalls and loft. e. Typical stable as for plan a. f. Stable with pitching eyes to loft. g. Simple stable and loft for one hackney pony. h. Elaborate stable and loft for several carriage and riding horses.

Farm Buildings: Granary/Cart Shed

As its name suggests, the granary was intended principally for the storage of grain which had been threshed but not milled. The grain was stored sometimes in chests but more commonly in heaps on the floor. It was believed that movement of air below the floor would help to keep the grain sweet, while, at first floor level, spoilage by rats could be reduced. The walls and ceiling were sometimes plastered, and the floor carefully boarded.

The cart shed was provided to protect the carts and farm machinery from the worst of the weather. The earlier timber jointed implements suffered from both rain and sunshine and covered accommodation was desirable. This usually took the form of an open fronted shed, though sometimes a draw through was provided in one bay. The cart shed might be a separate single-storey building but very often was combined with a first-floor granary. Access to the granary was usually by an external staircase rising up the side of the cart shed but sometimes a front or internal staircase was installed.

There were two particular structural problems to this building type, one was the support of the granary wall over the open front of the cart shed, the other was the inconvenience of a tie beam below head height in the granary. The one problem was solved by the use of piers of stone, brick, or heavy timber posts, together with lintels or arches, the other led to the use of various roof trusses which omitted the tie beams, e.g. the post and pad.

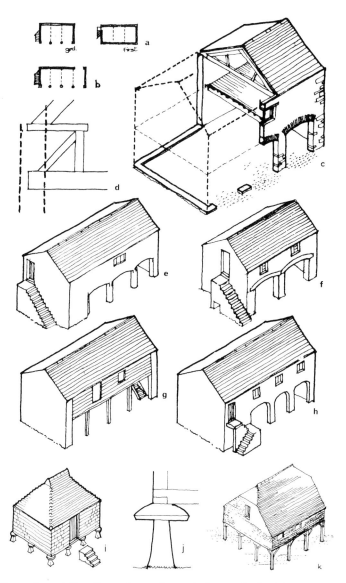

a. Ground- and first-floor plans of a typical cart shed with granary over. *b*. Cart shed with draw through. *c*. Cutaway isometric showing cart shed and granary. *d*. Detail of post and pad truss; the tie beam being truncated by a short post braced back to the floor beam. *e*. Granary/cart shed; stone piers, external gable stairs. *f*. Two-bay granary/cart shed, re-used crucks as lintels. *g*. Four-bay granary/cart shed, timber framed front wall, internal staircase. *h*. Three-bay granary/cart shed, external stair at front. *i*. Small granary raised on staddle stones, movable bridge from steps to door. *j*. Detail of two-piece staddle stone. *k*. Large granary of one and a half storeys raised over deep implement shed.

Farm Buildings: Shelter Shed

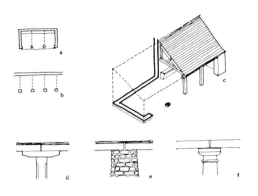

a. Plan of free standing shelter shed.
b. Plan of shelter shed attached to a wall.
c. Cutaway isometric, showing half-trusses and colonnade.
d. Beams carried on timber post.
e. Beams carried on stone pier.
f. Beams carried on cast iron column.

Where cattle were lodged in the farmyard during winter it became customary to provide an open-fronted shelter shed in which the cattle could be fed and also could shelter from the worst of the weather. Such a shed might be a separate building or back on to an existing wall. Timber or cast iron posts, brick piers, or stone columns have been used for the colonnade which supports the roof. Late 19C. and early 20C. developments included the transformation of the shelter shed into an entirely covered foldyard.

Farm Buildings: Linhay

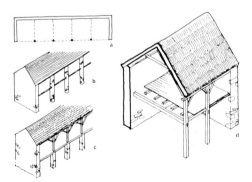

a. Plan of lower part of linhay.
b. Isometric showing full height stone piers.
c. Isometric showing timber posts at upper level.
d. Cutaway isometric showing method of support of the loft floor.

In lowland Devon and occasionally elsewhere a more elaborate shelter was provided. This, called locally a linhay, consisted of an open fronted shelter on the ground floor with a hay loft (tallet) above. In earlier examples the loft was open fronted, but later weatherboard protection to the hay was provided.

Farm Buildings: Hay Barn

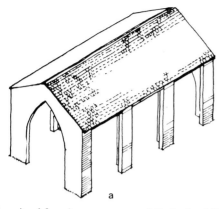

a. Brick-wall, tiled roof, hay barn as found especially in Staffordshire, Cheshire and South Lancashire.

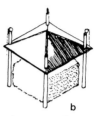

a

b

In mixed farming areas, especially in the Midlands, covered accommodation for the hay crop was sometimes provided in the form of a 'Dutch Barn'. For ease of access and benefit of ventilation the roof was carried on piers of stone or brick. The outer piers sometimes had 'Gothic' arches while the intermediate trusses might be carried by timber posts or, in later examples, by cast iron columns. *b.* Dutch style barns with rise and fall roofs were used in the 19C.

Farm Buildings: Field Barn

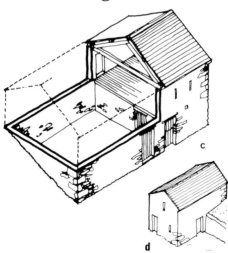

c. Cutaway isometric showing the use of the slope, the 'sink mow' with hay swept in at high level and removed for consumption at low level, also loft over loose box for young cattle.

d. Field barn across slope.

c

d

In upland districts greater protection was given to the hay. At the same time the practice developed in many areas of erecting a field barn on newly enclosed land, distant from the farmstead, and housing young cattle below and hay above. Such field barns are especially prominent in the Yorkshire Dales.

Farm Buildings: Pig-Sty

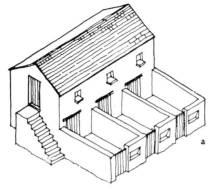

a. A rather elaborate triple pig-sty with a hen house up above; feeding troughs are incorporated in the walls of the exercise yards.

Many farmsteads still include, but rarely utilize, a pig-sty. In the traditional arrangement the sty consisted of a covered portion and a walled yard. Often a loft served as a hen house with a ramped access plank; the yard sometimes incorporated an ingenious feeding trough.

Farm Buildings: Dovecot

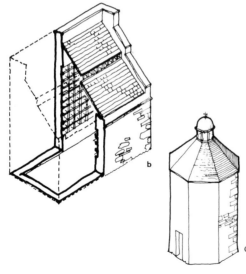
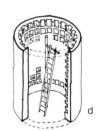

b. A rectangular dovecot with nesting boxes in each wall and access for the birds through a sort of clearstorey.
c. Octagonal dovecot.
d. Cylindrical dovecot, cutaway diagram.

Before the improved feeding stuffs simplified the problem of fattening stock through winter, pigeons and doves were considered a useful source of fresh meat. Their manure was also highly valued. Dovecots were for long restricted to the gentry but later examples are found on large farms. They are usually either rectangular or are a variation on the cylinder. Access for the birds was usually through a lantern, while eggs were collected with the aid of a revolving ladder.

Farm Buildings: Corn Drying Kiln

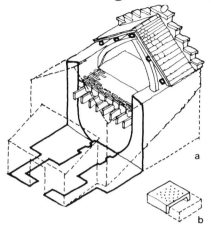

a. In the cutaway isometric is shown a corn kiln used, it is assumed jointly, in hamlets in the Lake District. The grille was based on specially shaped pieces of slate.

b. Perforated tile often used for floor of drying chamber.

Corn drying kilns were formerly common in the wetter agricultural regions. Although eventually associated with the mills such kilns had previously been erected for individual farmsteads or small farming groups. The parts consisted of a drying chamber in which the damp corn was spread on a horse hair blanket over a grille of stone or slate slats, or directly on perforated tiles, and a heating chamber sometimes served by a chimney but more commonly without.

Farm Buildings: Oast House; Maltings

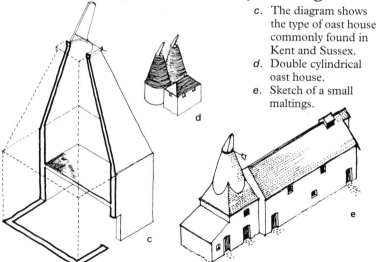

c. The diagram shows the type of oast house commonly found in Kent and Sussex.

d. Double cylindrical oast house.

e. Sketch of a small maltings.

The oast house was a kiln designed for drying hops. Most are circular and have a cowl over the vent and adjustable to the wind. Other examples are square.

6. URBAN VERNACULAR AND MINOR INDUSTRIAL BUILDINGS, CHAPELS

The domestic vernacular of the countryside and the vernacular buildings of the farmstead are linked by a common dependence on agriculture. While such probably represent the majority of vernacular buildings and comprise those which are most picturesque and richest in regional variation, the vernacular field is also occupied by buildings linked in their dependence on commerce and industry – the urban houses of the medieval merchant and the Victorian artisan, and the buildings, both urban and rural, designed for primitive industrial processes. This chapter, therefore, brings together notes on a number of widely differing building types, mainly urban, from various periods, but dependent in some way on commerce and industry.

The design of the urban equivalents of the Large Houses, Small Houses, and Cottages of the countryside was governed like that of their rural counterparts by the functional demands on plan and sectional form, the limitations of available building materials, and the dictates of architectural fashion; but their design was also governed to a much more substantial extent by the problems of restricted sites and the regulations necessary for neighbourly design. Although few British towns developed within so tight a strait-jacket as most towns on the Continent, pressure on the most desirable land within a city boundary meant that plots had to be filled and volume gained by upward building during medieval and later times. When changes in commercial organization and improvements in transport, particularly during the 18C., led to an increase in the size of many towns this took the form of more intensive use of existing urban land – building on gardens for instance, as well as expansion of towns along the roads, and by formation of suburbs. But the vast transfer of population from country to town which took place during the 19C. was a result of the operation of industry of all kinds – mining, manufacturing, transporting – on an unprecedented scale.

a. Urban vernacular before the Industrial Revolution: Louth, Lincs.

b. Urban vernacular after the Industrial Revolution: Sandbach, Cheshire.

Urban Vernacular: Medieval

In spite of the Roman origin so often claimed for the street pattern of any ancient town in which two streets cross at right angles, few towns retain an earlier layout than the medieval, and even then regular planning was probably exceptional, the layout of most medieval English towns being dependent on local topography rather than on human foresight.

However, development based on a market place, a quayside, or a grid-iron pattern of streets can often be detected. The market place was often an elongated rectangle (e.g. St. Albans) but subsequent encroachment has, in many places, obscured the original shape. The quay side development may be seen at ancient ports such as Southampton, or Kings Lynn, where merchants' warehouses and domestic quarters lined the quay; but shifts in water channels and later urban developments have usually left the early quayside high and dry. Grid-iron development was characteristic of the many medieval New Towns (such as Salisbury, Winchelsea and Conway) in which houses lined the rectangular streets, and churches or public spaces occupied island blocks left open for the purpose; but the many advantages of a grid-iron street pattern, especially in measurement, definition, and conveyance of land, led to its use in most towns from the medieval period almost to the present day.

Even when confined by a wall, a medieval town included a wide range of densities. The most important streets and the most valuable sites might be crowded, but the remainder of the town was occupied by separately walled enclosures, such as a monastery or cathedral close with a spacious setting to important buildings, or by individual houses, each set in a garden, much as they would be placed in a country village. Between and around the more permanent houses occupied by the wealthier land-owners and tradesmen, were the simple and flimsy cottages of the poor, of which very few remains survive.

For this period, the most characteristic urban vernacular is represented by the houses of merchants and tradesmen of which quite substantial portions remain in use in many of our older towns.

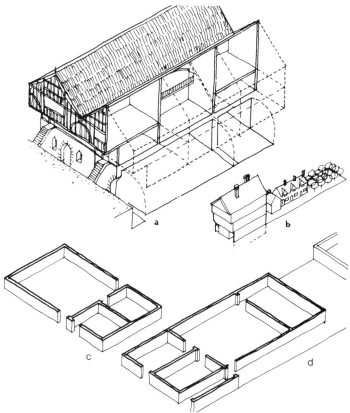

a. In the centre of a typical medieval market town, the front of each long narrow plot of land would be occupied by a house and workshop, the rear by kitchens, other service rooms, garden, well, and cesspool. A stone vaulted cellar was sunk half into the ground and reached by a short flight of steps. Here goods were manufactured, displayed, and sold – as they continue to be in Middle Eastern countries. Another short flight rose up to the house which might well have two-storey ends to a single storey hall in the medieval rural manner but roofed with a gable facing the street. Most town houses were timber framed above the cellar. Temporary booths between the two flights of steps were often roofed and incorporated in the main building to produce an upper gallery as in the 'Rows' of Chester.

b. During the latter part of the Middle Ages, the half-subterranean cellar appears to have passed out of favour. Instead, storage cellars were sometimes provided below ground and the shop rose to ground-floor level where it occupied the front portion of a house. As the shop might be separately let, there was often no intercommunication with the house. At this time pressure on the most valuable land was leading to multi-storey development, especially making use of jettied construction, and development within the gardens was beginning.

c. Wide frontage house with passage across hall giving access to rear of site.

d. Narrow frontage house with passage alongside front rooms giving access to the courtyards and further buildings within the site.

Urban Vernacular: 16th and 17th Centuries

During this period medieval urban house plans were transformed through greater attention to heating, to privacy, and to access from floor to floor as houses grew ever taller.

Open hearths and charcoal braziers were replaced by fireplaces, flues and chimney stacks, reducing danger from fire and asphyxiation and increasing the number of rooms which could be heated. Both back-to-back fireplaces and those on party walls were used; the former gave a compact plan, retained heat within the house and gave a good distribution of warmth within narrow rooms; the latter simplified planning but sometimes gave problems in the design of party walls and took valuable space within the width of narrow sites. The open hall was finally abandoned and the practice of opening one room off another fell out of use, rooms being reached from corridors or internal lobbies. At the same time pressure on space within valuable sites encouraged development on several storeys on as much of the site as could be daylit. The winding staircase remained in use but placed centrally within the building and with fairly generous dimensions; such a staircase could be placed neatly against the jambs of back-to-back fireplaces but easier newel and dog-leg staircases were also used, and the position at the rear of the building finally became most popular.

Towards the end of the 17C. the universal terrace house plan was developed. Having a lobby and staircase against the two rooms on each floor it could be used singly, in pairs or be repeated in terraced rows. This plan remained popular throughout the 18C. and 19C.

At the beginning of the 16C. most urban houses were timber framed and many had thatched roofs; at the end of the 17C. nearly all newly-built town houses were of brick or stone walls and a slate or tiled roof. Such materials were both fashionable and fire-resistant and many of the older houses were modernized and given fire-protection through the use of them: timber panelled gables towards the street were replaced by hipped roofs half-hidden behind a brick parapet, though often the timber framed party walls remained and, visible along the passages which led to the rear of each site, served as a reminder of the more ancient buildings underneath.

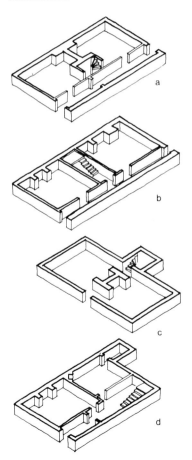

a. Narrow frontage house with back-to-back fireplaces and staircase against the fireplace jambs; corridor giving access to the rear of the site.

b. Narrow frontage house with party wall fireplaces, central staircase and longitudinal passage.

c. Wide frontage house with back-to-back fireplaces and rear staircase projection.

d. Narrow frontage terrace house plan of late 17C. with one party wall fireplace and one corner fireplace; projecting closet at rear; no means of access through house to remainder of site.

Urban Vernacular:
18th and 19th Centuries

These notes outline developments in urban vernacular architecture between the close of the medieval period, towards the end of the 16C. and the beginning of the transformation of towns in the 19C. During this period market towns benefitted from the general increase in population and agricultural productivity and, especially towards the end of the 18C., from improvements in transport. The coming of the railways from 1830 onwards meant rapid development of those served by the main lines but slow decay of the towns by-passed. The rise of factory based industry meant the establishment of some new towns and the transformation of many villages and some small market towns into tightly built settlements.

During the early part of the period, urban vernacular was characterized by the development of long thin buildings or rows of houses along the length of narrow medieval plots. A passage through the completely built-up front of the plot led to a footpath or alleyway; facing on to the footpath, and so at right angles to the street, new buildings occupied the former outbuildings and garden of the medieval house.

But during the later years of the period the most characteristic urban vernacular was in the development of terraces and squares, and in the grounds of the large houses which had been built as the town houses of country landowners. The most spectacular examples of such development in, e.g., London, Edinburgh and Bath, were architect-designed and out of the vernacular field, but few towns are without the provincial craftsman's version of these fashionable terraces. Some of the new towns of the early Industrial Revolution (e.g. Whitehaven) are built entirely in this manner.

At the same time, there was a great deal of reconstruction and refacing on the original sites in medieval towns to produce a narrow, tall, single fronted building – house or shop – or a similar façade on an earlier plan.

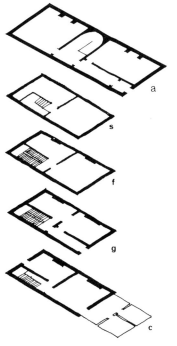

The typical town house of the 18C. combined the arrangement of rooms on several levels connected by a staircase with the newly fashionable horizontal grouping of individual houses to produce a unified elevation. Service rooms, even in vernacular buildings, might be confined to the basement, sometimes the principal rooms were at first-floor level, but usually the ground floor provided living-rooms, the first floor bedrooms, and the second floor or garret space was available for the bedrooms of children and servants. At this time most new houses were built of brick with tiles or slated roofs, though other materials continued in use.

a. Alternative with central staircase.

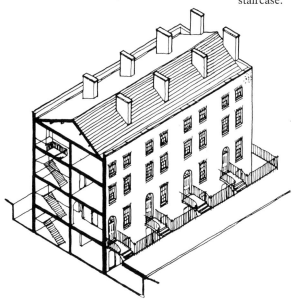

Minor Industrial Vernacular: Early Cottage Industry

For as long as domestic manufacture continued at subsistence level throughout the country, we could not expect to see any reflection of manufacture in the form of the dwelling house. But as machinery was gradually introduced and improved, as manufacturing operations became more specialized, and as changes in industrial organization led to larger scale operations, so these developments came to be reflected to a greater and greater extent in buildings. In some parts of the country, domestic manufacture never developed beyond the subsistence level, but in others especially in the Southern Pennines and in the Eastern Midlands the manufacturing processes left the home and became concentrated in factories.

During the early part of this development two stages may be distinguished: modification of a living-room for the accommodation of simple machinery, and provision of a separate room as a work place. Both developments could occur as modification or extension of an existing house, or could form the basis of new construction.

In the textile industries at least, these early industrial adaptations were more likely to occur in rural rather than urban situations. As the hand loom weavers of Oldham found to their cost, a life dependent on one trade was too uncertain, and those with the luxury of choice preferred to be able to switch between manufacture and agriculture according to the season and the state of trade. In rural locations these early industrial cottages might be built singly or in pairs, but in both country and towns cottages were also built in blocks of four or in terraces.

Construction was of brick or stone, according to locality, though modification of earlier timber framed houses may sometimes be seen.

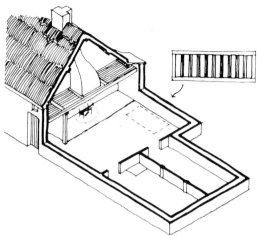

In this example, apparently of the late 16C., an extension of the main living-room provided space which was near the heat and winter light of the fire on the hearth, but was out of the way of domestic activities. This space was lit by a long window of ten lights divided by diamond mullions, which was quite the largest window of the house. It seems more than likely that the extension represents an early adaptation of a house for cottage industry.

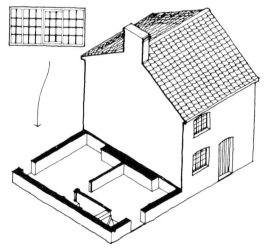

In the examples illustrated, based on early 19C. cottages at Hathern, Leicestershire, the front ground-floor room and the two first-floor rooms provided domestic accommodation while the rear ground-floor room accommodated stocking frames and was lit by a large, four-light window. The position of the staircase, rising from the living-room, meant that the work-room could be separately let without loss of privacy in the cottage.

Minor Industrial Vernacular: Later Cottage Industry

Such was the erratic progress of invention in the textile industry during the late 18C. and early 19C. that increased capacity in one part of the trade entailed shortage of capacity and therefore industrial prosperity in some other part. As an example of this situation, factory based and water powered cotton spinning placed such demands on the hand loom weavers that their prosperity was unprecedented, and they could afford to invest in specialized buildings for their craft, though still operating on a domestic basis.

Even when production of the coarser textiles had become concentrated in factories, the finer qualities, and work in more expensive materials and processes, continued on hand-powered machinery operated by craftsmen at home.

For the industrial parts of the house most textile trades at least had the following requirements:–

good daylight – e.g. from windows extending as far along the wall as structural stability would allow; *controlled ventilation* – e.g. where a smoke and dust free atmosphere was essential, and only a few small lights were made openable; *unobstructed space* – e.g. a space unobstructed by walls or piers most easily obtained under the roof; *provision for storage* – e.g. a loft in the attic space above the machinery; *access for goods and workers* – in some trades a hoist and 'taking-in hole' was necessary for raw material. As the work room might be let separately from the house, and as non-resident labour might be employed, access was arranged to intrude as little as possible on the privacy of the house; *heating* – e.g. a fireplace or brazier, but varied with the trade.

In the residential parts of the house, the artisan would have a kitchen and scullery on the ground floor and two bedrooms above; but, sometimes, one of a small group of such industrial houses would have larger and slightly more pretentious accommodation.

These buildings were erected both in the country and in the expanding towns, sometimes in groups of two or four, but more commonly in short terraces. They continued to be built until about the middle of the 19C., long after the factory-based textile industry had become established, but some of the later examples were so designed that they could alternate between purely domestic and partly industrial use according to the state of trade.

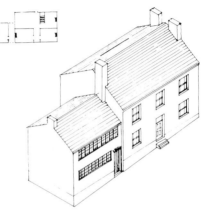

A master hosier's house from Wigston Magna, Leicestershire, consists of a two-storey building with fairly conventional domestic accommodation, but attached to it there is a two-storey workshop, both floors being well-lit by very long mullioned windows, the upper being approached by ladder and trap door from the lower, and both provided with fireplaces.

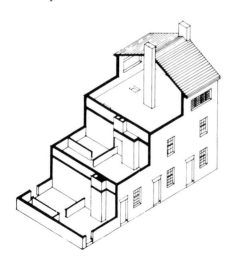

The old-established silk-manufacturing town of Macclesfield in Cheshire includes scores of examples of buildings designed for cottage industry as well as several elegant factories. In the terrace illustrated, the cutaway diagram shows the conventional 'two up and two down' of the domestic accommodation and the well-lit unobstructed floor space of the weaving loft. The rear staircase provided access to the loft in a relatively discreet manner and sometimes party walls were modified to allow several lofts to run together.

Urban Industrial Houses: Earlier

We have seen that from the latter half of the 18C. onwards it became normal for even the poorest families to be housed in dwellings built of materials permanent enough to survive to the present day. During this period, cottages were built by land-owners for the labourers on their tenants' farms, by the owners of mines and quarries which were located so far away from existing settlements that new construction was unavoidable, by mill-owners when, in the days of water-power, sites on streams in remote valleys were customary for factories, and by private landlords for the workers in the towns. Throughout the period it was customary for lodgers to be boarded by working class families, and many of the complaints of overcrowding sprang from this practice, which was, of course, largely unavoidable during this period of swift industrialization. At the same time, the ancient process of 'filtering down' continued, whereby large houses built for wealthier families were later divided and occupied by the poor. But also, both in town and country, a certain amount of philanthropic provision of 'model' or 'improved' dwellings for the poor helped to ensure an eventual and general improvement.

Throughout the period the plan and sectional form, and the material and construction of cottages, did not differ substantially between rural developments, urbanized miners' villages, and entirely urban situations. The difference was more a matter of location and degree, the 'two up and two down' appearing quite different in a terrace of three in a pretty village than in a long roadside terrace on a bleak moor.

Regional variations in plan form and materials emphasize the vernacular qualities of these cottages. For instance, miners and quarry-men tended to have single-storey dwellings, hence the long low terraces of the Pennines, of Northumberland, and of Devon, and the 'Croglofft' cottages of Caernarvonshire; while textile workers tended to have two-storey houses, the residue of design for cottage industry. The steep sided valleys of the Lancashire and Yorkshire Pennines led to the development of the extraordinary 'houses-on-top-of-houses'; Leeds and Sheffield preferred the back-to-back. And yet the non-industrialized communities of East Anglia and South-Eastern England continued to build cottages in timber and clay, closely following their own traditions.

The individual cottage was a perfectly adequate setting for contemporary family life, but when multiplied beyond count and unsupported by the services which community life required, it was inadequate and developed the bad reputation which it now endures.

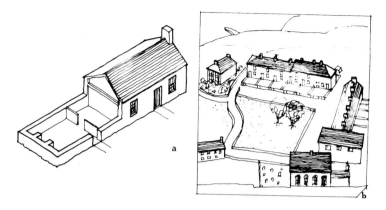

a

b

Part of the surrealist quality of a mining village, all the more extreme now that so many have been abandoned, come from the use of long terraces or courtyards of tightly packed cottages to give a curiously urban character to an isolated rural community (*b*). Often the effect is heightened by the use of single-storey cottages each consisting of two rooms, a living-room and a partitioned bedroom, in reincarnation of a medieval plan (*a*).

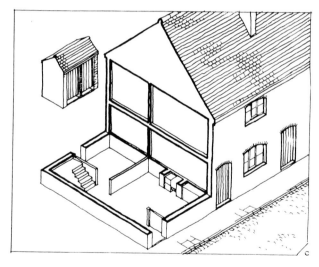

c

The two-storey workers' cottage which preceded the Public Health Act of 1875 usually consisted of a living kitchen and scullery/wash-house on the ground floor and two bedrooms above. Access was by a door opening directly off the street, with the living kitchen screened only by a timber 'speer'. At the rear a short yard, sometimes individual, sometimes communal, contained earth closet and coal store (*c*).

Urban Industrial Houses: Later

Various lines of development converged to ensure that the terraced row of cottages became the urban domestic vernacular of the second half of the 19C. But while the form of the individual dwelling had been crystallized the form of the terraced layout took longer to establish and depended at least partly on developments in sanitation.

As long as cottages were erected in twos and threes in scattered villages no serious sanitary problems arose and if rooms were tiny, space around buildings was plentiful, while fresh air was plentiful and unpolluted. Even when terraces of cottages were built to serve isolated mines or mills the sanitary problems, though more severe, were still at the village scale and capable of solution by traditional methods.

In the rapidly expanding towns, however, the scale was unprecedented and new solutions were necessary. In the older parts of towns, the ground available in long medieval plots for sanitation and water supplies diminished until cesspool and well occupied adjacent holes. In the newer parts, terraces and courts were built by developers who had neither powers nor incentive to ensure adequate water supply and sanitary arrangements. Disease and epidemic were the inevitable result and the reports of the 19C. Committees of Inquiry are full of detailed accounts of revolting conditions around the dwellings and overcrowding within.

The method of sanitation eventually adopted was based on the regular removal of night soil, neutralized by earth or ashes, from individual privies located at the rear, at an appropriate distance from each dwelling. Convenience and economy suggested the back alley and a grid-iron street layout, and it was not until waterborne sewage systems brought the

WC within the house that the back street, for sanitary purposes, could be eliminated and alternative layouts adopted.

Thus the design of the cottage had developed, typologically, from two rooms and a loft on a piece of the village common to the four rooms and two full storeys of high density urban development. The reaction which followed began with a return to an idealized village of one and a half storey cottages.

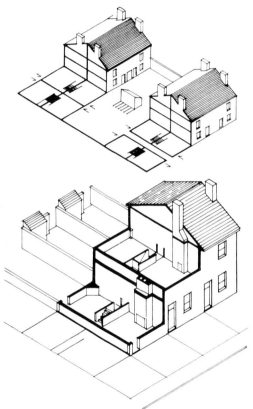

The true back-to-back houses had only one wall exposed to light and air, and, from their absence of through ventilation have gained a reputation as the most unhealthy of the 19C. slums. Once again it is the repetition and concentration of quite a normal vernacular domestic plan which was really at fault. In the most extreme examples, houses facing on to the streets were backed by other houses facing each other over a narrow courtyard containing the earth closets and reached by way of narrow passages through the buildings.

The Public Health Act of 1875 having required local authorities to make bye-laws to govern standards of construction and space about dwellings and having established effective enforcement machinery, a uniform pattern of housing began to spread over the country and to supersede local variations. In the houses illustrated, based on examples dated 1883, the traditional two-storey cottage plan was maintained but with tall rooms and large windows providing ventilation and short front gardens and long backyards providing the required space about dwellings. Back streets or alleys enabled the improved sanitation of the period to be adopted.

187

Minor Industrial Vernacular: Windmills and Watermills

Until the coming of the steam engine, power was available from wind, water, or muscle. The use of each power source has left its mark in the form of vernacular buildings.

The use of the muscular power of the horse to drive farm machinery has already been described and illustrated. Similar motive power was used for industrial purposes in mines and a few early factories, and indeed the horse engine known to have been employed in the coalfields of Northumberland, Durham and West Cumberland in the early 18C., may have provided the inspiration for the horse powered versions of the first threshing machines when employed in those districts. But virtually nothing remains of buildings to house industrial horse engines.

Wind and water driven mills have a long history and many examples still survive. Their use was largely though not entirely complementary, windmills serving the low-lying corn growing countryside of East Anglia, the Fylde, etc., where rivers are wide and sluggish, watermills serving the rest of the country where a regular and reliable flow of water was combined with a useful head. There were also a few mills operated by tides. Windmills were chiefly used for grinding corn or pumping water, watermills were used for these purposes and for an increasing range of industrial processes from fulling cloth to slitting iron.

The design of the actual machinery driven by wind and water power is far beyond the scope of vernacular architecture and its study has been carefully undertaken and well reported, but the buildings containing this machinery exercised the design and constructional ability of the vernacular craftsmen and a note is included here as a reminder of the range of design ability and constructional skills needed by these untutored members of the rural community.

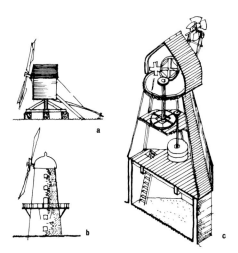

a

b

c

Most windmills were either post mills (*a*) or tower mills (*b*). In the former, the whole chamber containing gears and millstones could be rotated according to the direction of the wind and therefore a light, usually weatherboarded, timber framed structure was carried on an open timber base or a squat brick tapered cylinder. In the latter only the cap could be turned and the machinery was contained within a brick or weatherboarded tower. The cutaway isometric shows a typical smock mill (*c*).

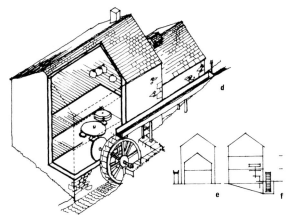

d

e

f

The usual arrangement in a watermill was to enclose the milling machinery and other ancillary accommodation in a weatherboarded, brick, or stone building alongside the mill race which turned the one or two wheels which projected from the building. Except when undershot wheels were used this meant that the building had to master the slope between headrace and tailrace. *d*. Cutaway view showing mill with attached corn-drying kiln; *e*., *f*. Diagrammatic section through kiln and mill.

Minor Industrial Vernacular:
Smithies, Kilns and Textile Mills

Among the most ubiquitous of vernacular industrial buildings are the smithies; among the most aesthetically pleasing are the kilns and furnaces; and among the most massive and structurally adventurous are the textile mills.

The smithy was usually a small rectangular building open to the roof and with space for storage, space for working and space for the hearth. At one end of the building was the hearth with its bellows and fuel store; at the other end were the racks for tools, items of equipment and part finished metal; in between was the working area, well-lit and ventilated from the open door and big enough for horse shoeing in wet weather. Outside was another working area including space for shrinking tyres on wooden wheels. Most surviving smithies are fairly late in date – mid- to late 19C., built of brick or stone and virtually without ornament; many have been lost in later garages and light engineering works.

Kilns included those in which limestone was converted into lime, those in which pottery was baked, those used in glass-making and those used in firing bricks or tiles. Limekilns were usually built into a slope, often an outcrop of limestone itself, so that alternate layers of limestone and fuel could be fed from the top and lime drawn out from the aperture at the bottom. The great arch over this aperture was made out of crude but massive stone voussoirs and the hidden shape of the kiln chamber was often gracefully formed. Pottery kilns made of brick and bottle-shaped were once common in the Stoke area but most have been destroyed; however, many country potteries still remain with small kilns of the same type. Pottery kilns were hollow, almost invariably made of brick, and usually reinforced with iron bands to counteract the cracks inevitable when one hot dry surface on the interior married with the cold wet external surface. Glass kilns were somewhat similar in principle but cone-shaped and with a furnace for heating the molten glass in the middle. Brick and tile kilns were squat or cupola-shaped.

The iron furnaces of the 18C. consisted of a stone surface tower fed with fuel and ore from storage sheds at an upper level, and attended by great water powered bellows at a lower level.

Water-powered textile mills made use of some of the devices and designs of watermills for corn grinding and developed designs and constructional methods used in later steam-powered factories. The corn mill was a compact building making use of several levels to take off the power as close as possible to the water-wheel itself; similarly the textile mill used several storeys just long enough to take power by way of a shaft from the wheel without too much loss in efficiency and just wide enough to take several machines in depth without losing too much daylight from the outer walls. Even with the light machinery of the period it was impossible to span from wall to wall, and slender cast-iron columns were devised to give intermediate support to the timber beams. Mills had windows of domestic proportions and domestic details which helped to give a dignity rarely found in other industrial buildings.

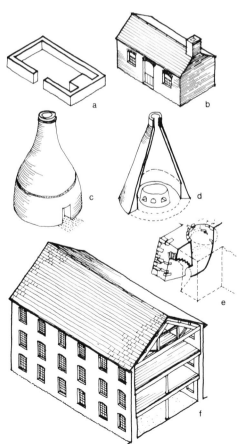

a. Smithy plan.
b. General view of smithy.
c. Pottery kiln.
d. Glass cone.
e. Lime kiln.
f. Textile mill with domestic proportions, cast iron intermediate columns, roof truss giving space on top floor.

Textile Mills and Workshops (continued)

As has already been mentioned and illustrated, the textile industry was originally home-based and went through a phase, especially during the 18C., when cottages were designed to accommodate small items of hand-powered machinery and this continued after some parts of the textile industry had already been powered by horse engines, water-wheels or steam engines. However, there was also a period when hand-powered machines were gathered into small factory-like structures.

In the silk industry, which was dispersed – though with concentrations in Derby, Congleton, Leek and Macclesfield – the early hand-throwing process required a 'shade' or shed usually at least 25 yards long, well-lit on two slides, in which the silk filament could be carried from a 'gate' to a fixed bar or cross and then twisted into thread. Generally this took place on the ground floor with other processes housed on one or two storeys above.

In the cotton and woollen industries, loomshops between two and five storeys high were built to house hand-powered machinery such as the spinning jenny or the mule. Unlike the rather later powered mills these loomshops were very narrow, only about 16 ft. wide and with plenty of windows.

In the hosiery industry the stocking frames continued to be housed until fairly recently in back-yard workshops as well as in powered mills. These workshops were usually two storeys high, each storey being quite tall to accommodate the stocking frames, and had continuous glazing to light the process. Once common in the Leicester area, very few now survive.

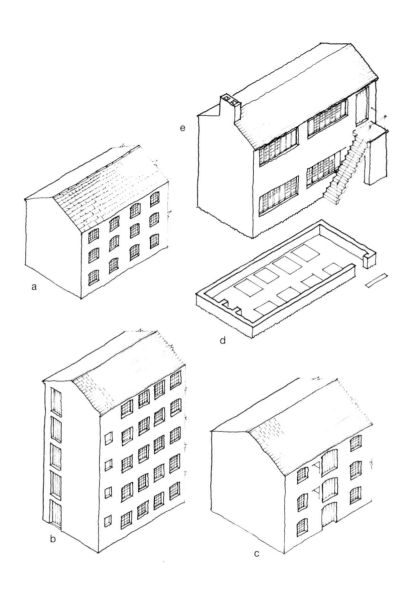

a. Mid-18C. silk factory for hand throwing and use of hand-powered machines. *b*. late 18C. hand-powered cotton factory with taking-in doors. *c*. Early 19C. woollen warehouse with goods access doors. *d*. Framework knitters' shop, ground floor, showing positions of stocking frames. *e*. Sketch of back-yard framework knitters' shop.

Chapels

Although churches have been excluded from this handbook on the grounds that most are polite rather than vernacular, it seems a pity to exclude the chapels of Nonconformist denominations since probably the majority of their buildings are vernacular rather than polite. Early Nonconformists such as the Separatists flourished in the 16C. but had to worship privately and could not build their own church buildings. In spite of periods of repression, Nonconformist persuasions attracted more adherents in the reign of the Stuarts and developed during the Commonwealth but it was not until the Toleration Act of 1689 that they gained the right to build their own places of worship. Even then it seems that congregations felt it best to build simple, unobtrusive chapels – vernacular buildings, in fact.

Apart from the Quakers who required little more than a room with benches around, most denominations wanted auditory chambers, rooms in which the worshippers could hear the preacher in his pulpit. The congregations sat in box pews or later on benches and, to increase accommodation in all but the smallest chapels, galleries were provided. They might be at each end or on three sides and were reached by internal staircases or by external flights of stairs.

Most chapels were arranged with the side to the approach and with two entrances and two tall windows in this wall. Some chapels, especially in Wales, presented a gable end with one entrance to the approach. Both models were developed into quite elaborate architectural façades in the larger chapels of the 19C. Cottage type accommodation was included (especially in Wales) alongside the chapel and was used by the minister or the chapel-keeper. Materials and construction were those of the locality and decoration was at first minimal.

194

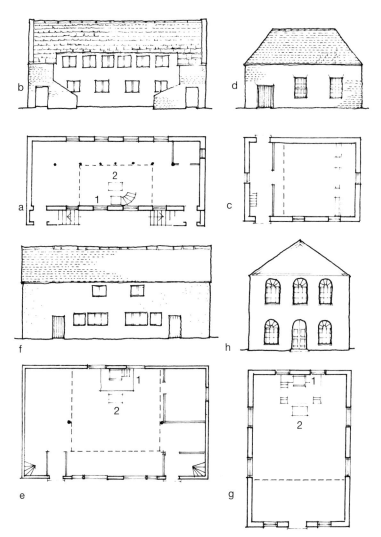

a. Presbyterian, later Unitarian, chapel of late 17C. with pulpit (1), position for communion table (2), three-sided gallery with external stairs, entrances in front side wall. b. elevational sketch of a. c. Friends Meeting House, early 18C.; plan showing platform with benches and internal access to single gallery. d. Sketch of (c). e. Plan of mid-18C. Congregational chapel with three-sided gallery and interior access from twin doors in front side wall; pulpit (1), position for communion table (2). f. Elevation sketch of (e). g. Presbyterian chapel of c. 1800; plan showing single gable entry and pulpit at far end (1), position for communion table (2) in front. h. Welsh Baptist chapel of early 19C. with gable entry.

7. COMPARISONS AND CONCLUSION

Walling and Roofing Materials: An Example of Local Distribution

The intricate pattern of the use of walling materials cannot yet be adequately demonstrated on a national scale, but sufficient work has been done in some districts for the local pattern to be shown. One such district, the Solway Plain, has been taken as an example. The position of the district is shown on the diagram and the scale is indicated by a grid of 10 km. squares. The maps are based on records made in the field of some 1,200 examples of domestic vernacular architecture built before about 1840.

The maps of walling material show how the basic geological formation of the district has determined the broad division between limestone, sandstone and clay, how the area of early use of clay roughly corresponds with that of the later use of brick, and how the use of the superior sandstone encroaches on those parts where the inferior limestone was the indigenous material.

The maps of roofing material show that thatching remained in use in districts which were distant from the quarries of the superior sandstone flags or Lake District slates. Nevertheless flags were used for superior buildings in all the lowland areas while Lake District slates came into universal use in the district once improved transport made them available.

196

Lowland and Highland Building Regions

The diagrammatic map (after P. Smith) shows a rich inner lowland region, a rather less rich outer lowland region, an intermediate region sharing highland and lowland characteristics, and an English and Welsh highland zone. Scotland and Ireland have further outer highland characteristics. Early farm-houses are rare in the highland zone; early farm-houses are plentiful in the inner lowland zone.

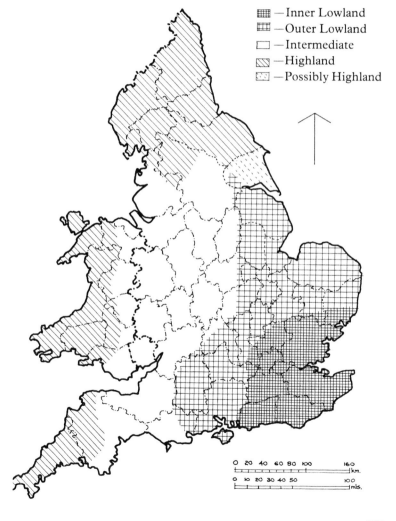

— Inner Lowland
— Outer Lowland
— Intermediate
— Highland
— Possibly Highland

Walling and Roofing Materials: Examples of National Distribution

Although no adequate national survey of vernacular architecture has yet been completed it is possible to illustrate in broad terms the pattern of use of certain walling and roofing materials, certain structural systems and certain plan types. The following very generalized maps are based on two sets of dot maps: one consisting of some 500 examples taken mainly from published sources and not evenly spread through the country and the other consisting of some 1200 examples evenly spread and taken partly from records of the Manchester University School of Architecture, partly from records of the Royal Commissions on Historical Monuments and partly from published sources. The map of cruck construction is based on those in Dr N. Alcock's *Catalogue of Cruck Buildings*. The tentative distributions of plan types depend on information which is not evenly available over the country; they depend partly on external observation and do not take into account the date or social level at which the plan-type was used.

Time Scales

An attempt (p. 211) has been made to show some time scales for window and door shape and mouldings. They are based on information from the North-West of England, the West Midlands, Monmouthshire and part of Oxfordshire only. Not all the information is available in a compatible form. Distinction between use of the various details at Large House, Small House and Cottage levels has been illustrated. Time scales for roofing materials have been prepared from the same information and shown in the same manner.

Walling Materials: Stone

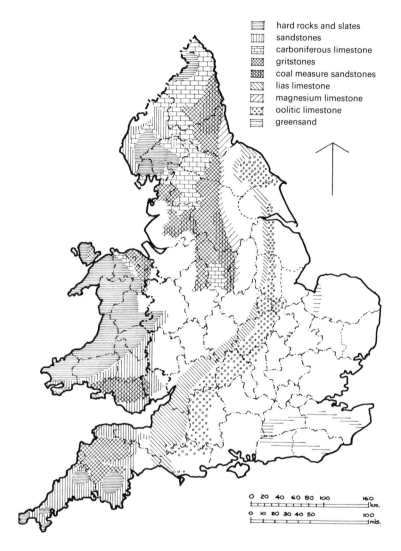

☰	hard rocks and slates
⫼	sandstones
⊞	carboniferous limestone
▨	gritstones
▦	coal measure sandstones
⧄	lias limestone
⧄	magnesium limestone
∴	oolitic limestone
☰	greensand

```
0  20  40  60  80  100        160
├──┼──┼──┼──┼──┤            ──┤km.
0   10  20  30  40  50         100
├───┼───┼───┼───┼───┤       ──┤mls.
```

Stone walling – shows the Pennine and Welsh mountain districts, the moorlands of South-West England, the limestone belt, and the Weald, but there are many other smaller patches of use. The building stones are indicated in a very general way, they combine some stones which appear similar but are geologically different, and they take no account of the intricate local variations found in many parts of the country.

199

Walling Materials: Flint, Pebble and Cobble

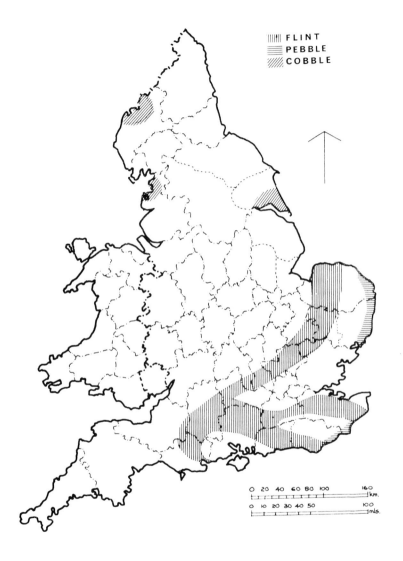

FLINT
PEBBLE
COBBLE

0 20 40 60 80 100 160 km.
0 10 20 30 40 50 100 mls.

Flint, pebble and cobble – the flint belt of the East and South-East is shown; pebble and cobble walling is found in many small patches of which only some of the most important can be shown.

Walling Materials: Brick

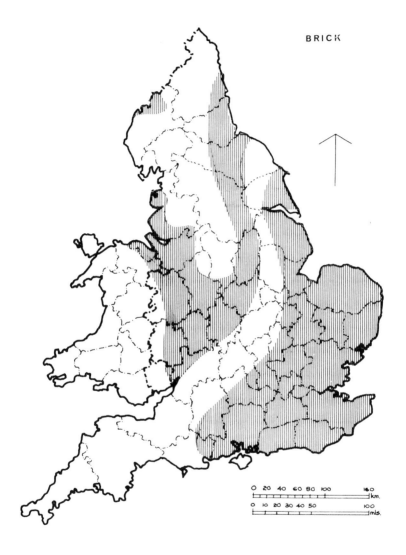

BRICK

Brick – generally the areas of brick walling complement those of stone; brick usually replaced timber frame.

Walling Materials: Clay, etc.

Clay, *etc*. – the map shows the districts in which substantial numbers survive and distinguishes the clay lump technique of East Anglia. Local names are indicated.

Timber Frame: Cruck Construction

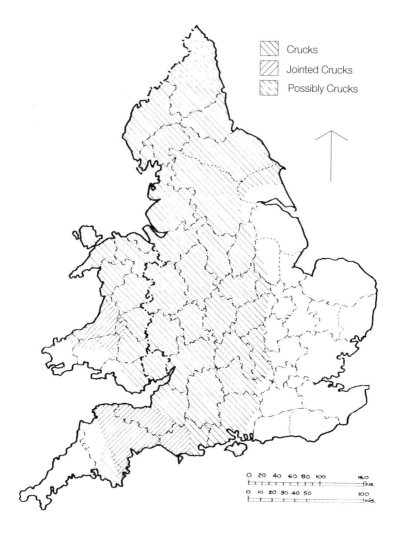

Crucks

Jointed Crucks

Possibly Crucks

Cruck construction – areas where jointed crucks are found are distinguished from those with true crucks.

Timber Walling

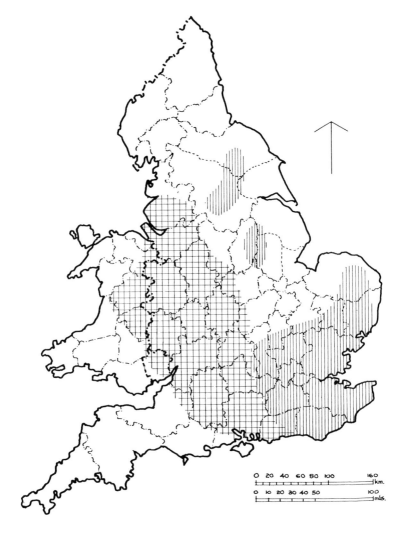

Exposed timber frame (half timbering) – the map shows areas in which half timbering is commonly found and distinguishes between areas in which narrow panels predominate (vertical hatching) and areas in which square panels predominate (cross hatching). Extensive areas of overlap in south-central counties are not indicated.

Timber Walling: Cladding Materials

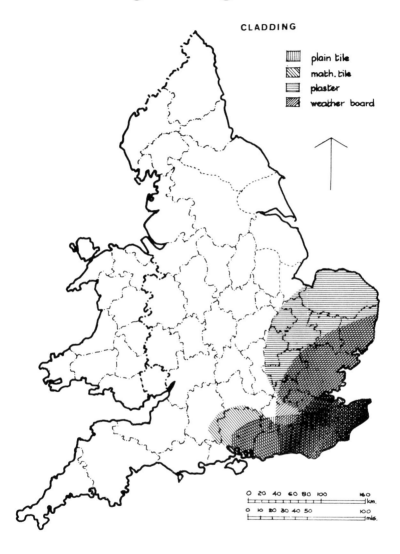

CLADDING

▥ plain tile
▧ math. tile
▤ plaster
▨ weather board

Cladding materials to timber frame are virtually confined to the East and South-East, districts vary somewhat, though all materials are found in east Kent.

Roofing Materials: Thatch

THATCH

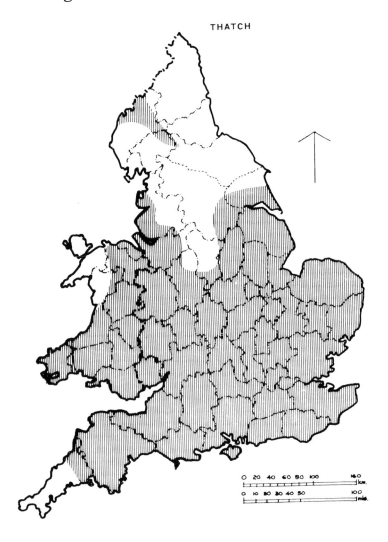

Thatch roofing – though varying in density, most parts of the country retain some thatched buildings.

Roofing Materials: Stone Flags and Stone Tiles

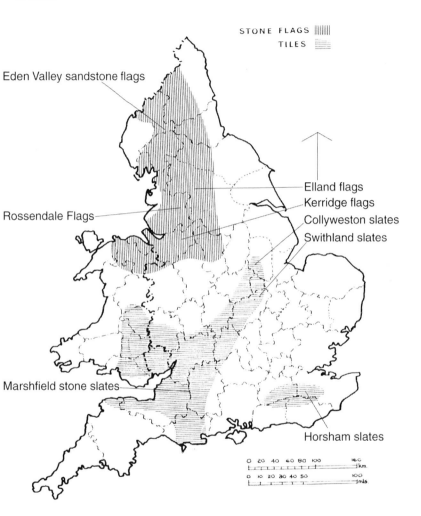

STONE FLAGS |||||||
TILES ≡≡≡

Eden Valley sandstone flags

Elland flags
Kerridge flags
Collyweston slates
Swithland slates

Rossendale Flags

Marshfield stone slates

Horsham slates

0 20 40 60 80 100   16 C
                   km.
0 10 20 30 40 50   100
                 mls.

Stone flag and tile roofing – the map distinguishes between the stone flags of the Pennines and the stone tiles of the Cotswolds, Wales, and the Weald. Some local names for stone 'slates' are indicated.

Roofing Materials: Plain Tiles and Pantiles

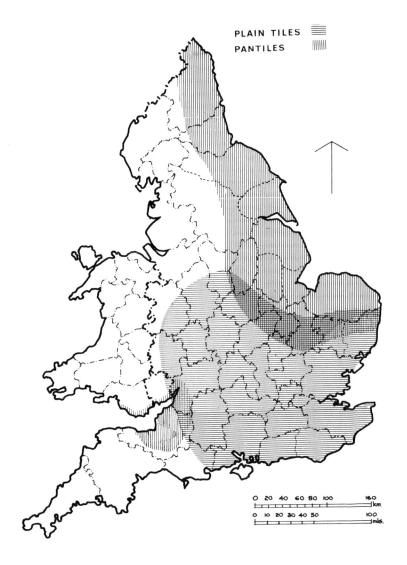

PLAIN TILES
PANTILES

Pantiles and plain tiles – the former are generally confined to the East and North-East, the latter to the South-East, South, and Midlands of England.

208

Fireplaces

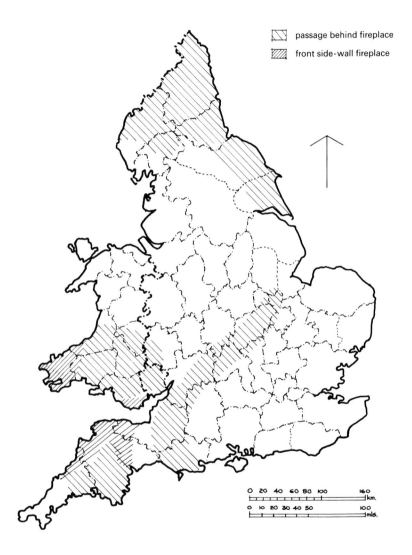

Two-unit and cross-passage houses – areas of common use are shown. *Fireplace in front side wall* – areas in South-West Wales and South-West England where these may be seen are shown; no attempt has been made to indicate halls with side-wall fireplaces at the rear.

Fireplaces (continued)

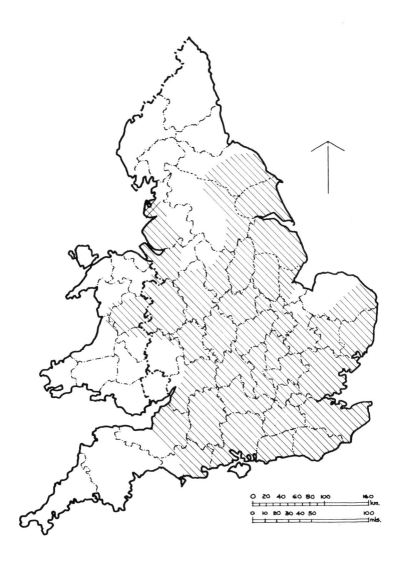

Central fireplaces plan (lobby entrance) – areas where these houses may be found are indicated.

Time Scales: Windows, Doors, Roofing

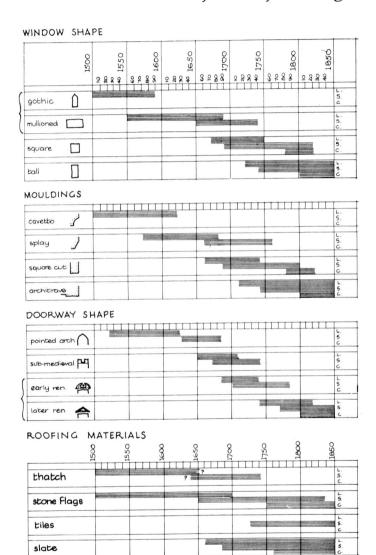

WINDOW SHAPE

	1500	1550	1600	1650	1700	1750	1800	1850	
gothic									L. S. C.
mullioned									L. S. C.
square									L. S. C.
tall									L. S. C.

MOULDINGS

cavetto									L. S. C.
splay									L. S. C.
square cut									L. S. C.
architrave									L. S. C.

DOORWAY SHAPE

pointed arch									L. S. C.
sub-medieval									L. S. C.
early ren.									L. S. C.
later ren.									L. S. C.

ROOFING MATERIALS

	1500	1550	1600	1650	1700	1750	1800	1850	
thatch				? ?					L. S. C.
stone flags									L. S. C.
tiles									L. S. C.
slate									L. S. C.

Vernacular Architecture in North America: A Note on English Influence

The next few pages include a few comments on the vernacular architecture of North America considered as a regional variation of English vernacular.

English influence on American vernacular was never without challenge. During the colonial period, the English colonists shared the settled territory with Dutch, Swedes, and Spaniards on the Eastern Seaboard, with the Spanish and French in the Gulf of Mexico, and with the French over most of Canada; the colonists of each nationality looked to their own homeland for architectural inspiration and their craftsmen brought over the traditional skills of each separate country. After the Revolution, the influence of supporting European nations, especially France, was naturally preferred to that of England and it is generally assumed that the greater significance of the Greek Revival in American domestic vernacular has some political basis. The great period of expansion in the later 19c. reinforced the influence of Central Europe which had begun to show itself in Pennsylvania during the early 18C. Nevertheless, the English has probably been the greatest single contribution to American vernacular.

Since there are several notable scholars working in the field, the current wave of interest in vernacular architecture has now gained the impetus in the United States which it has in this country. Domestic vernacular is still partly a study of individual monuments; in spite of the image only recently lost of America as a nation of farmers, only now has such work begun to be published on farm buildings; while, again, with a few important exceptions, systematic study of early industrial buildings has been neglected. On the other hand the preservation of material in the form of buildings in situ or moved together as open-air museums is very extensive and strikes a nostalgic chord in the mind of the American tourist.

For the English student of vernacular architecture, North America can provide valuable comparative material. In the first place it can show, for a short period at least, another English region, one which was culturally English, climatically not radically different but was subject to special local influences. This other English region is comparatively well documented – the measured drawings of the Historic American Buildings Survey are usually convincing and comprehensive, and genealogical self-interest as well as historical sense has provided documentary history for individual vernacular buildings not commonly available on this side of the Atlantic.

Secondly, it can show parallel and divergent development of planning and construction from common origins. The house plans recently classified in Cambridgeshire were employed in New England and developed simultaneously for a period, the corresponding constructional forms had a similar development except that in East and South-East England lightweight framing was developed for domestic use in a very small area even though widely adopted for industrial and transport buildings, while in America, lightweight framing became universal and is still the normal method of constructing all low buildings.

Thirdly, the larger country and greater population has led to preservation of vernacular practices through geographical isolation or deliberate cultural isolation. Thus the student of English vernacular architecture ought to be able to profit just as much as the student of English vernacular speech from the inbred communities of the Appalachians; and the strict puritan sects of Pennsylvania preserve to the present day the communal erection process and appropriate constructional forms which were once normal here on this side of the Atlantic.

However, it would be quite wrong to give comparative American material disproportionate weight. The great vernacular tradition of the hewn log construction in America appears to owe nothing to English influence though it may speak volumes for British adaptability. It is only claimed that for a hundred years or so after the middle of the 17C. there was yet another Great Rebuilding of England, but this time on the other side of the Atlantic.

Vernacular Architecture in North America: English Influence on the Northern Half of the Colonies

The groups who formed most of the original English colonies north of the Dutch settlements on the Hudson River were deliberately attempting to create a society which was not a copy of the stratified society they had left. Their homes, therefore, tended to be more uniform in size than in the districts they had left, Large Houses and Cottages being few, Small Houses, appropriate to yeoman status being the normal.

As the names of many of their settlements suggest, East Anglia and the South East provided the early immigrants. They brought over the plan types to which they had been accustomed; one room deep, two storeys in height, central chimneys placed back to back, and the corresponding structural forms, box-frame of heavy timber sections, light studded wall and independent roof construction. The surviving buildings show that the early wattle and daub panels proved inadequate for severe winters and were quickly replaced by weatherboards (or clapboards). To the two fireplaces of the original plan two further fireplaces for first-floor chambers were added, and often a heated extension or 'ell' was added at the rear.

During the period in question (late 17C. and early 18C.) plans with a continuous outshut at the rear, roofed by an extension from the main roof were often found on the English side of the Atlantic as well as the American, where they were called 'saltbox'. The double pitch, or gambrel roof was also used in common. Again the widespread use of masonry details imitated in painted timber on the fronts of timber framed houses recalls similar practices in South-Eastern England.

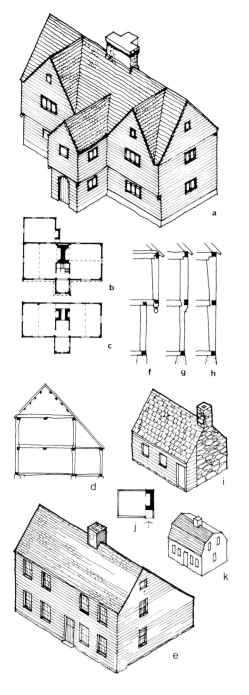

a. The illustration shows an example of a 17C. house in New England. The Ironmaster's House, at Saugus, Massachussetts, was built about 1640 as part of the development of a water powered ironworks on the site. The house has been altered and restored at various times but survives as a good example of the American equivalent of contemporary work in Eastern and South-Eastern England.

b., *c*. Ground floor and first plans of the Ironmaster's House.

d. Cross-section through 'saltbox' house with main roof extending down to cover rear outshut.

e. Isometric of saltbox house.

f., *g*., *h*. Details of upper floor construction (after Kelly). *f*. True jettied first floor, with pendants; *g*. false jettying; *h*. hewn post without jettying.

i., *j*. Sketch and plan of single-cell house.

k. Sketch showing commonly used gambrel roof.

Vernacular Architecture in North America: English Influence in the Southern Colonies

The earliest permanent English settlement on the Atlantic coast was made in 1607 at Jamestown, Virginia. Intensive excavation of the long-abandoned site of the colony, together with the many surviving examples of 17C. and 18C. domestic architecture in the South have combined to build a picture of a vernacular different from that of New England. This difference reflected a different social organization. Most of the Southern colonies were plantations made by individual proprietors or companies of investors as commercial enterprises and reflected all the grades of wealth and social status to be found in England. But beneath this social ladder was another formed of the slaves who were a vital part of the special agricultural and domestic economy. Thus, examples of domestic architecture range from the pretentious Palladian compositions of, e.g., Westover, Charles City County, Virginia, to the flimsy slaves' quarters of which only fragments remain. Only a proportion fall within the vernacular range. Of these many preserve a plan one room in depth but with gable chimneys, and some retain the projecting porch and staircase common throughout England at the turn of the 17C. Although most homes were timber-framed, a good proportion of the surviving examples are of brick with similar elaboration of chimney stack and gable wall to contemporary work in Eastern and South-Eastern England.

Further developments reflected the more temperate climate of this part of the Continent. In the summer and on the coastal plain breezes were to be attracted and shade sought, therefore the plans developed in forms extended and protected by verandahs rather than as compact blocks and with multiple fireplaces as further north.

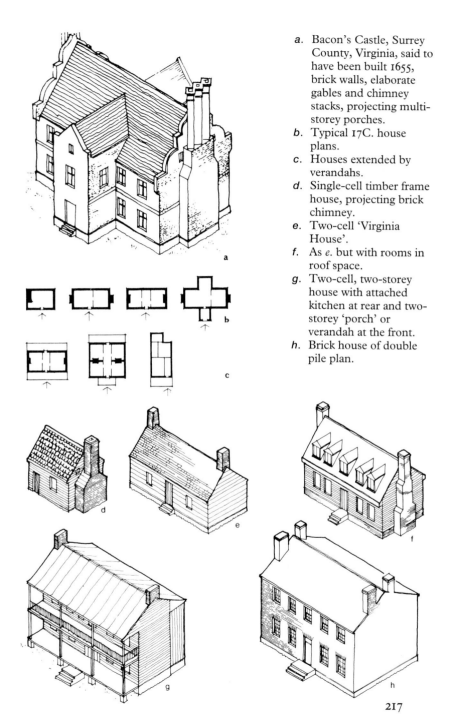

a. Bacon's Castle, Surrey County, Virginia, said to have been built 1655, brick walls, elaborate gables and chimney stacks, projecting multi-storey porches.
b. Typical 17C. house plans.
c. Houses extended by verandahs.
d. Single-cell timber frame house, projecting brick chimney.
e. Two-cell 'Virginia House'.
f. As e. but with rooms in roof space.
g. Two-cell, two-storey house with attached kitchen at rear and two-storey 'porch' or verandah at the front.
h. Brick house of double pile plan.

217

Vernacular Architecture in North America: English Influence in Eastern Pennsylvania and the Appalachians

Three aspects of the vernacular architecture of Eastern Pennsylvania and the Appalachians are noted here: the use of the I-house plan, the use of the one-room cottage plan and the development of the bank barn. The I-house (so-called because it was first noted in Indiana) consists of two rooms on the ground floor, both heated and with chimney stacks usually projecting from the gable wall, and a bedroom storey above. The plan was in use for a long time and there were several detailed variations but the plan seemed to have been inspired by the two-unit plan of England and Wales, which was itself much used in the counties from which so many emigrants to this part of the United States originated. The one-room cottage has a single room with door, window and a hearth or fireplace projecting from a gable wall; above was a loft space reached by an internal ladder. The plan was presumably based on the one-roomed cottages of England and Wales but the construction was usually of horizontal logs, a technique introduced from Bohemia, Moravia and Silesia and unknown in Britain.

The bank barns resembled those of Cumbria in that they had a barn for hand flail threshing placed over a range of stables and cow-houses, and in that they were built into a slope and had a ramp or bridge to give access to the upper level but direct access to the lower level. The fundamental difference to be seen in the Pennsylvania barn was the provision of a forebay, an extension of the threshing barn, projecting over the lower level. The forebay was usually of timber-frame construction and cantilevered but some were carried on posts or stone arcades. An extension of the pitched gabled roof of the threshing barn covered the forebay. Early bank barns were of log construction; most, however, were of heavy timber-frame construction; some had stone walls and a few had brick. The Pennsylvania bank barn had developed into a recognizable form by the 1780s and in certain circumstances they continue to be built according to the traditional techniques right up to the present day. The source area of the Pennsylvania bank barn has been placed in the Pratigau Valley of South-East Switzerland but the similarity with the Cumbrian bank barn may not be coincidental.

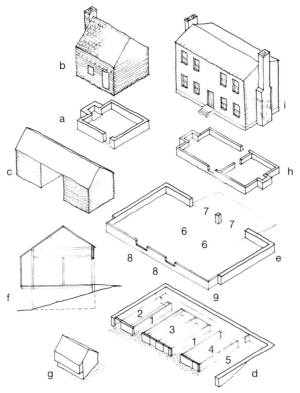

a. One-room cottage or cabin with loft above; horizontal log construction. b. Sketch of cottage or cabin. c. Double-pen barn, log construction, with central floor giving effect of 'English' barn. d. Pennsylvania bank barn, lower level showing feeding passage (1), cow stalls (2), steers, calves, sheep (3), horse stalls (4), cart shed (5). e. Pennsylvania bank barn, upper level with two threshing floors (6), each with barn door (7) and with winnowing doors (8) in forebay (9). f. Cross-section showing projecting forebay. g. Sketch showing projecting forebay. h. I-house with two ground-floor rooms and bedrooms above, may have outside kitchen at rear. i. sketch of I-house of clapboarded timber frame and stone chimneys.

Vernacular Architecture in Scotland

The vernacular architecture of Scotland developed differently from that of England and recent advances in its study suggest that some note should be included here by way of comparison.

Outside the towns, rural settlement over much of Scotland was based on *fermtouns*, townships of half a dozen families who tilled their land in common according to the 'run-rig' system of intensive cultivation of a well-manured infield and occasional cultivation of part of the rough pasture outfield. In the *fermtouns* the landlord–tenant relationship as well as the poverty of the people perpetuated the use of primitive structures of short life. From about 1750 to 1880, however, there was a great wave of 'improvement' whereby the *fermtouns* were replaced by individual farm-steads serving large farms of land enclosed in fields and including farm-houses, farm buildings and labourers' cottages. All the new structures were substantially built and provided living conditions much better than those they had replaced. Some farmsteads were designed by professional architects or agriculturalists and were in the forefront of farmstead design but others perpetuated the plans of earlier buildings. In parts of the Highlands and Islands, nevertheless, the traditional plans and methods of construction persisted until quite late in the 19C.

Within the bigger towns, medieval systems of land-holding perpetuated the use of tall multi-storey buildings, often retaining timber frame at least on the street frontage. The smaller towns took part in the architecture of the agricultural revolution and over 100 new planned villages and towns were founded and built.

Many tower-houses were built in the countryside of Lowland Scotland between the 12C. and 14C. As with their English counterparts, the Scottish tower-houses had a stone-vaulted ground floor, a hall at first-floor level and one or two storeys above; they usually had a first-floor entrance and internal winding staircases. Later examples had a projecting wing with a more generous staircase, a 'caphouse' above and a lively skyline of turrets, crow-stepped gables and chimney stacks. The final flourish of the late 16C. had a more elaborate Z-plan. The smaller and later bastle house with a first-floor hall and chamber above a defensible ground-floor cow-house and stable has recently been recognized. Before the Improvements of the 18C. the typical Scottish farm-house was an elongated single cell open to the roof with a common entrance for humans and animals but no cross-passage. A peat fire burned on a stone hearth in the middle of the building. Sleeping accommodation was in a bed recess or, later, in a box-bed. Little remains of these houses except in the Hebrides but travellers of the 17C. and 18C. commented unfavourably on them. From the mid-18C. they were succeeded by substantial stone-walled houses, also of elongated rectangular shape with a living room and parlour, both heated, and bedrooms lit by dormers in the roof space, though the tradition of sleeping in box-beds lingered, especially in the small, cottage versions of the plan.

Early cottages, rarely surviving, had only one room open to the roof and with no accommodation for animals. In the Improvement period of the later 18C. and 19C., day labourers on the new farms were provided with substantial cottages of one and a half rooms in a single storey or one room with a bedroom loft above. The developing textile trades, especially in linen manufacture, called for cottages with an unheated ground-floor workshop.

In the towns there was a long-standing tradition of multi-storey houses with domestic accommodation raised over ground-floor shops and reached by an external 'forestair'. In the Old Town of Edinburgh there was a tightly packed development of very tall buildings or 'lands' with layers of separate dwellings reached by a winding 'turnpike' staircase. This arrangement developed into the 'tenement flats' of the big towns such as Glasgow, Dundee and Aberdeen, as well as Edinburgh. Each tenement was a self-contained dwelling of one or more 'apartments' containing box-beds. They were set in buildings four or more storeys high with an internal common staircase reached from a single front door. The most substantial tenement blocks were mostly constructed in the period from about 1890 to 1914.

The well-known 'blackhouse' of remote Scotland consisted basically of a single rectangular room reached through a single door and accommo-

dating humans and animals under the same roof. The houses and cottages of the Improvement period usually had two habitable rooms on the ground floor, one or both containing box-beds. From the mid- to late 19C. rooms in the roof space were brought into use as bedrooms and lit by roof lights or dormer windows. Heating developed from the use of an open hearth set against a low fireback wall under a suspended chimney hood, via the 'hanging lum' of a hood cantilevered from a gable or transverse wall, to the use of a conventional fireplace, flue and chimney stack, nearly always set in a gable wall.

a. Clay-walled, thatched roof single-storey house as found in Dumfries-shire.

b. One-and-a-half storey house, widespread but here from Aberdeen-shire.

c. Horse-engine house, type widespread in the Lowlands.

d. Two-storey house with pantile roof as found in Fife.

e. Aberdeen Bond of large blocks of stone separated by small stones.

f. One-and-a-half storey house with dormers and roof light, widespread but here from the Borders.

g. House with rough boulder walls and corrugated galvanized roof replacing thatch; as to be seen in the Western Isles.

h. Upper-storey town house as found in Fife and Perthshire.

i. Blackhouse as re-erected at Kingussie in the Grampians.

j. Tower-house.

a

b

c

d

e

f

g

h

i

j

223

Although the buildings of Scotland now appear as solidly built of dressed stone, such substantial construction was confined to a relatively small number of important buildings such a churches and defensible dwellings until about 200 years ago. Most houses and farm buildings were built of clay, wattle, or various combinations of field stones and turf. Solid clay-walled structures, comparable with those of Cumberland survive here and there, especially in South-West Scotland. Clay and timber were used as 'stake and rice' in walls comparable with the mud and stud of Lincolnshire. 'Clay and bool' walls alternated stones or cobbles with clay and turf. Brick walls were used in the Central Lowlands and parts of the North East from the late 18C. but sometimes as an inner lining to a wall of some other material. Thick walls of outer and inner skins of rough stone with an interior of two or three feet of turf were characteristic of the 'blackhouses' of North and West Scotland. Conventional masonry walls of the late 18C. and 19C. included the techniques of pointing in lime mortar and harling, a roughcast with dry dash which concealed the stones behind a whitish surface.

Cruck construction was once widespread in Scotland though surviving examples are few and usually of rough and spindly timber. Jointed crucks were common and the upright parts often survive in ruined buildings which have lost their roofs. End crucks were used to produce the rounded hipped-roof shape. For although most of the buildings of the Scottish countryside now present gabled slated roofs to the observer, the use of hipped roofs of thatch was normal before the late 18C.

There were many regional variations but thatch of wheat or rye straw over a turf underthatch was commonly used. In the South-West and North-East heather was often used in place of straw. Broom or whin was a cheaper substitute while divots or squares of turf laid diamond fashion were used to cover inferior buildings. In the Northern Isles, especially, the thatch was kept in position with weighted nets of rope. Everywhere thatch was a material which required constant attention and frequent replacement. From the early 19C. on, slate quarried locally or imported from the Lake District or Snowdonia and carried on roofs of sawn softwood superseded the thatch. Flagstones of sandstone were an alternative available here and there. Felt roofs of cloth dipped in tar were a later Scottish development.

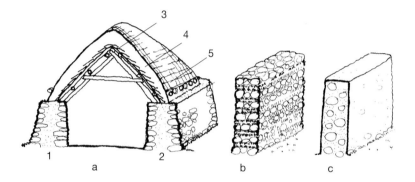

a. Wall of double thickness stone (1) and infill (2) with turf (3), thatch (4) and a net (5) weighted by stones. *b*. Wall with alternate layers of stone and turf. *c*. Wall of stone and clay.

Conclusion: The Vernacular Revival

We have seen that the closing years of the 19C. marked the end of any substantial vernacular content in even the humblest dwelling houses, farm buildings, or minor industrial buildings in this country. By 1900, the rich, middle classes, and poor alike could afford substantial dwelling houses in permanent materials; their houses were subject to building regulations national in origin even if local in administration; the choice of materials and constructional methods was wider than ever, but walls of mass-produced bricks and roofs of easily quarried slate were so cheap and universally available that any other choice was almost wilful; while large architectural practices operating nationally, their innovations immediately published in magazines of wide circulation, left little demand for regional variation.

And yet if one were to count separately many of the architectural details mentioned in this book, they could be shown to have been used more frequently in the fifty years after 1900 than the centuries before that date. The housing estates of the 1930s display more half-timbered gables than will ever be recorded in Worcestershire or Kent for they represent the ill-digested, speculative builder's version of the Vernacular Revival style which was dominant in English – and indeed in American – domestic architecture from about 1860 to 1914.

Minor domestic architecture had previously given inspiration to sophisticated designers as part of the Picturesque Movement of the late 18C. and early 19C. Details only just passing out of use – such as decoratively thatched roofs – were adopted by the fashionable designers and multiplied and magnified to produce vast 'cottages' for their clients. When picturesque qualities provided the criteria and the demands of a selected external appearance were paramount, then details from many periods and locations could legitimately be combined in the same building. But the Vernacular Revival of the later 19C. was quite differently based. In 1861, J. L. Petit, becoming disillusioned with a Gothic Revival which conformed to medieval types rather than developed medieval principles, suggested that the basis of a living architecture was 'our ordinary or vernacular architecture'. He thus gave to minor domestic architecture something of the rank formerly restricted to churches, temples, palaces and tombs and related architecture to the everyday world of speech and the vulgar tongue at that, rather than the esoteric worlds of sculpture, painting or poetry. At the same time, William Morris and his colleagues in the Arts and Crafts Movement had been looking back to what they believed had been an age of simple unaffected craftsmanship. Honesty in materials and techniques was held to apply equally to architecture as to the related crafts of furniture making, fabric weaving, glass painting, etc. The result was a style of architecture in which some practitioners at least felt they were returning to the down-to-earth, vernacular spirit of the Middle Ages.

The principal architects working in the Vernacular Revival were Philip Webb, W. R. Lethaby, C. F. A. Voysey, M. H. Baillie Scott, Edgar Wood, and, from time to time, R. Norman Shaw and Sir Edwin Lutyens. Their opportunities came in the design of those medium sized country houses demanded by the members of the middle class who had been made rich enough by the Industrial Revolution to afford country retreats in the newly accessible Downs or Lake District. Their characteristic designs were for long, low, sprawling houses set beneath wide spreading roofs, broken with gables, emphasized by deep eaves, with long bands of mullioned windows, plain rendered wall surfaces, spidery wrought iron brackets, diamond paned lattices, and so on. An appearance of age and history was built into the houses by the incorporation, presumably deliberate, of details from several periods in the same building, and premature repair work in, e.g., the use of sloping buttresses on exposed corners. Many architects in the school, and especially E. S. Prior with his Norfolk flint houses, made conscious use of local materials. Some, Edgar Wood for instance, filled their sketchbooks with details of local cottages and farm-houses; and in some parts of the country the literature of vernacular architecture still relies on the published notes and drawings of such architects.

And so the Vernacular Revival, to judge from its completed monuments, appears to have taken its place in the ranks of architectural revivals of the 18C. and 19C., though further research will no doubt show to what extent it was differently based from the Greek, Gothic, and Italianate Revivals. Sensitive architects had felt the need for a style appropriate to the domestic circumstances of their clients, had seen the ingredients for such a style in the manor houses and farm-houses of various periods up and down the country, and combined these ingredients each one according to his own recipe, and, in most cases, had served up the results without much account of where they were to be enjoyed. The results were, indeed, usually as charming as they were comfortable, but they could not, by any classification, be called vernacular architecture.

Indeed it is hard to visualize any circumstances, short of the nuclear holocaust, which can possibly revive vernacular architecture in the country. The simple, unaffected, method of building which we call vernacular has been employed and then discarded at all levels of the social scale. The results of its employment make up a large but swiftly diminishing part of our present environment, they must be studied now, by this generation, or never.

(*Opposite*)

The illustration is of the set of drawings prepared by Edgar Wood in 1894 for a house, 'Barcroft' to be built in Bolton Road, Marland, Rochdale. Edgar Wood was an enthusiastic student of the vernacular architecture of the countryside around Manchester and prepared many sets of measured drawings and sketch-books of details.

Rochdale lies on the boundary zone between the timber frame and brick vernacular of the Lancashire Plain and the millstone grit vernacular of the Pennines and authentic details of both techniques have been included, e.g., from the Lowlands, shallow brick arches, brick string course with dentils, diaper work in projecting brick headers, thin millstone grit transomes and mullions, and from the Uplands, stone flagged roof, door with false three-centred arched head and carved device on the lintel, raised lintel over centre of gable window.

However, neither plan nor section appear to embody any local vernacular precedent, the particular mixture of brick arched heads and stone lintels appears wilful, the boldly projecting bay window at the north-west corner is not a local detail.

The drawing shows the house as it would appear in its old age with ridge-line sinking and chimneys leaning. It was not built so, but the desire of the architect to make his building of its own time and yet timeless, appears to have dominated his thinking.

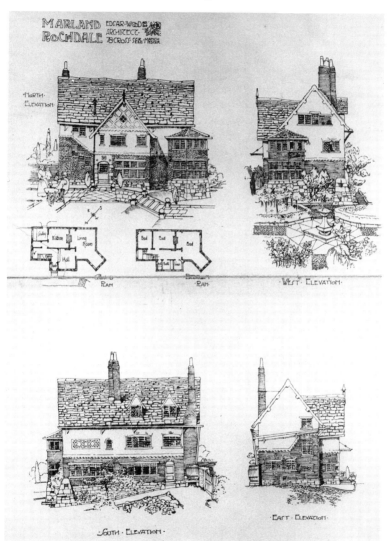

(from *British Architect* Vol. 14, 1894, p. 382)

APPENDIX 1

How to Study Vernacular Architecture

General

The full fascination of vernacular architecture can only be enjoyed by study of a selected area or subject; and such study is likely to be most rewarding if conducted in a systematic manner. In the field of vernacular architecture perhaps more than in some other fields of study there is a constant temptation to explore the by-ways of folklore, dialect, country crafts, humble genealogy, water-colour sketching, etc. etc., but the ruthless and single-minded student will find ample reward in concentration on the buildings, their setting and the related documents.

In this field, as elsewhere, the scope of any study must be defined at the outset. The actual geographical area selected should be severely restricted in size; even the smallest and most unlikely community is likely to reveal an iceberg of information beneath the visible tip of a few unpromising buildings. The building type selected must be carefully defined; normally one starts with houses, but farm buildings or minor industrial buildings have the advantage that no one's privacy is impaired and, once the mystified owners have given access, repeated visits to deal with uncertain points do not usually present any difficulty. The period of study should also be firmly defined. There will usually be no difficulty in fixing the earliest date, but the choice of terminal date may be more debatable; dates of 1840 for houses and 1880 for farm buildings have been found useful in the past, but at this distance in time a continuation to, say, 1914, in both cases has a good deal to recommend it.

A complete study will result from simultaneous operation at three levels; extensive recording in some systematic manner, covering all relevant examples but in a superficial way; intensive recording of examples selected from the extensive survey as being typical or, in some other way likely to repay closer investigation; and documentary study, illuminating the surviving buildings and giving information on their forgotten predecessors.

Extensive Recording

A systematic procedure for the extensive study of examples of minor domestic architecture was in use in the School of Architecture of the University of Manchester for some 20 years. It was devised by Professor Cordingley to assist in the speedy collection of survey material in the field, and, by reducing the subjective element as far as possible, to assist in the comparison of material between different parts of the country. The system was only intended to collect basic architectural information as revealed on the exterior of buildings and depended on intensive and documentary investigation to complete the study. The system has been reasonably successful in meeting its limited objectives but does require a certain amount of experience and technical knowledge for satisfactory use. For the present purposes a simplified version based on the same principles is presented. In future, systems based on hand-held computers may well be devised.

PROCEDURE

1. *Define the Survey Area.* A civil parish provides a convenient area, and in most parts of England, at least, will include a village and some isolated houses.

2. *Assemble Materials.* A $2\frac{1}{2}$ in. Ordnance Survey map, a field notebook, ball-point pens, preferably with separate colours for separate sets of notes, pencil for diagrams, camera and black-and-white film, and, if possible, field-glasses for reading datestones. The ideal method of transport is the pedestrian but bicycle, motor scooter, and motor car, in that order, would usually be used.

3. *Decide on the Relevant Period of the Building.* Some houses will be entirely of one build, but many will show evidence of work of several periods; it is important to decide which is the significant period – not necessarily the oldest – and note variations separately.

4. *Decide on Size-Type.* Ignoring Great Houses, each house will be either a Large House, a Small House, or a Cottage according to the wealth and status of its original occupant. One should distinguish between, say, Large Houses which have been subdivided, and Cottages built originally for cottagers. One should also bear in mind that the considerable variations in wealth between regions of the country meant that quite a small building might be a Large House in a poor district.

5. *Identify the Building.* A street address, if available (and many houses in villages have no permanent address), the parish and county should be noted. A six-figure map reference as explained on the Ordnance Survey map should be given; this will include the reference letters of the 100 km. square (e.g. NY) and the reference of the 100 m. square in which the building is located (e.g. 325·501),

the total reference being, e.g. NY – 325·501; it is also convenient to have a serial number for the surveyor's own use.

6. *Note Down the Aspect*. i.e. In what direction the front door is facing, e.g. S.E.; this may be obtained by compass or, accurately enough for the present purpose, from the Ordnance Survey map.

7. *Note Down the Principal Walling Material*. i.e. stone, flint, cobble etc., brick, clay, etc., timber frame (half-timbered, or with plain tile, math. tile, slate, weatherboard, plaster, cladding).

8. *Note Down Any Reliably Dated Feature*. Many stone-walled buildings bear an inscribed date either on a door lintel, in a plaque over the door, or alongside a chimney stack. Brick walled buildings might have a date scratched on a brick, in a diaper pattern, or on stone dressings. Timber framed buildings sometimes have dates carved on the main bressummer of a jettied projection; or modelled in a plaster cladding. Any building may have a date cast in a lead rainwater head or cistern. None of these dates necessarily relates to the original construction, but all relate to some period in the life of a building and, taken with other evidence are of obvious importance.

9. *Note Down Salient Features According to the Code*. From each line of the code sheets illustrated on pages 234–5 select the appropriate alternative.

10. *Add a Photograph and Diagrammatic Sketches*. A photograph alone is an inadequate record of a building. No single photograph can show enough of the exterior of a building nor, in fickle circumstances of light can quality be reliable. Diagrammatic sketches, however crude, are always useful and, really, indispensible

11. *Note Down Initials and Date of Survey*. For comparative purposes the date at which a record is made is significant – and during the present wave of destruction and alteration of country property important for historical record.

DEVELOPMENT:

Any surveyor can develop any part of the code to meet his own requirements. For instance if there were a special interest in brickwork then A2 could be developed to record eight different bonds, e.g. A2.1 for English Bond, A2.2 for English Cross Bond and so on. Further codes could be developed for pointing whatever the bond, e.g. A2.11 for English Bond with a struck joint.

	LARGE HOUSE		SMALL HOUSE		COTTAGE	

LOCATION		COUNTY		ADDRESS		MAP REFERENCE	FILING

SURVEYOR	SURVEY DATE	FILM No.	EXPOSURE No.	ELEV. PHOTO	ASPECT	WALLING MATERIAL	DATE

CODED DESCRIPTION	PHOTOGRAPH

A record card made from an 8 in. by 5 in. filing card.

	(LARGE HOUSE)	SMALL HOUSE	COTTAGE

LOCATION		COUNTY	ADDRESS	MAP REFERENCE	FILING
BURGH-BY-SANDS		CUMBERLAND	Low Moorhouse	NY 334.566	· 367

SURVEYOR	SURVEY DATE	FILM No.	EXPOSURE No.	ELEV. PHOTO	ASPECT	WALLING MATERIAL	DATE
RWB	July 1956	SD	21		S E	brick, s.s. dressings	lintel 1734

CODED DESCRIPTION

	1	2	3	4	5	6	7	8	9	0
A		✓								
B		✓								
C			✓							
D			✓							
E						✓				
F								✓		
G					✓					
H				✓						
J				✓						
K							✓			

A completed record card. The coded description shows the house to have brick walling (A2), with a mixture of other materials (B2), a gabled roof (C3), of thick slate (D3), to have tall windows (E6), with vertically sliding sashes (F8), a doorway with a renaissance type surround (G5), be two-storey (H4), to have the two-unit and cross-passage plan (J4) and to have a barn attached, laithe-house fashion (K7).

233

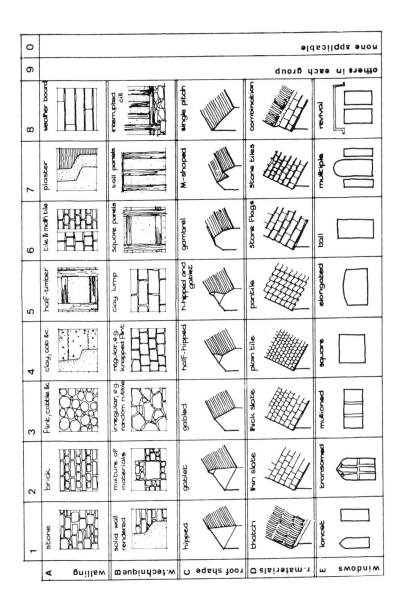

The following is the content of the coded description table:

	1	2	3	4	5	6	7	8	9	0
A walling	stone	brick	Flint, cobble &c.	clay, cob &c.	half-timber	tile & math tile	plaster	weather board	others in each group	none applicable
B w.technique	solid wall rendered	mixture of materials	irregular, e.g. random rubble	regular, e.g. knapped flint	clay lump	square panels	tall panels	interrupted cill		
C roof shape	hipped	gablet	gabled	half-hipped	h-hipped and gablet	gambrel	M-shaped	single pitch		
D r.materials	thatch	Tun slate	Trick slate	plain tile	pantile	stone flags	stone tiles	combination		
E windows	lancet	transomed	mullioned	square	elongated	tall	multiple	revival		

Diagram for coded description. Sheet 1.

234

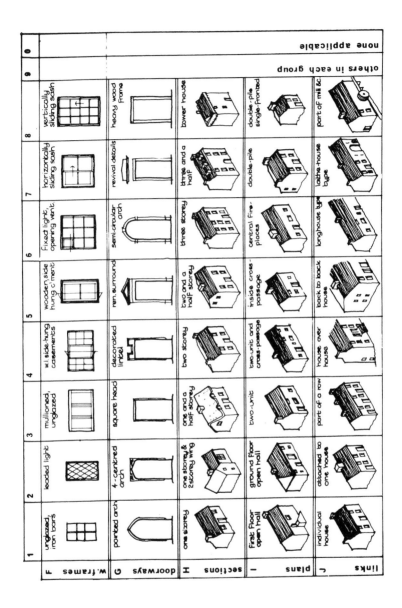

	1	2	3	4	5	6	7	8	9	0
F W.frames	unglazed, iron bars	leaded light	mullioned, unglazed	w.l side-hung casements	wooden,side hung c'ment	Fixed light, opening vent.	horizontally sliding sash	vertically sliding sash		
G doorways	pointed arch	4-centred arch	square head	decorated lintel	ren. surround	semi-circular arch	revival details	heavy wood frame		
H sections	one storey	one storey & 2 storey wing	one and a half storey	two storey	two and a half storey	three storey	three and a half	tower house	others in each group	none applicable
I plans	First floor open hall	ground floor open hall	two-unit	two-unit and cross-passage	two-unit and cross-passage	central fire-places	double-pile	double-pile single-fronted		
J links	individual house	attached to one house	part of a row	house over house	back to back house	longhouse type	laithe-house type	part of mill &c		

Diagram for coded description. Sheet 2.

235

Intensive Survey

During the progress of an extensive survey, it will be seen that certain building forms recur even in the most picturesque village of apparently haphazard development as typical of a certain period or a certain level of society. Examples of such buildings should be selected for intensive study through the preparation of measured drawings. This is a procedure which requires comparatively little skill or experience providing it is done in a systematic way. The refinements of the measuring procedure and the separate procedure of drawing out from measured notes may be discovered from one of the several books on draughtsmanship available but an outline here of the basic points may prove useful.

There are two distinct processes involved; measuring and drawing. These should ideally, but not essentially, be carried out by the same person and as soon as possible after each other. When measuring care must be taken to avoid accidents or damage especially in empty property. One should be wary of surveying alone.

MEASURING

1. *Personnel.* An ideal team is three; one surveyor and two helpers.

2. *Equipment.* (Metric equivalents in brackets.) A hardbacked pad preferably of foolscap/A4 size, a cloth tape 66 ft. long (20 m.), an extending rod 6 ft. long (2 m.), a spring steel tape 6 ft. (2 m.) long, a simple weight and cord for a plumb line, a ball of plasticene, a camera with black-and-white film, a flashlight, pencils and coloured ball-point pens.

3. *Procedure (having obtained all necessary permissions).*
   (*a*) Prepare sketch plans, sections and elevations. These should be reasonably in proportion but should not attempt to show too much detail.
   (*b*) Prepare larger scale details in plan, section and elevation, using the sketch plans as a key and with cross-referencing.
   (*c*) Locate the building by triangulation from some base line, e.g. the front fence.
   (*d*) Proceed from room to room, take plan dimensions, including diagonals, and of rough openings, e.g. window jamb to jamb, ignoring window frames.
   (*e*) Take sectional dimensions using staircases to give overall heights, floor to ceiling heights for separate rooms, roof space for accessible roof construction, and angle of roof slope.

(*f*) Take dimensions of each elevation in turn. These should be related to a horizontal datum line (e.g. top of a plinth) not the varying ground line. At upper levels dimensions may have to be taken from open windows. In the absence of long ladders, dimensions of chimney stacks may have to be estimated, e.g. by counting brick courses.

(*g*) Take dimensions of selected details.

(*h*) Take photographs of elevations and details; a composite photograph may be useful on a cramped site.

4. *Taking and Noting Dimensions.* With a team of three, one helper should hold the fixed end of the tape, another should read off each dimension and the surveyor should book down on his pad. Running dimensions are to be preferred wherever possible (see diagram), and using a long run through doors, to take in several rooms, as a check. It will be helpful if the sketch plans are drawn in pencil, dimensions and dimension lines shown in some other colour and notes and cross references in other colours.

5. *Assembling the Survey Notes.* To avoid subsequent confusion, each separate sheet should bear the address of the building, the name of the surveyor, the date of survey, and a number (e.g. sheet 1 of 10).

DRAWING

1. *Personnel.* Although the measured notes should be prepared in such a way that anyone could draw them out, it is obviously preferable that the surveyor draws them, and when his memory is fresh.

2. *Equipment.* A drawing board, which need only be a piece of blockboard with 'formica' on one face and two adjacent edges, a simple T-square, an adjustable set-square, masking tape to hold the paper, good quality tracing paper, a Rexel type pencil with 4H and 2H leads, a soft eraser, an architectural scale divided into divisions of $\frac{1}{4}$ in., $\frac{1}{8}$ in., etc. (1:50, 1:100, etc.), ink pens (e.g. Rotring) of various thickness, a pair of simple ink and pencil springbow compasses.

3. *Procedure.*

(*a*) Choose a scale for each part of the drawing. This should be appropriate to the subject and to the possibility of reproduction. For most vernacular buildings, plans and elevations drawn out to a scale of $\frac{1}{8}$ in. to the foot (1:100) with sections at $\frac{1}{4}$ in. to the foot (1:50) and details of windows, etc., to $\frac{1}{2}$ in. or 1 in. to the foot (1:25 or 1:10) and site plans at $\frac{1}{8}$ in. (1:100) scale, will give the appropriate amount of detail and be suitable for reductions in block-making.

(b) Set out the various sheets using overall dimensions as a guide. It is customary to arrange a site plan with north at the top, the floor plans with the main entrance facing the bottom of the sheet and the main elevation above the ground-floor plan.

(c) Set out in pencil each part of the drawing using the compasses to establish triangulation. Running dimensions will be helpful in using the scale. If several parts of the drawing are worked up simultaneously mistakes can be found and corrected without too much waste of effort.

(d) When the whole of the work has been completed in pencil it should be inked in, using varying thicknesses for lines of varying importance.

(e) Lettering should then be added. Hand script is no longer fashionable but stencil or transfer lettering is readily available and easy to use.

(f) Finally, each sheet should be given a title and date, north points should be provided for the plans and written and drawn scales in both Imperial and metric measure included.

4. *Draughtsmanship.*

(a) The drawings are intended to communicate information. To this end the presence or absence of any line is significant and its thickness should be in relation to its importance. A plan is a horizontal section, the most important line being that which indicates the cut through the wall, within that cut line no information is available, and none should be invented. Looking downwards, the walls as seen at windows, the steps at the door, the hearth and any changes of level are important. Less important are lines indicating window frames, glass lines, fixed furniture, etc. Least important are lines indicating a floor pattern or material texture. Similar considerations apply to sections. In elevations the silhouette lines are most important, with openings, changes of plane, and jointing in decreasing order.

(b) Records of fact and items of interpretation should be separated. Ideally one set of drawings should show what existed at the time of survey and another should be hatched to indicate assumed periods of construction, but the two sets are often combined.

(*Opposite*) A typical measured drawing of a vernacular building. Below is an example of the measured notes with indication of the way measurements are taken: running dimensions, diagonals, dimensions through openings to join rooms together, setbacks in recesses, etc. Only a selection of the measurements is given.

238

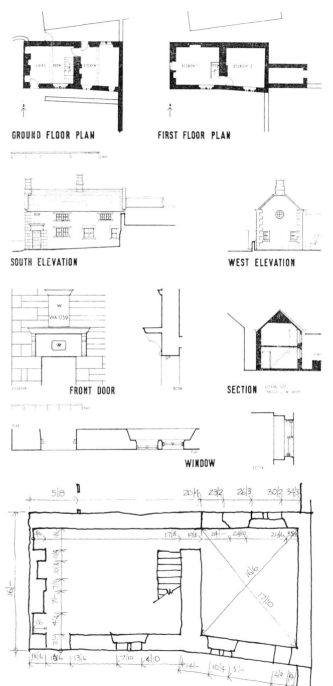

GROUND FLOOR PLAN

FIRST FLOOR PLAN

SOUTH ELEVATION

WEST ELEVATION

FRONT DOOR

SECTION

WINDOW

239

Documentary Investigation

If it is the hope that careful examination of examples of vernacular architecture will help to illuminate the activities for which the buildings were intended and the processes by which they were brought into existence; it must equally be acknowledged that careful examination of documents relating to the buildings, their owners, and occupiers should help to elucidate some of the mysteries presented by the physical remains. Alongside the development of archaeological examination of the buildings the historians have adapted their own methods of inquiry to provide information at the vernacular level.

Ideally, of course, one would want to identify a specific building with the documents which relate to it. The obvious link should be the *title deeds* of the property. The present owners may only have a recent summary of the various conveyances, but sometimes the archives of a local Solicitor, or a County Record Office can supply more complete deeds. These, however, relating to the land, will rarely be of much direct value in connection with a building, but in giving a history of the ownership may tie down pieces of information. Sometimes in deeds of the late 18C. or 19C. a site plan is included; sometimes covenants or leases may be helpful.

In the absence of title deeds, ownership or occupation may be established by reference to records of the *courts baron*, usually now held in a County Record Office, or to *surveys* made, often with maps, from time to time, and especially on change of ownership of an estate, to assist with administration. From the late 18C. onwards, *county directories* are very useful in relating people and occupations to addresses. *Glebe terriers* usually survive from about 1600 onwards and sometimes give quite detailed information on parsonage houses, their accommodation, building materials, and state of repair.

The various *taxation records* are useful in helping to give a general picture of a locality; but even when an individual piece of property can be identified the amount of actual information gained is not usually great. Nor can one expect any more reliable information to be volunteered by a property owner to a tax inspector in the past than at present. One very useful tax record, however, is the *tithe map*. These were prepared from about 1836 onwards and every Parish Church once possessed a copy of the map for its parish. The tithe maps normally show and name each individual field and many picture quite reliably and sometimes quite delightfully separate houses and farm buildings. There is usually some indication of the crops grown in the field at the time of survey and this information helps to establish the use of various farm buildings. Maps prepared in connection with enclosure awards from about 1750 onwards, and of which a copy was originally held by the Parish, the Lord of the Manor and the Enclosure Commission may be helpful in identifying separate tenements and their owners at the time.

Having identified ownership of buildings, records may help to show how they were used. By far the most helpful documents in this respect are the inventories made by neighbours to help in establishing the estate of a deceased person. These probate inventories were made during the three centuries roughly from 1539 to 1839, but most survive from about 1650 onwards. They have been held in the various Diocesan Registries, but are, in most counties, being moved to the Record Office. The inventories vary a great deal in their completeness; some of them simply give a lump sum value to the moveable possessions of the deceased; but many list item by item and, systematically, room by room, the furniture, household equipment, farm animals, unconsumed fodder, farm implements, etc., as well as recording his monetary wealth.

For later periods, descriptions of buildings in general and their use may be made in the various *reports and surveys*. These include county reports to the Board of Agriculture, Prize Essays of the Royal Agricultural Society of England, contributions to the *Gentleman's Magazine*, the accounts of late 18C. and early 19C. travellers such as W. Pennant and Arthur Young as well as some of their predecessors like Celia Fiennes and William Harrison. Guide-book writers – such as Wordsworth – sometimes note the buildings half-hidden by the scenery; while observant clergymen, such as Rev. T. D. Whittaker of Whalley in Lancashire, provide information about the buildings of their parishes.

More detailed information on the buildings, their construction, and appearance, may be obtained from *building accounts* preserved with estate documents in agents' offices or in County Record Offices. Sometimes the accounts are set out in such a way that actual building quantities can be read off and an approximate size and form of the building deduced. Sometimes also diagrams or even plans accompany the accounts. Building contracts when surviving are less useful than might be expected, but until the general contractor emerged as an individual it was the practice for the building owner to let out contracts by trades and sometimes (as does happen in the country at the present time), making no reference to the labour or materials he supplied himself.

Finally, *contemporary drawings and photographs* intended for other purposes must not be neglected for the sake of the vernacular buildings forming the topographical background.

Patience and persistence as well as a keen eye and a nose for detail are really essential in documentary investigation of vernacular buildings. Considerable effort with little reward is common experience and when effort is rewarded it is usually by an excess of information in one direction and scarcity in another. But even where actual identification of record and building cannot be made, the background information gained is quite unobtainable from the buildings themselves.

An attempt is made here to deduce the general lines of a house plan from the evidence given in an inventory, as affected by general knowledge of house types in that part of the country and of the early 18C.

It is assumed that the appraisers entered by the front door, turned right to the 'kitchen', then back along a lobby to the 'house' off which opened a 'dining room' and 'pantry'. They then retraced to the lobby, went downstairs to the cellar, then upstairs to the first floor where they visited, in the same order, the 'chambers' over kitchen, house and dining-room (this last also extending over the pantry); finally they ascended to the garrets. An idea of the dimensions of the house can be obtained from the furniture contained in the various rooms.

The information is, of course, limited and should be considered alongside other known information for someone of similar wealth and social status in a similar time and place.

AN INVENTORY OF THE GOODS OF MRS. PHILLIPSON &C OF THE TOWN OF ALMONDSBURY IN THE COUNTY OF YORK DECEASED (1740)

	£ s. d.
Purse	1. 10. 0.

Goods in the Kitching

A Jack	12. 0.
A range end irons tongs coal rake fire point	15. 0.
A bakeing stone and cover 10s. 5 spits & rakes ⎫	16. 6.
A fire shovel ⎭	
A tin(?) dripping Pan and standard 10s. a warming pan 3s.	13. 0.
Pot hooks a chopping bill a shreding Knife a brass ladle	2. 6.
2 iron pots three brass pans a bell a mortar & pestel	1. 18. 6.
2 sauce pans an iron bill 2 frying pans a toasting jack	7. 0.
2 water kits 1.6 an ax 3d. a stone 1s. a Draesar and case 4	6. 9.
4 chairs a buffet an oval table 10s. a bread creech 2	12. 6.

Goods in the House

7 chairs 14s. a craddle 2s an oval table 12 a long table 2s	1. 11. 0.
2 square tables 5 a range fire point and tongs and fire shovel 10	15. 0.
6 pictures 2 a fender 1.6 window curtains & rod 3	5. 6.

242

In the dining roome
A range tongs and fire shovel and point 4 a buffet 20s a glass 10   1. 14. 0.
in pewter 2. 10. 6 chairs 12s and oval table 12   3. 14. 0.
a square table a little oval table 3s 5 pictures 5s   8. 0.
12 pictures 6s window curtains and rod 7s and 10 cushions   18. 0.
4 Candlesticks and snuffers 7s a coffee pot 3s a box 6   10. 6.

In the pantery
A chest 5 6 barrels 6s Delf and case 6s a cupboard 4   1. 1. 0.
a napkin press a kneading kit a stand 1   2. 0.

In the Cellar
A stone and stand 2.6 1 Barrel 1s a Salting fat   6. 6.

In the kitching chamber
A bed and bedding £4.4. in silver plate 2.10   6. 14. 0.
A pair of chest of drawers and a box   1. 1. 0.
A desk and frame 2s   2. 0.

In the house chamber
A bed and bedding £4.4. in silver Plate 2.10   6. 14. 0.
A pair chest of drawers 15s a coach chair 10s three chairs 3   1. 8. 0.
Window curtains and rods 5s a table and range 3s and a glass 2   10. 0.
Linnen   1. 0. 0.

In the dining Roome chamber
Bed and Bedding 4 1 pair chest of drawers 1.1 2 tables 4s   5. 5. 0.
5 chairs 2 buffets a Range a tea table   16. 0.
A parcel of glasses and delf 3s a standard 1s   4. 0.
A press bed and close stool 10 a quilting frame 6   10. 0.

In the garrets
3 chests 18 3 wheelers 2 a pair bedstocks 2 bottles   1. 8. 0.
A pull of slate and laths 3s a stone trough   5. 0.
The hustements in an about the house   5. 0.
                                                        _____
                                                        £37. 7. 0.

(from p. 202 Transac. Cumb. & Westm. Antiq. and Arch. Soc. N.S. 64, 1964,
article on the Phillipson family by T. G. Fahy)

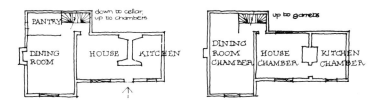

APPENDIX 2

Glossary Notes

In the hope that the various illustrations and captions will serve to explain the terms commonly used in the study of vernacular architecture no separate glossary has been prepared.

For architectural terms used in both vernacular and polite architecture see J. S. Curl (1992). More specialized illustrated glossaries appear in R. W. Brunskill (1985 and 1992), N. W. Alcock and others (1989 and 1997, both for timber building), and R. W. Brunskill (1990, for brick building). A comprehensive illustrated glossary of terms used in the architecture, including vernacular, of the southern United States appears in C. Lounsbury, ed. (1994). An *Illustrated Dictionary of Vernacular Architecture* is in preparation by the present author for future publication.

Two sets of glossary notes are, however, included here: one is a summary of room names used in the past and based on Barley (1963) but extended with the help of later publications, especially N. W. Alcock (1993), and information collected from probate inventories; the other is based on one originally prepared by J. E. C. Peters (1963) but extended through later study.

Room Names

Bedroom (bower, chamber) A room used mainly for sleeping but may in addition have been a work room or used for storage.

Boulting house (bake-house) Associated with the larger farm-houses, this room was devoted to sieving and storing flour and preparing food such as bread for the oven.

Brew house (back-house, kiln-house, malt-house) The room in which beer was brewed for household use. It might be equipped with a copper boiler and contain vats.

Buttery (spence, drink-house, dish-house) A cool storage space in which drink was kept; normally on the ground floor. However, buttery and pantry were alternative names for a storage room partitioned off the parlour of a Small House but separately entered.

Cellar A storage room – on the ground floor unless otherwise specified.

Chamber A general-purpose room name, supplanted in the 17C. by the term 'room'; in the South of England it meant at first a ground-floor room for sleeping; first-floor great chambers used for sleeping were found from the later 16C. onwards. Sometimes a distinction was made between upstairs store-chambers and upstairs bed-chambers. A chamber might also be used for cottage industry.

Cheese room (cheese chamber) A room, usually on the first floor or in a garret storey, in which cheeses were stored and cured. During the period of the Window Tax a cheese room was exempt if the words 'Cheese Room' were painted on the lintel of the window.

Croglofft The Welsh term for a loft over the inner room of a house or cottage reached by a ladder and where the main room remained open to the roof.

Dairy (milk-house) A room for storage of milk and its separation into cream and whey and conversion into butter; a cool room sometimes with running water from a spring. On larger farms the dairy might be a separate wing or a building between house and farm buildings. In smaller houses of the late 17C. the term might refer to the only service room in the house.

Downhouse In Cumbria, a service room below a cross-passage; it served as a brewhouse or scullery but often became a kitchen.

Garret (cockloft, loft, vance) A room within the roof space of a house two or more storeys high; mainly for storage but could provide sleeping accommodation for servants and children.

Hall Originally the principal living-room of a medieval Large House; a general-purpose room housing the lord's civic activities as well as the more public domestic activities. Later the term was applied to the principal living room of a Small House. An *open hall* was on the ground floor and open to the roof. A *first-floor hall* was for similar activities and might be open to the roof but was raised to first-floor level.

House As well as its current meaning of a dwelling the term was used in Yorkshire and some other parts of the North of England as a general term for an enclosed structure, thus *calf-house, cow-house, dwelling-house*. It was also used for the principal living-room as *house, house-body, house-part*, etc. The *fire-house* might be either the living-room or the complete dwelling.

Kitchen A room for cooking and for food preparation unless this was done in the *back kitchen* or *scullery*. In early Large Houses the kitchen was a separate building later incorporated in the main block and in the late 17C. and early 18C. often in a basement or semi-basement. In late 18C. Cottages the living-room (in which food was also cooked) was often called the kitchen or *living kitchen*.

Living-room (bodystead, fire-house, forehouse, hall, house, house-body, house-part, house-stead, living kitchen) The chief room for general domestic activities and the one which contained the principal or only hearth or fireplace. A multi-purpose room, it was the lesser equivalent of the superior hall. It was normally used at least in part for cooking unless there was a separate kitchen.

Loft A subsidiary bedroom or a storage room within the roof space whether at first-floor level or above.

Men's end A Yorkshire term for the part of a farm-house that was allocated to unmarried labourers. It might consist of a ground-floor kitchen and upper-floor bedrooms in which case it would have its own staircase.

Outshot (outcast, outend, outshut) or *lean-to* (toofall, turf-house) A room or rooms at the rear or end of a house covered by an extension of the main roof (sometimes called a catslide roof). The turf-house or toofall was a low outshut in which peat was stored.

Pantry A store room for dry foodstuffs (as distinct from a buttery, though in Small Houses the terms were interchangeable). The *larder* had a similar use but originally was for storage of meat.

Parlour (bower) A ground-floor room, usually opening off the hall, which was the principal retiring room. It served as the principal bedroom but also could be a dining room and a store for the most valuable possessions. At first the parlour was usually unheated but when no longer used primarily as a bedroom it was provided with a fireplace though with no provision for cooking. Hall and parlour (like the Scottish but and ben), public and private rooms, made up the basic Small House.

Privy (outhouse, necessary house, netty) An earth closet distant from the house near the garden or the midden.

Service room (back house, low end, low-house, nether end, also down-house) A term used to describe a ground-floor storage room such as a buttery or pantry or a ground-floor working room such as a scullery or brewhouse, as distinct from a living-room such as a hall or parlour.

Solar (soller) The principal bedroom (also sometimes called the Great Chamber) normally on the first floor of a house.

Store room (cellar, sellar) A storage room other than a buttery, pantry or larder usually on the ground floor but from the late 17C. possibly in a basement or semi-basement.

Farm Building Terms

Bank barn A two-level barn building placed along or across a slope with the barn at the upper level entered by way of a ramp and with stables, cow-house, cart shed, etc., below and entered at farmyard level.

Barn A building in which unthreshed sheaves of corn, straw or hay may be stored; usually there is a threshing floor. Other accommodation such as a stable or cow-house may be incorporated.

Barrack An American term for a hay barn with a rise and fall roof.

Bay A unit of the length of a building usually marked by a roof truss but alternatively by a stone or brick transverse wall.

Belfry A term sometimes used for a hay barn with a rise and fall roof.

Byre see Cow-house.

Cart shed (helm, wainhouse, waggon shade) An open-fronted building for housing carts and implements.

Chaff Husks of grain removed at winnowing. Hay or straw cut to short lengths.

Corn The name given in any region to the principal local grain crop, e.g. oats, wheat, barley, rye, in an unthreshed state whether cut or growing in the field. In North America the term refers to maize (known here as Indian corn).

Corn-hole see Granary.

Cow-house (byre, cow-shed, mistal, shippon) A building in which cows are kept tied up in stalls.

Dovecot (dovecote, doocot) A building containing nests for pairs of pigeons with louver access for the birds and a low access door for collecting eggs and manure.

Dutch barn An open-sided structure for the storage of hay.

Farmstead (farmery) Farm-house and farm buildings as a group around a farmyard.

Field barn (fieldhouse) An isolated cow-house or shelter shed, usually with a hayloft over. It may have a threshing floor and storage space for corn in addition to the cow-house.

Foldyard An open yard in which livestock are free to move about. A covered foldyard or covered yard has a roof over.

Gin case, Gin gang, Ginny ring see Horse engine house.

Grain Threshed ears of corn.

Granary A room in which grain is stored whether in sacks or in bulk; not a *corn hole*, which is a small room opening off the threshing floor of a barn for temporary storage of threshed grain. A granary is usually raised above the ground either on staddle stones, or over a cart shed.

Hackney stable A stable for horses that are used for riding or to pull traps or carriages rather than to work the land or pull wagons.

Hammel A loosebox for between two and four cattle.

Hay Cut and dried grass.

Hay barn A barn without a threshing floor and intended for the storage of hay rather than the storage and processing of corn crops.

Hay rack A railed shelf projecting from a wall or partition and containing hay to be fed to cattle or horses.

Helm see Cart shed, but could also be an open-sided timber barn raised on staddles, or a hay barn with rise and fall roof.

Hemmell An open-fronted shelter shed for cattle.

Hog-house (hogg-house) A low room for sheep with a hay loft above.

Horse engine (gin, ginny ring) A horse-driven source of rotary power.

Horse engine house (gin gang, gin case) A building to house a horse engine.

Hovel An ephemeral structure such as a temporary shelter shed.

Loft An upper-floor room or floored space in a roof, usually associated with a barn, cow-house or stable as a hayloft.

Loose box A compartment in which livestock can move about.

Manger A trough for food for livestock located on the floor and at a lower level than a hay rack.

Midstrey The bay of a barn which contains the threshing floor.

Mistal see Cow-house.

Pig-sty A building for pigs, each compartment usually including a small room with an adjoining exercise yard.

Pitching hole (pitching eye) Opening in a wall, usually serving a barn or loft, for unloading corn or hay, often closed by a sliding or hinged door or shutter; may be square or rectangular. Called a pitching eye if circular.

Rick (stack) A carefully arranged pile of sheaves of corn or trusses of straw. It may be circular, square or rectangular on plan and may be thatched or covered with tarpaulin.

Rickyard (stack yard, stackgarth) A yard in which ricks (stacks) of corn or hay are made and remain until threshed or consumed.

Scaffold A stack base raised high on posts with space for cattle or carts below.

Shelter shed (hovel) A completely or partially open-fronted building for loose cattle, horses or sheep free to enter or leave at will.

Shippon see Cow-house.

Stable A building in which horses are accommodated either tethered in stalls or loose in a loose box.

Stack see Rick.

Stack base (rick base) A framework raised on staddles acting as a base for a stack or rick of corn sheaves or occasionally hay. A solid stack base is a platform of stone on which a stack or rick is raised.

Stack yard (stackgarth) see Rickyard.

Staddle A low pillar in two parts intended to protect a rick or stack from the depredations of rats. Staddles may be of stone or brick, cob or cast iron.

Stall A compartment in which cattle or horses are tied.

Straw The stems of corn separated from the ears in threshing.

Threshing floor A pavement or platform of stone, timber or beaten earth on which sheaves of corn are threshed by hand with flails.

Trap-house A shed with doors intended to house a trap or small carriage.

Waggon shade see Cart shed.

Wainhouse see Cart shed.

Initial Example Reconsidered

This shows items which have been observed in the order in which comments appear in this handbook: walling material and construction, roof shape and materials, plan and sectional form, window and door details, and relation to farm buildings.

Fan-isaf, Merthyr Cynog, Breconshire

EXTERNAL DETAILS

a. Sandstone random rubble, irregular shape, wide joints, widely spread mortar, quoins not stressed, colourwashed overall.

b. Gabled roof.

c. Plain close verge.

d. Plain close eaves, cast iron rain water goods added.

e. Roof at present of Welsh Slate, regular courses, thin slates, steep pitch (over 45°) suggests replacement of thatch.

f. Tile ridge.

g. Chimneys at each gable, plain square stacks, one larger than the other

h. Water tabling remains to protect junction with lower roof.

i. Three dormers, all entirely in roof space, Welsh Slate roofs and cheeks, tile ridges, wooden barge boards, in present form probably date from re-roofing in slate.

j. Plan form: basically two-unit, subsidiary unit divided between parlour and pantry.

k. Sectional form: basically one storey with a continuous loft, this loft now lit by prominent dormer windows.

l. Present straight flight staircase, originally probably spiral alongside fireplace, no window or other outside indication.

m. Window shape: essentially squarish, wooden lintels, no architraves.

n.. Window frames, probably vertically sliding sash, may have been renewed.

o. Door shape, no dressings.

p. Door details, simple four panelled door in conventional door frame.

q. Farm building attached at lower end, no sign of intercommunication, plinth stones run through, straight joint above, farm buildings may have been rebuilt and possibly heightened, roof pitch lower, more consistent with slate covering.

r. Attached cow-house.

SKETCH PLAN

1. hall, 2. parlour, 3. pantry, 4. former stair? 5. later scullery, 6. possible stable, 7. cow house with central feeding passage, loft above, 8. calf pen, 9. loose box, 10. barn, two-storage bays each side of, 11. threshing floor, 12. cart shed below, granary above, internal wooden staircase access, 13. garden, 14. orchard, 15. foldyard.

(based partly on sketch plans by S. R. Jones, extended by R. W. B. on the site, July 1967)

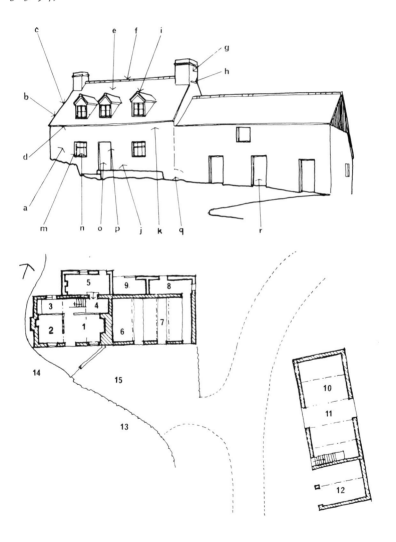

NOTES, REFERENCES AND RECOMMENDATIONS FOR FURTHER READING

Introduction

Bibliographies

One of the main activities of the Vernacular Architecture Group has been the preparation of bibliographies in the various aspects of the subject. The first bibliography was published in 1972 (R. de Z. Hall, 1972). A supplement was published in 1979 (D. J. H. Michelmore, 1979). A third volume was published to bring the references up to 1989 (Pattison, Pattison and Alcock, 1992).

A very interesting account of the development of the study of vernacular architecture in this country has been published by Anthony Quiney (A. Quiney, 1994) and this includes quite an extensive bibliography.

The following list of general, regional and local works, mostly about England and Wales, includes those that are generally available (in libraries at least as many are out of print) and which have been particularly useful in the preparation of this book. The list is limited and worthwhile books may have been omitted.

General Books (though many with regional sections)

Addy, S. O., *The Evolution of the English House*, 1898, 3rd edn revised by (Sir) John Summerson, 1933 – still a basic work though the author's views on the link between British and German plans and the particular significance of certain dimensions related to house plans are no longer generally accepted.

Ayres, J., *The Shell Book of the Home in Britain*, 1981 – the decoration, design and interiors generally of vernacular houses and cottages between 1500 and 1850.

Barley, M. W., *The English Farmhouse and Cottage*, 1981 – still one of the most valuable books on the subject, based on both fieldwork and documentary investigation, covering mainly the period 1500–1700 but with links back to medieval precedents.

Barley, M. W., *Houses and History*, 1986 – includes further thoughts.

Batsford, H. and Fry, C., *The English Cottage*, 1938 – deals with Small Houses as well as Cottages and is still useful as a record of buildings, many of which have now been demolished or altered out of recognition.

Brunskill, R. W., *Traditional Buildings of Britain*, 1981, 2nd edn 1992 – contains some introductory material and expands on other matters considered here.

Brunskill, R. W., *Houses and Cottages of Britain*, 1997 – describes and illustrates type plans of rural and urban houses and cottages. It supersedes R. W. Brunskill, *Houses*, 1982.

Clifton-Taylor, A., *The Pattern of English Buildings*, 1972 edn – deals comprehensively and with many illustrations with walling and roofing materials mainly, but not entirely, as found in vernacular buildings.

Hoskins, W. G., *Provincial England*, 1963 – a collection of essays including the important 'Rebuilding of Rural England 1570–1650', which introduced the concept of the Great Rebuilding.

Innocent, C. F., *The Development of English Building Construction*, 1916, re-issued with an Introduction by Sir Robert de Z. Hall, 1975 – has yet to be superseded as a general book on vernacular building construction, though, based mainly on evidence from northern England, may appear rather ill-balanced; further edition 1999.

Jones, S. R., *English Village Homes*, 1936 – like the Batsford and Fry book includes many useful photographs and drawings.

Lloyd, N., *History of the English House*, 1931, reissued 1975 – though dated, puts some vernacular houses in a wider context.

Mercer, E., *English Vernacular Houses*, 1975 – an authoritative work comprising an inventory of some 500 examples, a detailed commentary, and many plans and photographs.

Peate, I. C., *The Welsh House*, 1940, 1944, 1946 – a pioneering work dealing with houses as an aspect of folk culture.

Penoyre, J. and Penoyre, J., *Houses in the Landscape*, 1975 – has many sketches, photographs and regional maps of buildings materials.

Potter, M. and Potter, A., *Houses*, 3rd edn 1973 – a brief summary, well illustrated by cutaway drawings.

Prizeman, J., *Your House, the Outside View*, 1975 – has many coloured elevational drawings.

Quiney, A., *The Traditional Buildings of England*, 1990 – has many carefully selected photographs in colour and black and white.

Salzman, L. F., *Buildings in England down to 1540*, 1952, reissued 1997 – based on documents and, though dealing mainly with superior architecture of the medieval period, has much on vernacular building.

Smith, P., *Houses of the Welsh Countryside*, 1975, 2nd edn 1988, subtitled *A Study in Historical Geography* – this is the definitive work on its subject and has many plans, maps, sketches and other illustrations making effective use of cutaway perspectives and sketches of the interiors of houses.

Thirsk, J. (ed.), *The Agrarian History of England and Wales*, Vol. IV, 1500–1640, 1967, and Vol. V, 1640–1750 Pt. (i) 1984, pt. (ii) 1985 – has among the many relevant contributions important ones by M. W. Barley and P. Smith on English and Welsh houses, respectively. Subsequent volumes such as Vol. VI for 1750–1850 (G. E. Mingay, ed.) and Vol. VIII for 1914–1939 (E. H. Whetham, ed.) have less about vernacular buildings.

Wood, M. E., *The English Medieval House*, 1965, reissued 1981 – deals mainly with superior houses but does extend into the vernacular range.

Regional Books (though many contain sections of general significance)

Brunskill, R. W., *Vernacular Architecture of the Lake Counties*, 1974 – about the present Cumbria, incorporating Cumberland, Westmorland, and Lancashire North of the Sands.

Caffyn, L., *Workers' Housing in West Yorkshire 1750–1920* – deals with the houses and cottages of urban and rural industrial workers.

Chesher, V. M. and Chesher, F. J., *The Cornishman's House*, 1968 – mainly about medieval to 17C. Cornwall.

Denyer, S., *Traditional Buildings and Life in the Lake District*, 1991 – based on a survey of the vernacular properties owned by the National Trust in the Lake District.

Fox, Sir Cyril and Lord Raglan, *Monmouthshire Houses*, 3 parts, 1951–4, reissued later as one volume – deals with upland Monmouthshire and established procedures and dating criteria followed by many later scholars.

Giles, C., *Rural Houses of West Yorkshire, 1400–1830*, 1986 – the counterpart to L. Caffyn above, deals with houses of various sizes outside the developing towns.

Hall, L., *The Rural Houses of North Avon and South Gloucestershire, 1400–1720*, 1983 – a detailed study of houses in parts of Somerset and Gloucestershire, including part of the Cotswolds.

Harrison, B. and Hutton, B., *Vernacular Houses in North Yorkshire and Cleveland*, 1984 – a comprehensive study of a large part of Yorkshire conducted by a local study group led and guided by the authors; a part of the area was surveyed in greater detail by RCHME, see below.

Johnson, M., *Housing Culture: Traditional Architecture in an English Landscape*, 1993 – here the author illustrates his theoretical approach by reference to a study of houses in part of West Suffolk.

Lowe, J., *Welsh Country Workers' Housing, 1775–1875*, 1985 – deals with cottages and is the counterpart to J. Lowe, 1977.

Mason, R. T., *Framed Buildings of the Weald*, 1964 – a study of typical houses of parts of Kent and Sussex.

Nevill, R., *Old Cottages and Domestic Architecture in South-West Surrey*, 1889 – the first regional study and established principles and procedures which have been followed in many subsequent studies.

Pearson, S., *Rural Houses of the Lancashire Pennines 1560–1760*, 1985 – deals with the period in which great prosperity in north-east Lancashire was reflected in house design and construction.

Pearson, S., *The Medieval Houses of Kent: an Historical Analysis*, 1994 – examines the evolution of medieval houses in the county based on a survey of some 450 houses, with accompanying documentary investigation and tree-ring dating. It is linked with P. S. Barnwell and A. T. Adams, *The House Within: Interpreting Medieval Houses in Kent*, 1994, both being supported by S. Pearson, P. S. Barnwell and A. T. Adams, *A Gazetteer of Medieval Houses in Kent*, 1994. All three are very well illustrated.

Pevsner, N. and others, *Buildings of England* series; the early county volumes scarcely touched on vernacular buildings but the most recent editions include examples as well as authoritative introductions by county experts, e.g. *Devon*, 2nd edn 1989, with notes on rural buildings by P. Beacham and on town houses by M. Laithwaite. The same applies to *Buildings of Scotland* and *Buildings of Wales*.

Quiney, A., *Kentish Houses*, 1993 – a very well-illustrated personal view of the houses of the county.

Royal Commission on the Ancient and Historical Monuments of Wales (RCAHMW) – the various county inventories have devoted an increasing proportion of their space to vernacular buildings; those of Anglesey and Caernarfonshire are especially useful while *Glamorgan* Vol. IV Pt. 2, *Farmhouses and Cottages*, 1988, is as detailed a survey of a county as we are likely to see for many years.

Royal Commission on the Historical Monuments of England (RCHME) – again, the most recent county inventories include much on vernacular architecture; those of *Dorset*, 1970–75, *Cambridgeshire*, 1968, and *Northamptonshire*, 1984, are most useful for rural vernacular; and *York*, 1972–81, *Stamford*, 1977, and *Salisbury*, 1980, for urban vernacular. *Houses of the North York Moors*, 1987, is a thematic survey of some 80 parishes lying roughly between Helmsley and the coast. It includes farm buildings, mill buildings and town houses as well as rural houses and cottages.

Slocombe, P. M., *Wiltshire Farmhouses and Cottages*, 1988 – a general study of the houses of the county.

Smith, J. T., *English Houses 1200–1800: The Hertfordshire Evidence*, and *Hertfordshire Houses a Selective Inventory*, both 1993 – based on examination of nearly 1000 houses in the county and on the information available for demolished houses the survey covers superior houses as well as smaller houses and cottages and relates conclusions for the county to the pattern in the country as a whole.

Some of the volumes of the *Victoria County History* of the past 20 years or so include contributions on vernacular architecture.

District and Local Books (though often containing material of regional significance)

Thorough studies of the vernacular architecture of a single parish or a small number of parishes are now being published, often by local societies or universities. Examples include the following, though this is by no means an exhaustive list.

Alcock, N. W., *Stoneleigh Villagers*, 1978, and *People at Home: Living in a Warwickshire Village, 1500–1800* (also about Stoneleigh), 1993.

Harding, J. M., *Four Centuries of Charlwood Houses*, Surrey, 1976.

Hutton, B. (ed.), *Hatfield and its People*, 1963 – a pioneering study.

Lacey, H. M. and Lacey, U. E., *The Timber-framed Buildings of Steyning* (Sussex), 1974.

Machin, R., *The Houses of Yetminster* (Dorset), 1978.

Martin, D. and Martin, B., *Historic Buildings in Eastern Sussex*, from 1977 – in this series of six volumes the authors provide a detailed and well-illustrated account of the development in planning, construction and detailing of vernacular buildings (including farm buildings) in part of the county. The work has extended to *Domestic Buildings of the Eastern High Weald 1366–1750*, 1989.

Smith, W. J., *Saddleworth Buildings*, 1987 – an account with many photographs and drawings of the houses and cottages in a scattered Pennine community on the border between Lancashire and Yorkshire.

The Somerset and South Avon Vernacular Buildings Research Group is publishing a series of detailed village surveys of the area.

Wade, J. (ed.), *Traditional Kent Buildings* – a series started in 1980 based on student-measured drawings of vernacular buildings in the county.

Walton, J., *Early Timbered Buildings of the Huddersfield District*, 1955 – a pioneering work still of interest.

Watson, R. C. and McClintock, M. E., *Traditional Houses of the Fylde*, 1979 – a study of houses in the low-lying area of Lancashire between the Lune and Ribble estuaries.

The Setting for Vernacular Buildings

Many books have recently been published as a result of the interest in local history and the history of the landscape; only a few have been selected.

Beresford, M. W. and Joseph, J. K. St., *Medieval England: An Aerial Survey*, 1958, 2nd edn 1979 – relates aerial photographs to historic maps and plans to illustrate the development of nearly 120 communities in England and Wales.

Hoskins, W. G., *The Making of the English Landscape*, 1970 – first published in 1955, this has been a most influential book. It was followed by a series of regional books such as R. Millward and A. Robinson, *Landscapes of Britain, South-East England – The Channel Coastlands*, 1973.

Rackham, O., *The History of the Countryside*, 1986 – of interest particularly for the meaning of field patterns and for the management of woodlands from which structural timber was extracted.

Roberts, B. K., *The Making of the English Village: A Study in Historical Geography*, 1987 – a tightly argued book, superbly illustrated by diagrams, that describes the theory and practice of village planning in England.

Roberts, B. K., *Landscapes of Settlement, Prehistory to the Present*, 1996 – extends the arguments to village planning in other parts of the world.

Taylor, C., *Village and Farmstead: A History of Rural Settlement in England*, 1983 – an authoritative and well-illustrated book dealing with periods from prehistory to the present day.

Vernacular Buildings in a World Setting

Most European countries and many countries in other parts of the world have developed studies in vernacular architecture and primitive building, sometimes as part of folk-life studies, sometimes by way of archaeology, history, geography or architecture, sometimes out of a feeling of nationalism or regional identity. Rather than single out any country the following general works are mentioned.

Oliver, P. (ed.), *Shelter and Society*, 1969 – contains a thoughtful introduction and contributions about several countries. More recently Paul Oliver has expanded this work into the monumental *Encyclopedia of Vernacular Architecture*, 1998.

Lord Raglan, *The Temple and the House*, 1964 – gives an anthropologist's view on the meaning of aspects of domestic architecture throughout the world.

Rapaport, A., *House Form and Culture*, 1969 – looks at the subject on a world scale and distinguishes between the primitive, the vernacular, the popular and the academic traditions.

Rudofsky, B., *Architecture without Architects*, 1964 – based originally on a catalogue for an exhibition held in the Museum of Modern Art in New York. This has been an influential book, though no examples are taken from Britain.

Smith, P., 'British Vernacular Architecture in a Continental Context', 1994. It appeared in *Archaeologia Cambrensis*, Vol. CXLII, 1993.

Periodicals

Vernacular Architecture (henceforth *VA*), the journal of the Vernacular Architecture Group, has been published annually since 1970 and is exclusively devoted to the subject. In Scotland the equivalent journal is *Vernacular Building*, published by the Scottish Vernacular Buildings Group. Articles on vernacular architecture appear in the Journals or Transactions of such national organizations as the Ancient Monuments Society, the British Archaeological Association, the Royal Archaeological Institute, the Society for Architectural Historians, the Society for Medieval Archaeology, the Society for Post-Medieval Archaeology and the Society for Folk Life Studies, together with the *Journal of the Historic Farm Buildings Group* and the *Industrial Archaeology Review*. In addition, articles on subjects of local or regional interest usually appear in the Transactions of the appropriate county archaeological societies. Some of the local recording groups such as the Domestic Buildings Research Group (Surrey) produce Newsletters devoted to vernacular architecture. The magazine *Period Home* included many short articles by experts in the field during its period of independent publication.

Theses and Dissertations

Many Ph.D., M. Phil., MA and BA theses and dissertations have been completed or are in progress. Some were listed in *VA*, Vol. 14, 1983, and others may be found in the *Research Register* published from time to time by the Society of Architectural Historians. Many of the reports or dissertations prepared in connection with postgraduate courses in building conservation offered by some universities, by the Architectural Association and by the College of Estate Management are on subjects related to vernacular architecture. The policy on retaining theses and dissertations in university libraries varies from institution to institution but Ph.D. and M. Phil. theses are usually deposited and so are accessible.

National Monuments Records and Statutory Lists

The National Buildings or Monuments Records for England, Wales and Scotland are maintained in Swindon, Aberystwyth and Edinburgh at the headquarters of the various Royal Commissions on Historical Monuments. All include many valuable records of vernacular buildings as well as others while the National Monuments Records for England, and increasingly for Scotland and Wales also, incorporates a large and growing collection of reports on vernacular buildings which include measured drawings – the Domestic Buildings Research Group (Surrey) alone has deposited over 3,500 such reports.

The statutory *lists* of buildings of 'special architectural or historic interest' were first compiled as an aid to local planning authorities by way of the Town and Country Planning Act of 1947. They have been amplified by re-survey and review so that the total for England alone approaches 500,000 buildings, of which a large proportion are works of vernacular architecture. The *List Descriptions* are now quite extensive for each building. Parish lists (so-called 'greenbacks') may be consulted at the offices of the relevant local planning authority and the National Monuments Record offices in Swindon, Aberystwyth and Edinburgh. The lists for England have now been computerized and it is hoped the national lists will become more accessible thereby.

Sites and Monuments Records (SMRs) have been developed in most counties. Although originally intended to record antiquities most now include many vernacular buildings, including those of local interest which are not 'listed'. In some counties and unitary authorities the records are held by the Planning Department, in others in the Archives or Records Offices and in yet others they may be part of the Library or Museum Service. In Wales the SMRs are generally maintained by the regional Archaeological Trusts.

Theory behind the Study of Vernacular Architecture

Most work so far has been devoted to collecting material in the field or from documentary sources, classifying the results and suggesting some interpretation. However, discussions towards general theory are advancing. The work of Lawrence (1983), Hillier and Hanson (1984) and J. Johnson (1990, 1993) is relevant here. See also *Planning Theory* below. For size-types, see Cordingley (1948).

The Vernacular Zone

The Great Rebuilding was described by W. G. Hoskins in his article 'The Rebuilding of Rural England, 1570–1640' which first appeared in *Past and Present* for November 1953 and was reprinted in Hoskins' *Provincial England*, 1963. The symbols in the diagram of the vernacular zone refer to dated buildings illustrated in the books listed below or taken from my own records: M. W. Barley, 1961; N. Lloyd, 1931; P. Smith in Thirsk (ed.), 1967; R. B. Wood-Jones, 1963. An article by R. Machin, 'The Great Rebuilding: a reassessment', in *Past and Present*, No. 77, Nov. 1977, suggests modifications to Hoskins' argument, though accepting that the late Middle Ages saw a change from impermanent building. Harrison and Hutton, 1984, question the idea of the Great Rebuilding. S. Wrathmell shares the doubts in 'The Vernacular Threshold of Northern Peasant Houses', *VA*, Vol. 15, 1984, but suggests that 'from the thirteenth to the seventeenth century the peasant farmers of Northumberland constructed low-cost buildings which would stand for centuries provided they were subject to a high degree of maintenance and repair'. It appears that they were succeeded by 'permanent dwellings which involved high cost and a low level of maintenance'. However, five years later (in M. Aston, D. Austin, and C. Dyer, *The Rural Settlement of Medieval England*, 1989), Wrathmell had come to the view that the concept of 'impermanent' late medieval houses intended to last for decades rather than centuries was no longer tenable. Nevertheless he continued to emphasise the late threshold (rather than the 'threshold of survival') when low-cost buildings needing a lot of maintenance and repair were replaced by high-cost low-maintenance buildings, single-storey cruck or post-built dwellings being replaced by substantial two-storey houses of timber-frame, masonry or brick. J. T. Smith in *VA*, Vol. 16, 1985 suggested that evidence for moving timber-frame buildings, as at Myddle in Shropshire, indicated that more or less 'impermanent' methods of construction persisted side by side with 'permanent' techniques for centuries. In a closely-argued article in *VA*, Vol. 19, 1988, C. J. C. Currie examined the varying survival rates of houses and suggested explanations. He is sceptical about insubstantial construction and believes that 'The earliest surviving houses in an area may not have differed significantly in construction and quality from their lost contemporaries and predecessors.' His thesis was questioned by E. Mercer and P. Smith in *VA*, Vol. 21, 1990. A new theory was put forward by R. Taylor in *VA*, Vol. 23, 1992 suggesting that in the period 1550–1850 population explosions in various regions were met: first by dividing up existing houses and building inexpensive and sometimes impermanent buildings but later by a process of replacement and building new houses on new sites. M. Johnson in *VA*, Vol. 28, 1997 refers to the 'so-called Vernacular Threshold'. The debate continues. See also Grenville, 1997.

To repeat the argument put forward here: casual observation of houses in England and Wales, at least, shows that from a date which varies with status and place, substantially constructed houses survive. These house may incorporate parts of their predecessors. They may be succeeded by other newly built houses. They may themselves display additions, modifications, items of modernization since their first substantial construction. They may repeat the plans of their predecessors because change of building material and methods of construction do not necessarily imply change of plan. The reasons for this substantial rebuilding may be many and may vary with circumstance, place and time: for instance earlier building might be structurally inadequate through short-lived materials, might require too much maintenance, there might be materials or constructional methods which were now available (such as the supply of bricks and tiles), there might be a sudden increase in prosperity which allowed money to be invested in rebuilding, there might be a change of tenure which justified investment in expensive buildings of indefinite life. As we discover more about the process of providing vernacular buildings we will understand why such a rebuilding took place but it is still too early to deny that something as recognizable as a vernacular threshold does exist and that it varies with status, time and place.

Organization of the Book

This handbook concentrates on the vernacular architecture of England and Wales. There is a different tradition in Scotland which is briefly noted. Ireland has a different tradition again mentioned but not discussed here.

The traditional county names and imperial measure have been retained in the text.

Walling

General

The distinction between the different walling and cladding materials follows that made by R. A. Cordingley and described and illustrated by R. W. Brunskill (1965–6). Distribution maps showing the use of the various materials appear in Brunskill (1979) and others have been placed in Chapter 8 to help comparisons. An interesting study of craft techniques appears in Wright (1991). See also Grenville (1997).

Stone, Irregular and Regular, Pebble, Cobble and Flint

The chapters in A. Clifton-Taylor (1972) have been expanded in A. Clifton-Taylor and A. S. Ireson (1983, 1994). Further information on masonry walling techniques, for instance, may be found in the older text books of building construction such as W. B. McKay's *Building Construction* (1938) and in the pre-WWII editions of *Mitchell's Building Construction*. There is a brief note on watershot masonry in the Pennines by Frank Atkinson (1959). A study of galletting was published by W. R. Trotter (1989).

Brick Walling

The original work on the subject is N. Lloyd, *A History of English Brickwork*, 1925, reissued 1983. Many of the examples are of 'polite' rather than 'vernacular' architecture and later research has qualified some of the conclusions. More generally available are R. W. Brunskill (1990), which includes an illustrated glossary, and G. Lynch (1994). J. Wight, *Brick Building in England*, 1972, deals with the period Middle Ages to 1550 but mainly in superior buildings. Dr Brian's two articles on brick bonding and the distribution of brick bonds (A. Brian, 1972, 1980) are fascinating. Much new material is appearing in *Information*, the Newsletter of the British Brick Society.

Earth Walling

A very good general introduction is provided by J. McCann (1983) and a more technical introduction by J. R. Harrison (1984). The various local techniques have been the subject of articles of which the most comprehensive are by J. R. Harrison (1989, 1991) on Cumberland. N. Jennings (1993, 1997) gives further information on the buildings using the technique in the county. M. Seaborne (1964) on earth walling in Northamptonshire is still relevant. Much work has recently been done on cob walling in the South West but little has been published, though there is a short contribution in P. Beacham (1990) on buildings in Devon. Welsh techniques are described in E. Wiliam (1988), Scottish in B. Walker (1996). Comparable Irish techniques are described in A. Gailey (1984). Some historical material was included in C. Williams-Ellis (1947). Clay lump is a technique explained in J. McCann (1987, 1997), and D. Bouwens (1988).

Timber-framed Construction

An excellent basic introduction to the subject is provided by R. Harris (1978). More introductory material, including an extensive illustrated glossary, appears in R. W. Brunskill (1985, 1992). Major works incorporating research over many decades include F. W. B. Charles (1967) on cruck construction and the historical parts of F. W. B. and M. Charles (1984), which is mainly on box-frame and post and truss construction. There are many books and articles by C. A. Hewett, concentrating on examples from Essex, though the wider-based Hewett (1980) is indispensible. N. W. Alcock's (ed.) lists of cruck trusses and their variations with distribution maps (1982) supersedes the same author's *Cruck Catalogue* of 1973 and extends his work by including contributions by others on various aspects of the subject. Among local publications those by H. M. and U. E. Lacey (1974) and D. and B. Martin (1977, etc.) have already been mentioned. Another example, from South Yorkshire, is P. F. Ryder (1978).

In recent years many articles on timber-frame and roof construction have been published in national and county journals. The following selection includes many useful in the study of vernacular architecture.

Charles, F. W. B., 'Post construction and the rafter roof', 1981 – suggests possible origins for some features of timber-frame and roof construction. Comments by P. A. Rahtz, J. T. Smith, G. Beresford and P. A. Barker in *VA*, Vol. 13, 1982, disagree with some of Charles's points.

Cordingley, R. A., 'British Historical Roof-Types and their Members', 1961 – gives a detailed description and classification of roof trusses together with a glossary. A distinction is made between rafter roofs, butt-purlin trusses and through purlin trusses.

Gee, E. A., 'The Chronology of Crucks', 1977 – considers methods of dating by reference to examples dated on documentary evidence; nowadays dendrochronology (tree-ring dating) provides new opportunities for more precise dating.

Harding, J. M., 'Timber-framed early buildings in Surrey: a Pattern for Development, c. 1300–1650', 1993 – draws on the recording work of the Domestic Buildings Research Group (Surrey).

Rigold, S. E., 'Timber-framed buildings at Steventon, Berkshire, and their regional significance', 1948 – a very early study and includes a brief typology of timber framing with regional distributions.

Smith, J. T., 'Medieval Roofs: a Classification', 1960 – introduced theories, terms and methods of study which are still generally accepted.

Smith, J. T., 'Cruck Construction, a Survey of the Problems', 1964 – another pioneering work of fundamental importance.

Smith, J. T., 'Timber-framed Building in England', 1966 – extensively illustrated by drawings and maps, makes a distinction in wall framing noted here and illustrated in a general way and based on the article.

Smith, J. T., 'The Early Development of Timber Building: the Passing Brace and Reversed assembly', 1974 – deals with the introduction of techniques from which conventional timber framing developed.

Webster, V. O., 'Cruck-framed buildings in Leicestershire', 1954 – an early work still not superseded for the county.

Williams, E. H. D., 'Jointed crucks', 1977 – deals with the technique which is localized but common in its locality.

Timber Walling and Cladding

Most of the references to timber-frame construction include details of the various half timber and cladding techniques. However, brick-tile or mathematical tile cladding has attracted a literature of its own. The original work was A. Arschavir, 'False fronts in Minor Domestic Architecture' (1956) but the study has been brought up to date by M. Exwood (1981a, b) and by T. P. Smith (1979, 1985). The earliest known mathematical tile has an inscribed date of 1724 and was discovered in Westcott, Surrey, by J. M. Harding and members of the Domestic Buildings Research Group (Surrey).

Dating by Dendrochronology (Tree-ring Dating)

At one time it was expected that pieces of structural timber could be dated by the carbon-14 method. This did not prove satisfactory for the historical periods during which timber was used. Instead, over the past 20 years or so there have been great advances in the use of dendrochronology or tree-ring dating. The technique is explained in D. Miles (1997). Dates for the oak timber used in over 650 buildings have been published in *Vernacular Architecture* and for some other vernacular buildings in other journals. The results have been reviewed for Kent in S. Pearson (1994) and generally in S. Pearson, 'Tree-Ring Dating: A Review' (1997). As well as dating the oak timber used in hitherto undated buildings, the evidence helps to confirm or correct the dates already suggested for buildings on other evidence. These in turn provide exemplars whereby other buildings may be dated. The evidence also sheds some light on the re-use of timber members and helps clarify the various periods of construction of individual buildings.

Roofing

General

The classification and terminology used here is based on R. A. Cordingley (1961). The references given under *Timber-frame Construction* above generally apply to timber roofs on solid walls as well as those which are part of total timber-frame construction. Developments which occurred as traditional timber construction was being super-seded by scientific design, incorporating iron straps, bolts, shoes and rods, are outlined in D. T. Yeomans (1985) and he deals in detail with king post roof trusses (Yeomans, 1992).

Single and Double Rafter Roofs

In addition to the other references listed above, see J. M. Fletcher and P. S. Spokes (1964). There is currently some confusion about the purpose of the collar purlin. It had been assumed that, supported by the crown post, it existed to provide the longitudinal restraint which in other roofs was provided by side purlins. One would therefore expect the collars to be pegged to the collar purlin. Close examination has shown that in some trusses at least, and perhaps in most, there are no such pegs.

Thatch Roofing

The techniques still in use are thoroughly described and illustrated in Rural Industries Bureau (1961). See also M. Billet (1979). Other techniques including use of sod (turf) underthatch were employed in Scotland, Ireland and Wales and were known in the North of England – see J. R. Harrison (1991) and under *Scotland* below. For 'rafterless roofs' of thatch carried on a roof-shaped heap of twigs see J. E. C. Peters (1977) and D. M. Smith (1978).

Stone Flags and Stone Tiles

In the past these materials have been collectively called 'stone slates' and 'grey slates' and these terms are still used, together with the clearer 'stone flags' and 'stone tiles'. As well as the familiar Cotswold stone tiles (such as those from Stonesfield) there are the Collyweston slates of Northamptonshire and the Swithland slates of Leicestershire. Isolated are the Horsham slates of Sussex. At the other extreme are, for instance, the heavy Kerridge slates of east Cheshire above Macclesfield. The *Stone Slate Roofing: Technical Advice Note*, 1998, of English Heritage has much useful information on stone roofing and its conservation. Traditional techniques are described in J. Walton (1975) and H. B. Sharp (1980). There is also much on the subject in A. Clifton-Taylor and A. J. Ireson (1983, 1994).

Plan and Section

General

The following are some of the works which include illustrations of the development of various forms of vernacular house plans: S. O. Addy (1898, 1933); N. W. Alcock series, 'Devonshire Farmhouses' (1962 on); M. W. Barley (1961, 1986); P. S. Barnwell and A. T. Adams (1994); R. W. Brunskill (1974, 1997); L. Caffyn (1986); C. Carson (1976); P. Faulkner (1960); Fox and Raglan (1951 on); C. Giles (1985); L. Hall (1983); J. Harding (1976, 1993); B. Harrison and B. Hutton (1984); S. R. Jones and J. T. Smith (1963 on); B. Martin and B. Martin (1977 on); E. Mercer (1975); S. Pearson (1985, 1994); I. C. Peate (1940, 1946); RCHME (1987); P. Smith (1975, 1988); J. T. Smith (1992); W. J. Smith (1987); M. E. Wood (1965).

Planning Theory

A debate on the theory behind the study of vernacular architecture was initiated by T. R. J. Lawrence (1983); it has continued since (e.g. E. Mercer and B. Hutton, *VA*, Vol. 15, 1984). Theories of house planning have been developed by F. E. Brown (1990), G. Fairclough, (1992), H. Glassie (1975), R. Hillier and J. Hanson (1984), M. Johnson (1990, 1993). The theorists are particularly interested in privacy and segregation through the ways in which rooms open off the outside, off passages and lobbies, or off each other. A different approach based on rules of proportion was taken by J. M. Jenkins (1967), and for some American Small Houses and Cottages by A. J. Lawton, 'Ground Rules of Folk Architecture', in *Pennsylvania Folk Life*.

Classifications

Various attempts at classification of plan forms in different localities have been made. An early example was P. Eden (1969), which developed from that in the RCHME *Inventory for West Cambridgeshire*, 1968, which itself was the model for that in the RCHME *Inventory for Dorset*, Vol. II Pt 1, 1970. Classifications for Wales were developed in P. Smith (1975, 1988). R. W. Brunskill (1982) and its successor of 1997 were written around classifications of rural and urban house plans.

First-Floor Family

Examples of tower-houses and bastle houses in Cumbria have been collected along with other house plans in D. R. Perriam and J. Robinson (1998). Very few self-contained tower houses were found; most towers now independent were formerly defensible solar wings with halls once attached, and were part of T-shaped or H-shaped houses. See G. Fairclough, 'Clifton Hall, Cumbria . . .' and R. W. McDowall, 'Wraysholme Tower' in *CW2*, Vols LXXX, 1980 and LXXVII, 1976, respectively.

Examples of what may have been first-floor halls are described and illustrated in T. L. Marsden (1962) and S. E. Rigold (1966). For first-floor halls in Wales see P. Smith (1975, 1988). For the special version of defensive first-floor halls – usually called 'bastle houses' – see H. G. Ramm, R. W. McDowall and E. Mercer (1970) (though P. Dixon considers the term inappropriate as mentioned in his article 'Tower-houses, Pelehouses and Border Society', 1979). See also P. F. Ryder (1990, 1992) and P. Dixon (1993).

The Hall Family

From the earliest days of the study of vernacular architecture there have been many articles on individual buildings of this type such as those by R. T. Mason in *Sussex Archaeological Collections* and by E. W. Parkin in *Archaeologia Cantiana*, while a classic example from the opposite end of the country is R. A. Cordingley and R. B. Wood-Jones on Chorley Hall (1959). For aisled halls see J. T. Smith (1956) and K. Sandall (1975, 1986), including distribution maps and inventory. Much has been written recently about houses of the hall family, e.g. in Kent (Pearson, 1994, P. Barnwell and A. T. Adams, 1994), Hertfordshire (J. T. Smith, 1992), North Yorkshire (B. Harrison and B. Hutton, 1984) and West Yorkshire (C. Giles, 1986), as well as in the general works listed above.

An interesting commentary on a group of houses which may include halls but which show evidence of design or extension for the use of two families on the 'unit system' appears in J. T. Smith (1970). This was pursued for smaller houses in RCHME (1987).

The Two-unit Family

Many examples of the various versions of this plan may be found in, e.g., RCAHMW, *Inventory for Glamorgan*, Vol. IV Pt. 2, *Farmhouses and Cottages*, 1988, and S. R. Jones and J. T. Smith (1963 on) as well as in S. Pearson (1985), B. Harrison and B. Hutton (1984) and W. J. Smith (1978). The term 'direct entry' has come into use to describe those two-unit houses in which the front door opens directly into the front of the principal ground-floor room without the intervention of any lobby or cross-passage.

The second group having this house plan is sometimes called the 'hearth passage' plan or the 'chimney backing on entry' plan. The agricultural use of space beyond the cross-passage or cross-entry meant that a longhouse plan was involved. See P. Smith (1963, 1975, 1988) and R. W. Brunskill (1974).

The Central Fireplaces Family

For the general discussion of the plan variously known as 'baffle-entry' and 'lobby-entry' see A. Quiney (1984). An early example, though hardly vernacular, is described in N. Summers, 'Old Hall Farm, Kneesall' (1972). The plan-type is also described in C. A. Hewett (1973). Examples are illustrated in many of the general works listed above as well as those for West Cambridgeshire (RCHME, 1968), Hertfordshire (J. T. Smith, 1993), the Lancashire Pennines (S. Pearson, 1985), North Yorkshire (B. Harrison and B. Hutton, 1984), West Yorkshire (C. Giles, 1986) and Glamorgan (RCAHMW, 1988).

Double-Pile Plans

The term 'double pile' was used by Sir Roger Pratt about 1675 for 'polite' versions of this plan (see R. T. Gunther, 1928), but this term is convenient in describing vernacular houses which are two rooms deep. For a full discussion see M. W. Barley (1979). Examples are illustrated in some of the regional studies noted above, especially in the Lancashire Pennines (S. Pearson, 1985) and West Yorkshire (C. Giles, 1986) as well as in the general books listed above. The double-pile plan was important in the design of town houses (see, e.g., RCHME, *Stamford*, 1977).

Rural Cottages

Most of the general books on vernacular architecture stop short at the design of rural cottages. P. Smith (1975, 1988) is an exception. There is a section in R. W. Brunskill (1997). Of the county volumes, RCHME, *North York Moors* (1987), includes a chapter on cottages (some of them in towns) and C. Giles, *Rural Houses of West Yorkshire* (1978) touches on the subject. For Wales, J. B. Lowe (1985) and E. William (1988) are devoted to the subject. For discussion of the late survival of the single-storey cottage type, see C. D. Newton (1976). See also under *Minor Industrial Vernacular, Cottage Industry* and *Urban Industrial Houses*, below.

The mystery of the 'invisible cottage' is discussed in C. Dyer (1997), who comments on the disparity between historical and architectural or archaeological evidence for cottages. The topic has been explored in more detail and especially in relation to impermanent construction in a typescript document by R. Machin (1997).

Staircases

Detailed drawings of various staircases of vernacular inspiration may be seen in Fox and Raglan (1951 on), especially in Volume III, and the subject is considered in P. Smith (1975, 1988, esp. pp. 251–260). A brief historical study of staircases in one city is F. F. Johnson, *Historic Staircases in Durham City* (1970). In York the RCHME volumes include something on staircases, e.g. Vol. V, 1981, where a variety of balusters are illustrated. In RCHME, *Stamford*, 1977, the subject is also noted.

Architectural Details

General

Most general books and articles on individual buildings include drawings and photographs of the architectural details and particular attention is drawn to J. Ayres (1981) and to comparative collections of such details in Fox and Raglan (1951 on), P. Smith (1975, 1988), M. Wood (1965) and R. B. Wood-Jones (1963), as well as C. Giles for RCHME (1986). The books produced by architects and antiquarians of the early

20C. also often include photographs and drawings of details; see, for example, Fletcher Moss (1901–20).

Windows and Doors

There are two chapters on this subject in C. F. Innocent (1916). W. O. Davies and H. Tanner, *Old English Doorways*, 1903, is an even earlier work on the subject. Details of window shape, mouldings, etc., are illustrated in the RCHME *Inventories* listed above and the subject of windows and doors is amply covered in RCAHMW, *Glamorgan*, 1988, as well as in P. Smith (1975, 1988). The development of the double-hung sash window is explained in detail by H. Louw (1983) while further articles by the same author cover metal windows and window glass manufacture and use.

Internal Ornament

Again, many *Inventories* of the Royal Commissions illustrate internal ornament. Illustrated examples in dated buildings appear in N. W. Alcock and L. Hall (1994).

Farm Buildings

General

General surveys include the following: R. W. Brunskill (1982, 1987, 1999); N. Harvey (1970, 1980, 1984); J. Lake (1989); J. E. C. Peters (1981); S. Wade Martins (1991); J. Weller (1982); E. Wiliam (1986). The national picture is illuminated by way of the sample districts surveyed and analysed by P. S. Barnwell and C. Giles (1997). Regional studies completed include the comprehensive survey of part of Staffordshire in J. E. C. Peters (1969) and the equally comprehensive survey of part of North Wales (E. Wiliam, 1982). There is also a section on farm buildings in R. W. Brunskill (1974). The annual *Journal* of the Historic Farm Buildings Group, published since 1987, covers vernacular buildings as well as planned farmsteads and professionally designed farm buildings.

For contemporary accounts of farm building design the *General Surveys* made county by county for the Board of Agriculture at the end of the 18C. and the beginning of the 19C. are sometimes useful, as are the *Prize Essays* published in the *Journal of the Royal Agricultural Society of England* from about 1850 onwards. The designs for model farmsteads initiated in D. Garrett (1748) and continued in, e.g., J. C. Loudon (1842) or collected in, e.g., J. Bailey Denton, *The Farm Homesteads of England*, 2nd edn, 1845, are not strictly vernacular but are useful in illustrating farming practice.

Location and Layout

For the siting of farmsteads in relation to villages and land settlement see B. K. Roberts (1987) and C. Taylor (1983). Useful also is M. W. Beresford and J. K. St. Joseph (1979). The combination of farmhouse and farm buildings in the longhouse form excited the early years of the Vernacular Architecture Group, e.g. P. Smith (1963). Comments on its archaeological significance in, e.g., G. Beresford (1979) have shown the importance and long persistence of the arrangement. See also E. Mercer (1975) and P. Smith (1975, 1988) for the importance of the longhouse form in any general survey of house plans. The combination of farmhouse and farm buildings in the laithe house form was explained in C. F. Stell (1965) and further examples have been illustrated in, e.g., C. Giles (1986). Farmstead layouts generally are discussed in P. S. Barnwell and C. Giles (1997) and in relation to the North York Moors in RCHME (1987).

Combination Arrangements

The bank barn was recognized as a building type by J. Walton (1950) and described by R. W. McDowall (1956). It was further described and illustrated in R. W. Brunskill (1974). I recognized the American relationship and brought over the American term in the first edition of this book (1971). For the American context see R. F. Ensminger (1992). The building type is called a 'chall barn' in Cornwall, see P. S. Barnwell and C. Giles (1997). It is also quite widespread in Devon, see P. Beacham (ed., 1990). M. Laithwaite gives a date range of c. 1755 through the 19C. in that county. For the variant bank barn see T. M. Whittaker (1989); for the Lancashire barn, see R. W. Brunskill (1982, 1987, 1999).

The Barn for Hand Threshing

Many studies of individual barns have been published, though they are mainly the superior barns of monastic estates. A fine collection appears in W. Horn and E. Born (1956). An important early study was S. E. Rigold (1966). A range of individual barn studies from different parts of England and Wales could include F. W. B. Charles and W. Horn, 'The Cruck-built Barn of Leigh Court, Worcestershire', 1973; S. Jones, 'Gunthwaite Hall Barn, South Yorkshire', 1980; J. E. C. Peters, 'The Tithe Barn, Arreton, Isle of Wight', 1964; Essex County Council, *Cressing Temple, A Brief Guide*, 1990; and E. Wiliam, 'A Welsh Cruck Barn . . .,', 1988. For the procedures and customs associated with hand flail threshing, see the works of G. E. Evans, e.g. *Ask the Fellows Who Cut the Hay*, 1956, and *The Farm and the Village*, 1969.

The Barn for Machine Threshing

For the machinery around which the later farm buildings were designed see G. E. Fussell (1952) and M. Partridge (1973). The design and development of the horse engine is described in F. Atkinson (1960–1). See also S. Macdonald (1975, 1978), and, for the distribution of horse engine houses, K. Hutton (1976). There are informative diagrams of horse engines and their housing in P. Barnwell and C. Giles (1997). See also J. Weller (1982).

The Shelter Shed and Linhay

N. W. Alcock (1963) gives a thorough and well-illustrated account of a building type since widely recognized. For the somewhat similar building type often called a 'Hammell' or 'Helm' see R. W. Brunskill, *Traditional Farm Buildings of Britain* (1999).

Kilns, Oast Houses and Maltings

Useful references include A. H. Burges (1964) and I. Homes (1970). For corn-drying kilns some information appears in D. H. Jones and J. K. Major (1973), while G. Beresford (1979) gives details of kilns used in a deteriorating climate on Dartmoor. The traditional layout of small maltings may be followed from C. J. Loudon (1836) and from J. Lugar (1807).

Urban Vernacular, Minor Industrial and Other Vernacular Buildings

Urban Vernacular Generally

A thorough introduction is provided by D. W. Lloyd (1984). Background material appears in M. Aston and J. Bond (1976). An interesting anthology of contemporary descriptions of urban life is contained in R. C. Richardson and T. B. James (1983). Among the more recent *Inventories* of the RCHME those of Salisbury, Stamford and York contain a great deal of urban vernacular while the RCHME volume on the North York Moors includes the urban vernacular of the small towns of the area. The RCAHMW *Inventory* for Glamorgan, Vol. IV Pt. 2, includes a chapter on Cowbridge, a town, and Llantwit Major, an urban village, also has a chapter.

Medieval Urban Vernacular

General studies include M. W. Beresford and J. K. St. Joseph (1967) and C. Platt (1976). For a thorough study of a town full of medieval buildings see V. Parker (1971) on Kings Lynn. Useful information on 16C. houses and cottages in London appears in J. Schofield (1984), and on earlier houses in J. Schofield (1994). The series on houses in Ludlow published by the Ludlow Research Group (e.g. D. Lloyd, 1979) are thorough studies of individual buildings or small groups of medieval houses, as are the series on Lincoln in the Survey of Ancient Houses in Lincoln. The work of M. Laithwaite in Devon is represented in P. Beacham (ed., 1990) and in P. Clark (ed., 1984). There is a chapter on medieval towns and town buildings in Hertfordshire in J. T. Smith (1992). Discussion of the Rows in Chester has been continued through the work of A. N. Brown and others published in the *Journal of the Chester Archaeological Society*. See also P. Short (1980) for 14C. houses in York. Other important articles include W. A. Pantin (1962–3), which established a typology of urban house plans, and R. A. Faulkner (1966), which explained the significance of undercrofts. See D. Portman (1966) for houses in Exeter 1400–1700. See also Grenville (1997).

Urban Vernacular of the Seventeenth, Eighteenth and Early Nineteenth Centuries

For the background see C. W. Chalkin (1974) and P. Clark (ed., 1981). S. Collier with S. Pearson (1991) traces the development of Whitehaven, Cumbria, from 1660-1800. Useful articles include A. F. Kelsall (1974) and R. F. Taylor (1974). The later volumes of the Survey of London series include houses of this period.

Cottage Industry and Industrial Housing

Housing conditions in the early 19C. have been amply, if sometimes partially, reported in the textbooks of town planning and social reform. A useful summary may be seen in W. Ashworth (1954). The importance of cottage industry and early industrial housing as both a rural and an urban phenomenon may be seen from S. D. Chapman (ed.), especially the chapter by W. J. Smith (1971). Another account of houses for domestic industry is given in Timmins (1979). The article by O. Ashmore (1963–4) on Low Moor, Clitheroe, Lancashire, was an early study of the link between factories and cottages. R. Leech (1981) for Frome, Somerset, and W. G. Muter (1979) (together with

J. Alfrey and C. Clark, 1993) for Ironbridge, Shropshire, deal with cottages in specific industrial communities, as does W. Barke (1979) for the Huddersfield area, H. Coutie (1992) for Stockport, Cheshire, N. Morgan (1990, 1993) for Preston, Lancashire, and J. Roberts for Manchester. S. Muthesius on the *English Terraced House*, 1982, and J. Lowe on *Welsh Industrial Workers' Housing*, deal with the topic more widely. E. Gauldie (1974) gives the background to workers' housing. Many books on regional industrial archaeology include chapters on cottage industry and industrial housing – D. M. Smith (1967) for the East Midlands is a good example. See also L. Caffyn (1986) for West Yorkshire. The process of land development, financing and construction of urban cottages is covered in M. Doughty (ed., 1986), and the transition to suburban cottage development is the theme of A. Sutcliffe (1981).

Minor Industrial Vernacular Including Windmills and Watermills

Here the literature of industrial archaeology forms the basis. Examples include R. A. Buchanan (1972), N. Cossons (1975, 1993) and K. Hudson (1963). For specific building types see R. T. Clough (1962) on lead smelting mills, L. Sysons (1965), R. Wailes (1948) and J. Reynolds (1970) on windmills and watermills. For the vernacular phase of textile mill design see the early chapters of A. Calladine and J. Fricker (1993) for East Cheshire, A. Williams with D. A. Farnie (1992) for Greater Manchester and C. Giles and I. Goodall (1992) for West Yorkshire.

Other Vernacular Buildings

The early Nonconformist meeting houses were unobtrusive in design and clearly related to traditional domestic buildings in many ways. See H. G. Arnold (1960) on early meeting houses generally, K. H. Southall (1974) for Quaker Meeting Houses and C. W. Dolby (1964) for Methodist Chapels; also A. Jones (1984, 1996) for Chapels in Wales. Three volumes of the definitive series on Chapels in England by C. F. Stell for RCHME were published in 1986, 1991 and 1994. Village schools may also be vernacular buildings and a well-developed example in Audlem, Cheshire, is described and illustrated in B. C. Redwood (1964). Almshouses may be vernacular or polite. A good general account appears in W. H. Godfrey (1955).

Comparisons and Conclusions

Distribution Maps and Time Scales

The maps of walling and roofing materials used in part of Cumberland are based on R. W. Brunskill, 'Traditional Domestic Architecture of the Eden Valley' and 'Traditional Domestic Architecture of the Solway Plain', unpublished theses, University of Manchester, 1952 and 1963 respectively. The map of building regions is based on that in P. Smith (1980). Similar but dot-type distribution maps as well as time scales may be found in other unpublished theses in the University of Manchester; M. E. Little (part of Shropshire), T. L. Marsden (Lower Trent Valley and Rutland), D. V. McCaig (Cheshire), J. E. Partington (North Lancashire and Lake District), R. S. Partington (South Lancashire), W. A. Singleton (parts of Cheshire and Derbyshire), P. Tolhurst (Norfolk), G. L. Worsley (Cotswolds). National distribution maps appear in R. W.

Brunskill (1978) and in P. Smith (1980). Regional distribution maps of building materials appear in J. and J. Penoyre (1978). There are several distribution maps in C. Giles (1986), L. Hall, (1983), B. Harrison and B. Hutton (1984), S. Pearson (1985, 1994), J. Warren (ed., 1990, contributions of K. Coutie and J. Harding). Time scales appear in P. Barnwell and A. T. Adams (1994), S. Pearson (1994), RCHME (North York Moors) (1987) and J. Warren (ed., 1990, contribution of P. Grey). There are many distribution maps of features in Wales in P. Smith (1975, 1988). For interpretation of evidence from inscribed dates see B. Hutton (1977), R. Machin (1977) and P. Smith (1988).

Vernacular Architecture and North America

Publication of books on the relationship between vernacular architecture in Britain and North America has reflected the various phases of the study. One phase is represented by such books as J. F. Kelly (1924) for Connecticut, F. Kimball (1922) for the American colonies generally, and H. C. Forman (1948) for 'The Old South'. The phase was summarized in H. Morrison's general book on early American architecture (1952). An early book devoted to links between the vernacular architecture of the two sides of the Atlantic is M. S. Briggs (1932). The academic approach to the subject was given a new impetus by A. L. Cummings (1979). A new phase and a different approach to the subject followed the article on source areas and routes of diffusion by F. B. Kniffen (1965) and with H. Glassie (1966) as well as by H. Glassie (1969, with a 73-page Bibliography) and further developed by Glassie (1975). Kniffen and Glassie (1977) developed the diffusion idea into a study of timber construction. A third phase has been marked by a vast expansion of interest in vernacular architecture in the USA and Canada, some of it devoted to aspects unrelated to British precedent, and much of it related to the wide definition of the term 'vernacular architecture' as understood in North America. A bibliography was published by H. W. Marshall (1981) but there are the ever-expanding bibliographies prepared by D. Upton and others in the *Bulletins* of the Vernacular Architecture Forum of the USA. D. Upton and J. Vlach (1986) have edited an anthology of articles on the subject. An anthology devoted to vernacular architecture in the western states was edited by T. Carter (1997). Vernacular buildings are placed in their architectural context by way of a field guide to American houses by V. and L. McAlister (1989), and by way of a sample survey of 20 small towns by J. A. Jakle, R. W. Bastion and D. K. Meyer (1989). They have been placed in their cultural context in D. Yoder (ed., 1976). Among the several books which take the subject into further depth is, e.g., the first two chapters in C. W. Bishir and others (1990) and the monumental glossary prepared by C. R. Lounsbury (1994).

Kniffen had suggested three source areas from which ideas in vernacular architecture had spread: New England, Middle Atlantic and Lower Chesapeake with the southern Atlantic seaboard. These three have been acknowledged here. The important book, *Albion's Seed* (D. H. Fischer, 1989), divides the settlement areas into four: Massachusetts by English Puritans from East Anglia, 1629–41, Virginia from the South of England, 1642–75, North Midlands to the Delaware, 1675–1725, and from North Britain (Scotland, Ulster and the North of England) to the back country of Pennsylvania and the Appalachians, 1717–1775. He shows that the culture of the Eastern colonies, including their vernacular architecture, was strongly influenced by the regions of Britain from which the colonists emigrated. Of course, by the 18C. colonists from Continental Europe, especially Germany, added their own influence, especially in timber-frame constructional methods. A suggestion, nevertheless, of British influence further afield appears in H. W. Marshall (1989–90).

A further dimension has been added by C. Carson and others (1981) showing that in Maryland and Virginia at least, colonists built first their temporary tents or 'English wigwams', then impermanent earth-fast post structures were used for several years before resources and adequate security allowed conventional timber-framed houses to be erected. This discovery has influenced English attitudes to archaeological evidence of medieval structures and to evidence, including documentary evidence, of some cottage construction extending to quite recent times.

The study of farm buildings has included the 'English Barn' of New York State and the New England States, and the Connected Farm Buildings of New England (see Hubka, 1989). Then there is the Pennsylvania Bank Barn with its origins in the Pratigau Valley of eastern Switzerland and its diffusion from Pennsylvania through the north central states of the USA as far west as Oregon and to Ontario and the Maritime Provinces of Canada. See Ensminger (1992). A summary with distribution maps is in A. G. Noble and R. K. Cleek (1995).

As well as books and articles by the increasing number of scholars devoted to the study of vernacular architecture in North America, and sometimes its British origins, the Vernacular Architecture Forum has published a series, *Perspectives in Vernacular Architecture*, devoted to papers read at the Forum's annual meetings.

Vernacular Architecture in Scotland

The characteristics of the vernacular architecture of Scotland are often different from those of England and Wales. Some of the basic material such as the *Reports* to the Board of Agriculture of the late 18C. and early 19C. are shared while the comments of travellers in the 17C., 18C. and 19C. are, if anything, more helpful. Scotland also benefits from the volumes of the *First Statistical Account* giving details of the various communities in the later 18C. and the *New Statistical Account* of c. 1845. For the rural setting see R. N. Millman (1975). For the setting of urban buildings see C. McWilliam (1975). For the architectural context see J. G. Dunbar (1966), H. Fenwick (1974) and (for the period 1371–1560) R. Fawcett (1994). The various county *Inventories* of the Royal Commission on the Ancient and Historical Monuments of Scotland, especially the volumes on Argyll published between 1971 and 1992, include works of vernacular as well as polite architecture. The most recent volumes in the *Buildings of Scotland* series include brief contributions about vernacular architecture. Two important comprehensive works have been published fairly recently: A. Fenton and B. Walker (1981) (which relates traditional buildings, especially farm buildings, to their social and economic setting) and R. Naismith (1985). The latter summarizes conclusions from a survey of the external appearance of Scottish rural houses based on a sample of 23,000 examples and culminates in the definition of architectural character zones.

For the special case of tower houses see Dunbar (1966), Fawcett (1994) and Fenwick (1974); as well as the Argyll volumes of RCAHMS. Bastle houses have recently been discovered between the Borders and the Glasgow area; see Ward (1988). The houses of the Improvement period of the late 18C. and 19C. comprise most of the evidence used in Naismith (1985). The 'black houses' of the western highlands and islands have interested travellers from the 18C. to recent times. One of the most expert observers was the Swedish scholar Ake Campbell and a summary from his field notebooks appears in B. Walker (1989a). For the black houses on the Uists see B. Walker (1989b).

The longhouse building type was discussed by Fenton (1985). Characteristic hearths have been noted in R. Marshall (1983–4) and also in Fenton (1981).

For the background to one period of agricultural change affecting the design of farm buildings see I. Whyte (1979).

The superbly illustrated volume by G. D. Hay and G. P. Stell (1986) includes some material on the vernacular architecture of industry and farming such as the detailed isometric drawing of a horse engine.

For materials and construction generally see, e.g., A. Riches and G. Stell (1992) and J. G. Dunbar and others (1976). For those of the farmstead see I. Maxwell (1996) and for clay building there is the detailed study by B. Walker (1996). For an experiment in turf walling see R. Ross Noble (1983–4).

There are many other articles now in print including those which appear in *Vernacular Building*, the Journal of the Scottish Vernacular Buildings Working Group, and in the *Journal* of the School for Scottish Studies of Edinburgh University.

A Note on Vernacular Architecture in Ireland

There is still no single substantial work on the subject but introductory material was included in E. E. Evans (1957). For Ireland generally there is an excellent brief account by C. O'Danachair (K. Danaher) (1975). Vernacular houses are set in their architectural context in B. de Breffry and R. ffolliott (1975) but without plans or sections. The northern part of the island (not solely Northern Ireland) has been admirably covered by A. Gailey including sections devoted to British influence where found. The close relationship between folk life and folk building is described in H. Glassie (1982). For study of houses of a rural community see F. H. A. Aalen (1970); and of an urban community see P. Robinson (1979).

The Vernacular Revival

The reference to Petit is taken from P. Collins (1965); Collins devoted a chapter to 'The Linguistic Analogy'. For an account of the work of Edgar Wood see J. H. G. Archer (1963–4). For a remarkable contemporary account see H. Muthesius, *Das Englische Haus*, Berlin, 1904–5 and 1908–11, re-issued as H. Muthesius, *The English House* (D. Sharp, ed.), 1979.

Appendix 1: How to Study Vernacular Architecture

General

Study depends on both fieldwork and library or archive work. While study can certainly be done individually, many beginners are introduced to the subject by way of evening classes or summer schools; others find it helpful to join one of the existing study groups. Affiliated to the Vernacular Architecture Group, as at June 1997, were groups connected with the Avoncroft Museum of Buildings, the Bedfordshire, Buckinghamshire and Cambridgeshire Historic Buildings Research Group, the Domestic Buildings Research Group (Surrey), the Essex Architectural Research Society, the Essex Historical Buildings Group, a group connected with the Gwynedd Archaeological Trust, the Norfolk Archaeological Unit, the North-East Vernacular

Architecture Group, the Petersfield Area Historical Society, the Suffolk Historic Buildings Group, the Somerset and South Avon Vernacular Buildings Research Group, the Traditional Architecture Group of Newcastle upon Tyne, a group connected with the Weald and Downland Open Air Museum, the Wealden Buildings Study Group, the Wiltshire Buildings Record, a group connected with the Yorkshire Archaeological Society and the Yorkshire Vernacular Buildings Study Group. Because of frequent changes it is not practicable to give addresses here but local libraries or record offices usually know of such groups.

A useful introduction to fieldwork is R. W. McDowall (1980) in which four levels of survey are distinguished: (a) superficial (external only), (b) superficial (external and internal), (c) measured, (d) destructive. RCHME, *Recording Historic Buildings, A Descriptive Specification*, distinguishes somewhat similar levels. C. Giles and S. Wade Martins (1994) is based on a conference at which various methods of study of farm buildings were described.

The study of vernacular architecture has obvious benefits at all levels of education but especially in connection with the National Curriculum for Schools. It is not feasible to give specific suggestions here.

Extensive Recording

The Manchester Method was briefly described by R. A. Cordingley (1948). It was thoroughly described and illustrated in R. W. Brunskill (1965–6). It represents level (a) in McDowall (1980) as does the simplified version described and illustrated here. For a development designed to cover farm buildings see R. W. Brunskill (1975–6); its use was described by E. Wiliam in C. Giles and S. Wade Martins (1994). It represents level (b) in McDowall (1980). A. Carter and S. Wade Martins (1987) described methods used in the Norfolk Farm Buildings Project.

Intensive Recording

A useful introduction for beginners was prepared by B. Hutton (1986). Measuring and drawing techniques have been described in various books on draughtsmanship for architectural students; R. Fraser Reekie (1946, and many subsequent editions) is one of the best known. J. K. Major (1975) is an excellent practical guide to measuring vernacular buildings as well as examples of industrial archaeology. R. Chitham (1980) is a thorough guide to measuring and drawing techniques for works of vernacular and polite architecture. L. Smith (1985) is another useful guide. P. Swallow, D. Watt and R. Ashton (1993) is a guide directed mainly at professional surveyors. T. Buchanan (1983) is devoted to the problems and opportunities in photographing historic buildings, including examples of vernacular architecture.

Documentary Investigation

A useful general guide is P. Cunnington (1980). W. G. Hoskins (1959) explains sources and techniques appropriate to this sort of investigation. J. H. Harvey (1947) is a brief guide prepared by another pioneer in the subject. Another useful brief introduction is D. Iredale (1968, 1977, 1991). Also by D. Iredale is a book on archives generally (1973).

Many of the recent studies of the vernacular architecture of districts or counties demonstrate the value of combinations of fieldwork and documentary investigation. Examples include B. Harrison and B. Hutton (1984), S. Pearson (1985), J. T. Smith (1993), S. Pearson (1994). Probate inventories have proved to be the most useful single type of document though Spufford (1990) warns of the limitations of use of probate inventories.

A remarkable series of articles by B. Tyson shows the understanding of vernacular buildings and the processes by which they were created which can come from the study of typical documents available in the County Record Offices. They have appeared in *Transactions of the Cumberland and Westmorland Antiquarian and Archaeological Society* since 1978, in the *Transactions of the Ancient Monuments Society* since 1982 and in *Vernacular Architecture*, 1987, and *Post-Medieval Archaeology* in 1981.

Destructive Recording

When, sadly, vernacular buildings have to be taken down there is a wonderful opportunity to record to a depth not possible in studying an existing building. One can record masonry techniques, timber jointing, details of plaster craftsmanship, etc., as the building is carefully taken down. The article by E. Wiliam (1976) relates the discoveries made when a barn was dismantled prior to re-erection at the Welsh Folk Museum. Similar intensive studies have been made by R. Harris in connection with buildings dismantled and re-erected at the Weald and Downland Open Air Museum.

Accessible Vernacular Buildings

J. R. Armstrong (1979) provided a very interesting and detailed account of vernacular buildings accessible at that time but it has not yet been brought up to date. Current information on vernacular buildings in the care of the National Trust (and the National Trust for Scotland) and accessible and of those in the care of English Heritage (and of Historic Scotland and Cadw-Welsh Historic Monuments) can be seen in the various visitor handbooks produced each year by these organizations. The national annual lists of buildings open to the public (and of museums) include vernacular buildings such as manor houses and barns, along with the major buildings and monuments, while open-air museums and small houses furnished as museums are listed in the appropriate publications. English Heritage publishes lists of buildings that have received grants in aid of repair and so are made accessible to the public, usually by appointment. Many of these are vernacular buildings.

BIBLIOGRAPHY

Abbreviations

Archl. J.:	*Archaeological Journal* – the Journal of the Royal Archaeological Institute.
CW2:	*Transactions of the Cumberland and Westmorland Antiquarian and Archaeological Society*, New Series.
JBAA:	*Journal of the British Archaeological Association.*
Journal HFBG:	*Journal of the Historic Farm Buildings Group.*
Med. Arch.:	*Medieval Archaeology* – the Journal of the Society for Medieval Archaeology.
TAMS:	*Transactions of the Ancient Monuments Society.*
VA:	*Vernacular Architecture* – the Journal of the Vernacular Architecture Group.

Addy, S. O., *The Evolution of the English House*, 1898.

Alcock, N. W., 'Devonshire Linhays', *Transactions of the Devon Association* Vol. 95, 1963.

Alcock, N. W., 'Devon Farmhouses', *Transactions of the Devon Association* Pt. I, Vol. 100, 1968; Pt. II, Vol. 101, 1969.

Alcock, N. W., *Stoneleigh Villagers 1597–1650*, 1975.

Alcock, N. W., *Cruck Construction: An Introduction and Catalogue*, CBA Research Report No. 42, 1982.

Alcock, N. W., 'The Great Rebuilding and its Later Stages', *VA*, Vol. 14, 1983.

Alcock, N. W., *People at Home: Living in a Warwickshire Village, 1500–1800*, 1993.

Alcock, N. W. and others, *Recording Timber-framed Buildings: An Illustrated Glossary*, 1989, 1997.

Alcock, N. W. and Hall, L., *Fixtures and Fittings in Dated Houses 1567–1763*, 1994.

Aldsworth, F. G. and Harris, R., 'A Medieval and Seventeenth Century House at Walderton, West Sussex, Dismantled and Re-erected at the Weald and Downland Museum', *Sussex Archaeological Collections*, Vol. 20, 1982.

Alfrey, J. and Clark, C., *The Landscape of Industry: Patterns of Change in the Ironbridge Gorge*, 1993.

Archer, J. H. G., 'Edgar Wood, A Notable Manchester Architect', *Transactions of the Lancashire and Cheshire Antiquarian Society*, Vols 73–4, 1963–4.

Armstrong, J. R., *Traditional Buildings Accessible to the Public*, 1970.

Arnold, Godwin H., 'Early Meeting Houses', *TAMS*, Vol. 8, 1960.

Arschavir, A., 'False Fronts in Minor Domestic Architecture', *TAMS*, Vol. 4, 1956.

Ashmore, O., 'Low Moor Clitheroe: a Nineteenth-Century Factory Community', *TAMS*, Vols 73–4, 1963–4.

Ashworth, W., *The Genesis of Modern British Town Planning*, 1954.

Aston, M. and Bond, J., *The Landscape of Towns*, 1976.

Atkinson, F., 'The Horse as a Source of Rotary Power', *Transactions of the Newcomen Society*, Vol. 33, 1960–1.

Ayres, J., *The Shell Book of the Home in Britain*, 1981.

Barke, W., 'Weavers' Cottages in the Huddersfield Area: A Preliminary Survey', *Folk Life*, Vol. 17, 1979.

Barley, M. W., *The English Farmhouse and Cottage*, 1961.

Barley, M. W., 'A Glossary of Names for Rooms in Houses of the Sixteenth and Seventeenth Centuries', in I. Ll. Foster and L. Alcock, *Culture and Environment*, 1963.

Barley, M. W., 'The Double-Pile House', *Archl. Journal*, Vol. 136, 1970.

Barley, M. W., *Houses and History*, 1986.

Barley, M. W., 'The Use of Upper Floors in Rural Houses', *VA*, Vol. 22, 1991.

Barnwell, P. and Adams, A. T. for RCHME, *The House Within: Interpreting Medieval Houses in Kent*, 1994.

Barnwell, P. and Giles, C. for RCHME, *English Farmsteads 1750–1914*, 1997.

Batsford, H. and Fry, C., *The English Cottage*, 1938, 1944, 1950.

Beacham, P. (ed.), *Devon Building*, 1990.

Beresford, G., 'Three Deserted Medieval Settlements on Dartmoor . . .', *Med. Arch.*, Vol. 23, 1979.

Beresford, M. W., *New Towns of the Middle Ages*, 1967.

Beresford, M. W. and Joseph, J. K. St., *Medieval England; An Aerial Survey*, 1958 and 1979.

Billet, M., *Thatching and Thatched Buildings*, 1979.

Bishir, C. W. and others, *Architects and Builders in North Carolina*, 1990.

Bouwens, D., 'Clay lump in South Norfolk: Observations and Recollections', *VA*, Vol. 19, 1988.

de Breffny, B. and ffolliott, R., *The Houses of Ireland*, 1975.

Brian, A., 'A Regional Survey of Brick Bonding in England and Wales', *VA*, Vol. 3, 1972; Vol. 11, 1980.

Briggs, M. S., *Homes of the Pilgrim Fathers in England and America 1620–1685*, 1932.

Brown, F. E., 'Analysing Small Building Plans', in R. Samson (ed.), *The Social Archaeology of Houses*, 1990.

Brunskill, R. W., 'A Systematic Procedure for Recording English Vernacular Architecture', *TAMS*, Vol. 13, 1965–6.

Brunskill, R. W., *Vernacular Architecture of the Lake Counties*, 1974.

Brunskill, R. W., 'Recording the Buildings of the Farmstead', *TAMS*, Vol. 21, 1975–6.

Brunskill, R. W., 'Traditional Domestic Architecture of South-West Lancashire', *Folk Life*, Vol. 15, 1977.

Brunskill, R. W., 'The Distribution of Building Materials and Some Plan-types in the Domestic Vernacular Architecture of England and Wales', *TAMS*, Vol. 23, 1978.

Brunskill, R. W., *Traditional Farm Buildings of Britain*, 1982, 1987, 1999.

Brunskill, R. W., *Timber Building in Britain*, 1985, 1992.

Brunskill, R. W., *Brick Building in Britain*, 1990.

Brunskill, R. W., *Houses and Cottages*, 1997.

Buchanan, R. A., *Industrial Archaeology in Britain*, 1972.

Buchanan, T. for RCHME, *Photographing Historic Buildings*, 1983.

Burges, A. H., *Hops*, 1964.

Caffyn, L. for RCHME, *Workers' Housing in West Yorkshire 1750–1920*, 1986.

Calladine, A. and Fricker, J., *East Cheshire Textile Mills*, 1993.

Carson, C., 'Segregation in Vernacular Building', *VA*, Vol. 7, 1976.

Carson, C., 'Impermanent Architecture in the Southern American Colonies', *Winterthur Portfolio*, Vol. 16, Nos 2/3, 1981.

Carter, A. and Wade-Martings, S., *A Year in the Field*, 1978.

Carter, T. (ed.), *Images of an American Land, Vernacular Architecture in the Western United States*, 1997.

Chalkin, C. W., *The Provincial Towns of Georgian England*, 1974.

Chapman, S. D. (ed.), *The History of Working-class Housing*, 1971.

Charles, F. W. B., *Medieval Cruck-Building and its Derivatives*, 1967.

Charles, F. W. B., 'Post Construction and the Rafter Roof', *VA*, Vol. 12, 1981.

Charles, F. W. B. and Charles, M., *Conservation of Timber Buildings*, 1984, 1995.

Charles, F. W. B. and Horn, W., 'The Cruck-built Barn of Leigh Court, Worcestershire', *Journal SAH (USA)*, Vol. 32, 1973,

Chesher, V. M. and Chesher, F. J., *The Cornishman's House*, 1968.

Chitham, R., *Measured Drawings for Architects*, 1980.

Clark, P. (ed.), *The Transformation of English Provincial Towns*, 1984.

Clifton-Taylor, A., *The Pattern of English Building*, 1972.

Clifton-Taylor, A. and Ireson, A., *English Stone Buildings*, 1983, 1994.

Collier, S. with Pearson, S. for RCHME, *Whitehaven 1660–1800*, 1991.

Collins, P., *Changing Ideals in Modern Architecture*, 1965.

Cordingley, R. A., 'Rural House Types', *Proceedings of the British Association for the Advancement of Science*, 1948.

Cordingley, R. A., 'British Historical Roof-Types and Their Members', *TAMS*, Vol. 9, 1961.

Cordingley, R. A. and Wood-Jones, R. B., 'Chorley Hall, Cheshire', *TAMS*, Vol. 7, 1959.

Cossons, N., *The BP Book of Industrial Archaeology*, 1975, 1993.

Cruden, S., *The Scottish Castle*, 1960.

Cummings, A. L., *The Framed Houses of Massachusetts Bay, 1625–1725*, 1979.

Cunnington, P., *How Old is your House?*, 1980.

Curl, J. S., *Encyclopedia of Architectural Terms*, 1993.

Danaher, K., *Ireland's Vernacular Architecture*, 1975.

Denyer, S., *Traditional Buildings and Life in the Lake District*, 1991.

Dixon, P., 'Tower-houses, Pele houses and Border Society', *Archl. J.*, Vol. 136, 1979.

Dixon, P., 'From Hall to Tower: The Change in Seignorial Houses on the Anglo-Saxon Border after c. 1250', in P. Coss (ed.), *Thirteenth Century England*, 1992.

Dixon, P., 'Mota, Aula et Turris: The Manor Houses of the Anglo-Scottish Border', in G. Meirion-Jones and M. Jones (eds), *Manorial Domestic Buildings in England and Northern France*, 1993.

Dolby, G. W., *The Architectural Expression of Methodism: The First Hundred Years*, 1964.

Doughty, M. (ed.), *Building the Industrial City*, 1986.

Dunbar, J., *The Historic Architecture of Scotland*, 1966.

Dunbar, J. and others, *Building Construction in Scotland. Some Historical and Regional Aspects*, 1976.

Dyer, C., 'English Peasant Building in the later Middle Ages', *Med. Arch.*, Vol. 30, 1986.

Dyer, C., *Standards of Living in the later Middle Ages: Social Change in England c. 1200–1520*, 1989.

Dyer, C., 'History and Vernacular Architecture', *VA*, Vol. 28, 1997.

English Heritage, *Stone slate roofing: Technical Advice Note*, 1998.

Ensminger, R. F., *The Pennsylvania Barn*, 1992.

Estyn Evans, E., *Irish Folk Ways*, 1957.

Exwood, M., 'Mathematical Tiles', *VA*, Vol. 12, 1981.

Exwood, M. (ed.), *Mathematical Tiles: Notes of the Ewell Symposium*, 1981.

Fairclough, G., 'Meaningful Construction – Spatial and Functional Analysis of Medieval Buildings', *Antiquity*, Vol. 66, 1992.

Faulkner, P. A., 'Domestic Planning from the Twelfth Century to the Fourteenth Century', *Archl. J.*, Vol. 115, 1960.

Faulkner, P. A., 'Medieval Undercrofts and Town Houses', *Archl. J.*, Vol. 123, 1966.

Fawcett, R., *The Architectural History of Scotland, 1371–1560*, 1994.

Fenton, A., *The Hearth in Scotland*, SVBWG, 1981.

Fenton, A., *The Shape of the Past*, Vol. 1, 1985.

Fenton, A. and Walker, B., *The Rural Architecture of Scotland*, 1981.

Fenwick, H., *Scotland's Historic Buildings*, 1974.

Fischer, D. H., *Albion's Seed, Four Folkways in America*, 1989.

Fletcher, J. M. and Spokes, P., 'The Origin and Development of the Crown Post Roof', *Med. Arch.*, Vol. 8, 1984.

Forsyth, R., *The Beauties of Scotland*, Vols I–V, 1805–8.

Fox, Sir C. and Raglan, Lord, *Monmouthshire Houses*, 1951–4.

Fussell, G. E., *The Farmer's Tools*, 1952.

Gailey, A., *Rural Houses of the North of Ireland*, 1984.

Gauldie, E., *Cruel Habitations: A History of Working-Class Housing*, 1974.

Gee, E. A., 'The Chronology of Crucks', *TAMS*, Vol. 22, 1977.

Giles, C. for RCHME, *Rural Houses of West Yorkshire 1400–1830*, 1986.

Giles, C. and Goodall, I. H. for RCHME, *Yorkshire Textile Mills*, 1992.

Giles, C. and Wade Martins, S. (eds), *Recording Historic Farm Buildings*, 1994.

Glassie, H., *Pattern in the Material Folk Culture of the Eastern United States*, 1969.

Glassie, H., *Folk Housing in Middle Virginia*, 1975.

Grenville, J., *Medieval Housing*, 1997.

Gunther, R. T., *The Architecture of Sir Roger Pratt*, 1928.

Hall, L., *The Rural Houses of North Avon and South Gloucestershire, 1400–1720*, 1983.

Hall, Sir Robert de Z. (ed.), *Bibliography of Vernacular Architecture*, 1972.

Harding, J. M., *Four Centuries of Charlwood Houses*, 1976.

Harding, J. M., 'Timber-framed Early Building in Surrey, A Pattern for Development', *TAMS*, Vol. 37, 1993.

Harris, R., *Discovering Timber-framed Buildings*, 1978.

Harris, R., 'The Grammar of Carpentry', *VA*, Vol. 20, 1989.

Harris, R., 'Jetties', *VA*, Vol. 21, 1990.

Harrison, B. and Hutton, B., *Vernacular Houses in North Yorkshire and Cleveland*, 1984.

Harrison, B., 'Longhouses in the Vale of York, 1570–1669', *VA*, Vol. 22, 1991.

Harrison, J. R., 'The Mud Wall in England at the Close of the Vernacular Era', *TAMS*, Vol. 28, 1984.

Harrison, J. R., 'Some Clay Dabbins in Cumberland: Their Construction and Form', *TAMS*, Vol. 33, 1989; Vol. 35, 1991.

Harvey, J. H., *Sources for the History of Houses*, 1974.

Harvey, N., *A History of Farm Buildings*, 1970, 1984.

Harvey, N., *The Industrial Archaeology of Farming in England and Wales*, 1980.

Hay, G. D. and Fell, G. P., *Monuments of Industry*, 1986.

Herman, B. L., *Architecture and Rural Life in Central Delaware 1700–1900*, 1987.

Hewett, C. A., 'The Development of the Post-medieval house', *Post-Medieval Archaeology*, Vol. 7, 1973.

Hewett, C. A., *English Historic Carpentry*, 1980.

Hewett, C. A., 'The Evidence for an Intermediate Stage between Earth-fast and Sill-mounted Posts', *TAMS*, Vol. 33, 1989.

Hillier, R. and Hanson, J., *The Social Logic of Space*, 1984.

Homes, I., 'The Agricultural Use of the Herefordshire House and its Outbuildings', *VA*, Vol. 9, 1970.

Horn, W. and Born, E., *The Barns of the Abbey of Beaulieu at its Granges of Great Coxwell and Beaulieu St. Leonards*, 1965.

Hoskins, W. G., *The Making of the English Landscape*, 1955, 1970.

Hoskins, W. G., *Provincial Building*, 1963.

Hoskins, W. G., *Fieldwork in Local History*, 1967.

Hubka, T. C., *Big House, Little House, Back House, Barn: The Connected Farm Buildings of New England*, 1984.

Hudson, K., *Industrial Archaeology*, 1963, 1965.

Hutton, B., *Hatfield and its People*, 1963.

Hutton, B., 'Rebuilding in Yorkshire: The Evidence of Inscribed Dates', *VA*, Vol. 8, 1977.

Hutton, B., *Recording Standing Buildings*, 1986.

Hutton, K., 'The Distribution of Wheelhouses in the British Isles', *Agricultural History Review*, Vol. 24, 1976.

Innocent, C. F., *The Development of English Building Construction*, 1916.

Iredale, D., *Enjoying Archives*, 1973.

Iredale, D. and Barrett, J., *Discovering Your Old House*, 1968, 1977, 1991.

Jakle, J. A., Bastion, R. W. and Meyer, D. K., *Common Houses in American Small Towns*, 1989.

Jenkins, J. M., 'Ground Rules of Welsh Houses: A Primary Analysis', *Folk Life*, Vol. 5, 1967.

Jennings, N., 'The Buildings of Moorhouse', *CW2*, Vol. XCIII, 1993.

Jennings, N., 'Two remarkable Cumbrian Clay Dabbins', *CW2*, Vol. XCVII, 1997.

Johnson, B., 'Not "Mansard" or "Gambrel" ', *VA*, Vol. 22, 1991.

Johnson, M., 'The Englishman's House and its Study', in R. Samson (ed.), *The Social Archaeology of Houses*, 1990.

Johnson, M., *Housing Culture: Traditional Architecture in an English Landscape*, 1993.

Jones, A., *Welsh Chapels*, 1984, 1996.

Jones, D. H. and Major, J. K., 'Drying Kilns Attached to Corn Mills', *Conference Proceedings, International Molinological Society*, 1973.

Jones, G. and Bell, J., *Oasthouses in Sussex and Kent*, 1992.

Jones, S., 'Gunthwaite Hall Barn, South Yorkshire', *Archl. J.*, Vol. 137, 1980.

Jones, S., 'Stone Houses in the Vernacular Tradition in South Yorkshire, 1600–1700', *Archl. J.*, Vol. 137, 1980.

Jones, S. R., *English Village Homes*, 1936, 1947.

Kelly, J. F., *Early Domestic Architecture in Connecticut*, 1924, 1963.

Kelsall, A. F., 'The London House Plan in the Late Seventeenth Century', *Post-Medieval Archaeology*, Vol. 8, 1974.

Kimball, F., *Domestic Architecture of the American Colonies and Early Republic*, 1924, 1963.

Kniffen, F., 'Folk Housing: Key to Diffusion', *Annals of the Association of American Geographers*, Vol. 55, No. 4, 1965.

Kniffen, F. and Glassie, H., 'Building in Wood in the Eastern United States: A Time–Place Perspective', *Geographical Review*, Vol. 56, No. 1, 1966.

Lacey, H. M. and Lacey, U. E., *The Timber-framed Buildings of Steyning*, 1974.

Laithwaite, M., 'The Building of Burford: A Cotswold Town in the Fourteenth to Nineteenth Century', in A. Everitt (ed.), *Perspectives in English Urban History*, 1973.

Lake, J., *Historic Farm Buildings*, 1989.

Lawrence, R. J., 'The Interpretation of Vernacular Architecture', *VA*, Vol. 14, 1983.

Leech, R. H. for RCHME, *Early Industrial Housing: The Trinity Area of Frome*, 1981.

Leech, R. H., 'The Prospect from Rugman's Row: The Row House in Late Sixteenth and Early Seventeenth Century London', *Archl. J.*, Vol. 153, 1996.

Lloyd, D., *'Broad Street'*, Ludlow Research Paper No. 3, 1979.

Lloyd, D. W., *The Making of English Towns*, 1984.

Lloyd, N., *The History of the English House*, 1931, 1975.

Loudon, J. C., *An Encyclopedia of Cottage, Villa and Farm Architecture*, 1836.

Lounsbury, C. D. (ed.), *Illustrated Glossary of Early Southern Architecture and Landscape*, 1994.

Louw, H. J., 'The Origin of the Sash Window', *Architectural History*, Vol. 26, 1983.

Louw, H. J., 'The Rise of the Metal Window During the Early Industrial Period in Britain', *Construction History*, Vol. 3, 1987.

Louw, H. J., 'Window-glass Making in Britain, c. 1600–c. 1860 and its Architectural Impact', *Construction History*.

Lowe, J. B., *Welsh Industrial Workers' Housing, 1775–1875*, 1977.

Lowe, J. B., *Welsh Country Workers' Housing, 1775–1875*, 1985.

Lugar, J., *The Country Gentleman's Architect*, 1807.

Lynch, G., *Brickwork, History, Technology and Practice*, Vols 1 and 2, 1994.

McAlister, V. and McAlister, L., *A Field Guide to American Houses*, 1989.

McCann, J., *Clay and Cob Building*, 1983, 1995.

McCann, J., 'Brick Nogging in the Fifteenth and Sixteenth Centuries . . .', *TAMS*, Vol. 31, 1987.

McCann, J., 'An Historical Enquiry into the Design and Use of Dovecotes', *TAMS*, Vol. 35, 1991.

McCann, J., 'The Origin and Use of Clay Lump in England', *VA*, Vol. 28, 1997.

McDowall, R. W., 'The Westmorland Vernacular', in W. A. Singleton (ed.), *Studies in Architecture History*, Vol. II, 1956.

McDowall, R. W., *Recording Old Houses – A Guide*, 1980.

Machin, R., 'The Great Rebuilding: A Reassessment', *Past and Present*, Vol. 77, 1977.

Machin, R., *The Houses of Yetminster*, 1978.

Major, J. K., *Fieldwork in Industrial Archaeology*, 1975.

McWilliam, C., *Scottish Townscapes*, 1975.

Malton, J., *Essay on British Cottage Architecture*, 1798.

Marsden, T. L., 'The Manor House at Donnington-le-Heath', *TAMS*, Vol. 10, 1962.

Marshall, H. W., *American Folk Architecture: A Selected Bibliography*, 1981.

Marshall, H. W., 'The British Isles Single-Cell House in the American Cultural Landscape', *Folk Life*, Vol. 28, 1989–90.

Marshall, R., 'The Ingleneuk Hearth in Scottish Buildings: A Preliminary Survey', *Vernacular Building*, Vol. 8, 1983–4.

Martin, D. and Martin, B., *Historic Buildings in Eastern Sussex*, Vol. I, 1977; Vol. II, 1981; Vol. III, 1982.

Martin, D. and Martin, B., *Domestic Building in the Eastern High Weald, 1300–1750*, 1989.

Mason, R. T., *Framed Buildings of the Weald*, 1964, 1969.

Maxwell, I., *Building Materials of the Scottish Farmstead*, 1963.

Mercer, E., *English Vernacular Houses*, 1975.

Michelmore, D. H. (ed.), *A Current Bibliography of Vernacular Architecture 1970–76*, 1979.

Miles, D., 'The Interpretation, Presentation and Use of Tree-ring Dates', *VA*, Vol. 28, 1997.

Millman, R. N., *The Making of the Scottish Landscape*, 1975.

Morgan, N., *Vanished Dwellings: Early Industrial Housing in a Lancashire Town*, 1990.

Morgan, N., *Deadly Dwellings . . .*, 1993.

Morrison, H., *Early American Architecture from the First Colonial Settlements to the National Period*, 1952, 1987.

Moss, J. Fletcher, *Pilgrimages to Old Homes*, 1901–20.

Muter, W. G., *The Buildings of an Industrial Community, Coalbrookdale and Ironbridge*, 1979.

Muthesius, H., *The English House*, 1979; translation of *Das Englische Haus* of 1904–5 and 1908–11.

Muthesius, H., *The English Terraced House*, 1982.

Naismith, R. J., *Buildings of the Scottish Countryside*, 1985.

Nash, G. D., 'The Historical Farm Buildings of Pembrokeshire', *Journal HFBG*, Vol. 3, 1989.

Nash, G. D., 'Up at Dawn: The Experimental Erection of a Squatter's Cabin', *Folk Life*, Vol. 27, 1988–89.

Nevill, R., *Old Cottages and Domestic Architecture in South-West Surrey*, 1889.

Newton, G. D., 'Single-storey Cottages in Yorkshire', *Folk Life*, Vol. 14, 1976.

Noble, A. C. and Cleek, R. C., *The Old Barn Book: A Field Guide to North American Barns and Other Farm Buildings*, 1995.

Noble, R. R., 'Turf-walled Houses of the Central Highlands', *Folk Life*, Vol. 22, 1983–4.

Oliver, P. (ed.), *Shelter and Society*, 1969.

Oliver, P. (ed.), *Encyclopedia of Vernacular Architecture*, 1988.

Pallister, A. and Wrathmell, S., 'The Deserted Village of West Hartburn . . .', in B. E. Vyner (ed.), *Medieval Rural Settlement in North-East England*, 1990.

Pantin, W. A., 'Medieval English Town-house Plans', *Med. Arch.* Vols 6–7, 1962–3.

Parker, V., *The Making of Kings Lynn*, 1971.

Partridge, M., *Farm Tools through the Ages*, 1973.

Pattison, I. R., Pattison, D. J. and Alcock, N. W. (eds), *A Bibliography of Vernacular Architecture, Vol. III, 1977–1989*, 1992.

Pearson, S. for RCHME, *Rural Houses of the Lancashire Pennines 1560–1760*, 1985.

Pearson, S. for RCHME, *The Medieval Houses of Kent: An Historical Analysis*, 1994.

Pearson, S., 'Tree-Ring Dating: A Review', *VA*, Vol. 28, 1997.
Pearson, S., Barnwell, P. S. and Adams, A. T. for RCHME, *A Gazetteer of Medieval Houses in Kent*, 1994.
Peate, I. C., *The Welsh House*, 1944, 1946.
Penoyre, J. and Penoyre, J., *Houses in the Landscape*, 1978.
Perriam, D. R. and Robinson, J., *The Medieval Fortified Buildings of Cumbria*, 1998.
Peters, J. E. C., *The Farm Buildings of Western Lowland Staffordshire up to 1880*, 1969.
Peters, J. E. C., 'The Solid Thatched Roof', *VA*, Vol. 8, 1977.
Peters, J. E. C., *Discovering Traditional Farm Buildings*, 1981.
Platt, C., *The English Medieval Town*, 1976.
Platt, C., *The Great Rebuilding of Tudor and Stuart England*, 1994.
Portman, D., *Exeter Houses 1400–1700*, 1966.
Potter, M. and Potter, A., *Houses*, 1948, 1960, 1973.
Prizeman, J., *Your House, the Outside View*, 1975.

Quiney, A., 'The Lobby-entry House: Its Origins and Distribution', in J. Newman (ed.), *Design and Practice in British Architecture*, 1984.
Quiney, A., *The Traditional Buildings of England*, 1990.
Quiney, A., *Kentish Houses*, 1993.
Quiney, A., 'Medieval and Post-medieval Vernacular Architecture', in B. Vyner (ed.), *Building on the Past*, 1994.

Rackham, O., 'Grundle House: On the Quantities of Timber in Certain East Anglian Buildings in Relation to Local Supplies', *VA*, Vol. 3, 1972.
Rackham, O., *The History of the Countryside*, 1986.
Ramm, H., McDowall, R. W. and Mercer, E., *Shielings and Bastles*, 1970.
Rapaport, A., *House Form and Culture*, 1969.
Reekie, R. F., *Draughtsmanship*, 1946, etc.
Reynolds, J., *Windmills and Watermills*, 1970.
Richardson, R. C. and James, T. B., *The Urban Experience: A Source Book*, 1983.
Riches, A. and Stell, G., *Materials and Traditions in Scottish Building*, 1992.
Rigold, S., 'Timber-framed Buildings in Steventon, Berkshire and their Regional Significance', *Transactions of the Newbury and District Field Club*, Vol. 10, 1958.
Rigold, S., 'Some Major Kentish Barns', *Archaeologia Cantiana*, Vol. 81, 1966.
Roberts, B. K., *The Making of the English Village*, 1987.
Roberts, D. L., 'The Vernacular Buildings of Lincolnshire', *Archl. J.*, Vol. 131, 1974.
Roberts, J., 'The Provision of Housing for the Working Classes in Manchester', *Journal of the Manchester Literary and Philosophical Society*, Vol. 24, 1986.
Royal Commission on the Ancient and Historical Monuments of Scotland, *Inventory for Argyll*, Vol. 1, 1971; Vol. 2, 1974; Vol. 3, 1980; Vol. 4, 1982.
Royal Commission on the Ancient and Historical Monuments of Scotland, *Eastern Dumfries-shire: An Archaeological Landscape*, 1997.
Royal Commission on the Ancient and Historical Monuments of Wales, *Inventory for Glamorgan*, Vol. IV Pt. 2, *Farmhouses and Cottages*, 1988.
Royal Commission on the Historical Monuments of England, *Inventory for the City of Cambridge*, 1959.
Royal Commission on the Historical Monuments of England, *Inventory for Dorset*, Vol. II, 1970; Vol. III, 1970; Vol. IV, 1972; Vol. V, 1975.
Royal Commission on the Historical Monuments of England, *Inventory for the City of York*, Vol. III, 1972; Vol. IV, 1975; Vol. V, 1981.

Royal Commission on the Historical Monuments of England, *Inventory for the Town of Stamford*, 1977.

Royal Commission on the Historical Monuments of England, *Inventory for the City of Salisbury*, Vol. I, 1980.

Royal Commission on the Historical Monuments of England, *Inventory for North Northamptonshire*, 1984.

Royal Commission on the Historical Monuments of England, *Inventories for West Cambridgeshire*, 1968; *North-east Cambridgeshire*, 1972

Royal Commission on the Historical Monuments of England, *Inventory of Nonconformist Chapels and Meeting Houses*, Vol. 1, 1986; Vol. 2, 1981; Vol. 3, 1994.

Royal Commission on the Historical Monuments of England, *Houses of the North York Moors*, 1987.

Rudofsky, B., *Architecture without Architects*, 1964.

Rural Industries Bureau, *The Thatcher's Craft*, 1961.

Ryder, P. F., *Timber-framed Buildings in South Yorkshire*, 1978.

Ryder, R. F., 'Vernacular Building in South Yorkshire', *Archl. J.*, Vol. 137, 1980.

Ryder, R. F., 'Fortified Medieval and Sub-Medieval Buildings in the North-East of England', in B. E. Vyner (ed.), *Medieval Rural Settlement in North East England*, 1990.

Ryder, R. F., 'Bastles and Bastle-like Buildings in Allendale, Northumberland', *Archl. J.*, Vol. 149, 1992.

Salzman, L. F., *Building in England down to 1540*, 1952, 1997.

Samson, R. (ed.), *The Social Archaeology of Houses*, 1990.

Sandall, K., 'Aisled Halls in England and Wales', *VA*, Vol. 6, 1975; Vol. 17, 1986.

Schofield, J., *The Building of London from the Conquest to the Great Fire*, 1984.

Schofield, J., *Medieval London Houses*, 1994.

Seaborne, M., 'Cob Cottages in Northamptonshire', *Northamptonshire Past and Present*, Vol. 3, No. 5, 1964.

Sharp, H. B., 'Collyweston Stone Slating Techniques', *Folk Life*, Vol. 18, 1980.

Short, P., 'The Fourteenth Century Rows of York', *Archl. J.*, Vol. 137, 1980.

Slocombe, P., *Wiltshire Farmhouses and Cottages*, 1988.

Slocombe, P., *Wiltshire Farm Buildings 1500–1900*, 1989.

Smith, D. M., *Industrial Archaeology of the East Midlands*, 1967.

Smith, D. M., 'Some Flat-roof Thatch Survivals', *Folk Life*, Vol. 16, 1978.

Smith, L., *Investigating Old Buildings*, 1985.

Smith, J. T., 'Medieval Aisled Halls', *Archl. J.*, Vol. 112, 1956.

Smith, J. T., 'Medieval Roofs: A Classification', *Archl. J.*, Vol. 115, 1960.

Smith, J. T., 'Cruck Construction: A Survey of the Problems', *Med. Arch.*, Vol. 8, 1964.

Smith, J. T., 'Timber-framed Building in England', *Archl. J.*, Vol. 122, 1966.

Smith, J. T., 'The Evolution of the English Peasant House to the Late Seventeenth Century: The Evidence of Building', *JBAA*, Vol. 33, 1970.

Smith, J. T., 'Lancashire and Cheshire Houses: Some Problems of Architecture and Social History', *Archl. J.*, Vol. 127, 1971.

Smith, J. T., 'The Early Development of Timber Buildings: The Passing Brace and Reversed Assembly', *Archl. J.*, Vol. 131, 1974.

Smith, J. T. for RCHME, *English Houses 1200–1800, The Hertfordshire Evidence*.

Smith, P., 'The Longhouse and the Laithe-House', in Ll. Foster and L. Alcock (eds), *Culture and Environment*, 1963.

Smith, P., *Houses of the Welsh Countryside*, 1975, 1988.

Smith, P., 'The Architectural Personality of the British Isles', *Archaeologia Cambrensis*, Vol. 129, 1980.

Smith, P., 'British Vernacular Architecture in a Continental Context', *Archaeologia Cambrensis*, Vol. 142, 1994.

Smith, T. P., 'Re-facing with Brick-tiles', *VA*, Vol. 10, 1979.

Smith, T. P., 'Brick-tiles (Mathematical Tiles) in Eighteenth Century and Nineteenth Century England', *JBAA*, Vol. 138, 1985.

Smith, W. J., *Saddleworth Buildings*, 1987.

Somerset and South Avon Vernacular Buildings Research Group: a series of publications, e.g. *Somerset Villages, The Vernacular Buildings of West and Middle Chinnock*, 1984.

Southall, K. H., *Our Quaker Heritage: Early Meeting Houses Built Prior to 1720 and in Use Today*, 1974.

Spufford, M., 'The Limitations of the Probate Inventory', in J. Charles and D. Hey (eds), *English Rural Society 1500–1800*, 1990.

Steer, F. W., 'Smaller Houses and their Furnishings in the Seventeenth and Eighteenth Centuries', *JBAA*, Vol. 20, 1957.

Stell, C. F., 'Pennine Houses: An Introduction', *Folk Life*, Vol. 3, 1965.

Summers, N., 'Old Hall Farm, Kneesall', *Transactions of the Thoroton Society*, Vol. 76, 1972.

Swallow, P., Watt, D. and Ashton, R., *Measurement and Recording of Historic Buildings*, 1993.

Sysons, L., *British Water Mills*, 1965.

Taylor, C., *Village and Farmstead*, 1983.

Taylor, R. F., 'Town Houses in Taunton 1500–1700', *Post-Medieval Archaeology*, Vol. 8, 1974.

Thirsk, J. (ed.), *The Agrarian History of England and Wales*, Vol. IV, 1500–1640, 1967; Vol. V, 1640–1740, Pt. I 1984, Pt. II 1985.

Timmins, J. G., 'Hand Loom Weavers' Cottages', *Post-Medieval Archaeology*, Vol. 13, 1979.

Trotter, W. R., 'Galleting', *TAMS*, Vol. 33, 1989; Vol. 35, 1991.

Tyson, B., 'Low Park Barn, Rydal: The Reconstruction of a Farm Building in Westmorland', *CW2*, Vol. LXXVIII, 1978.

Tyson, B., 'Rydal Hall Farmyard: The Development of a Westmorland Farmstead before 1700', *CW2*, Vol. LXXIX, 1979.

Tyson, B., 'Building work at Sockbridge Hall, its Farmyard and Neighbourhood, 1660–1710', *CW2*, Vol. LXXXIII, 1983.

Tyson, B., 'Two Appleby Houses in the 18th Century: A Documentary Study', *CW2*, Vol. LXXXV, 1985.

Tyson, B., 'Low Cost Housing in Cumbria, 1665–1721: Documentary Evidence for Three Cottages', *VA*, Vol. 24, 1993.

Upton, D. and Vlach, J., *Common Places, Readings in American Vernacular Architecture*, 1986.

Wade, J. (ed.), *Traditional Kent Buildings*, Vols 1–7, 1980–90.

Wade Martins, S., *Historic Farm Buildings*, 1991.

Wailes, R., *Windmills in England*, 1948.

Walker, B., 'The Vernacular Buildings of North-East Scotland: An Explanation', *The Scottish Geographical Magazine*, Vol. 95, 1979.

Walker, B., 'Some Regional Variations in Building Techniques in Angus, Fife and Perthshire', in *Building Construction in Scotland*, 1976.

Walker, B., 'Edited Notes on Hebridean Buildings . . .', *Vernacular Building*, Vol. 13, 1989.

Walker, B., 'Traditional Dwellings of the Uists', *Highland Vernacular Building*, 1989.

Walker, B. and others, *Earth Structures and Construction in Scotland*, 1996.

Walton, J., 'Upland Houses', *Antiquity*, No. 30, 1950.

Walton, J., *Early Timbered Buildings of the Huddersfield District*, 1955.

Walton, J., 'The English Stone-Slater's Craft', *Folk Life*, Vol. 13, 1975.

Warren, J. (ed.), *Wealden Buildings*, 1990.

Watson, R. C. and McClintock, M. E., *Traditional Houses of the Fylde*, 1979.

Ward, T., 'The Elusive Scottish Bastle House', *Vernacular Building*, Vol. 17, 1988.

Weller, J., *History of the Farmstead: Development of Energy Sources*, 1982.

Whittaker, T. J., *The Origins and Development of the Bank Barn in Cumbria*, unpublished M.Phil. thesis, University of Manchester, 1989.

Whyte, I., *Agriculture and Society in Seventeenth Century Scotland*, 1970.

Wiliam, E., 'A Cruck Barn at Hendre Wen, Llanrwst, Denbighshire', *TAMS*, Vol. 21, 1976.

Wiliam, E., 'Yr Aelwyd: The Architectural Development of the Hearth in Wales', *Folk Life*, Vol. 16, 1978.

Wiliam, E., *Home-made Homes*, 1988.

Wiliam, E., *Traditional Farm Buildings in North-East Wales*, 1982.

Wiliam, E., 'A Welsh Cruck Barn and the Study of Vernacular Architecture in Britain', *TAMS*, Vol. 32, 1988.

Wiliam, E., *Historical Farm Buildings of Wales*, 1986.

Williams, E. H. D., 'Jointed Crucks', *VA*, Vol. 8, 1977.

Williams, M. with Farnie, D. A., *Cotton Mills in Greater Manchester*, 1992.

Williams-Ellis, C., *Building in Cob, Pise and Stabilized Earth*, 1947.

Wood, J. (ed.), *Building Archaeology, Applications in Practice*, 1994.

Wood, M. E. (ed.), *The English Medieval House*, 1965, 1981.

Wood-Jones, R. B., *Traditional Domestic Architecture of the Banbury Region*, 1965.

Wrathmell, S., 'Peasant Houses, Farmsteads and Villages in North-East England', in M. Aston, D. Austin and C. Dyer (eds), *The Rural Settlement of Medieval England*, 1989.

Wright, A., *Craft Techniques for Traditional Buildings*, 1991.

Yeomans, D. T., 'Historical Development of Timber Structures', in J. Sunley and N. Bedding (eds), *Timber in Construction*, 1985.

Yeomans, D. T., *The Trussed Roof, its History and Development*, 1992.

INDEX